THE GUITAR REPAIR BOOK

A PRACTICAL GUIDE TO REPAIRING
AND MAINTAINING ACOUSTIC AND
CLASSICAL GUITARS

JAMES LISTER

THE GUITAR REPAIR BOOK

A PRACTICAL GUIDE TO REPAIRING
AND MAINTAINING ACOUSTIC AND
CLASSICAL GUITARS

✲ THE CROWOOD PRESS

Contents

	Introduction	7
	Audience	8
	Scope of the book	8
	Research	8
	Health and safety	9
	Terminology	9
CHAPTER 1	**Anatomy of an acoustic guitar**	11
	The components of an acoustic guitar	11
	Differences between classical and acoustic guitars	14
	Modern construction methods	15
CHAPTER 2	**Workshop facilities, tools and materials**	17
	The workbench	17
	Tools	18
	Measuring and marking tools	18
	Cutting tools	19
	Rasps and files	20
	Clamping	21
	Fretting tools	22
	Other tools	23
	Materials	24
	Glues	24
	Abrasives	25
	Finishing and cleaning materials	25
	Miscellaneous	26
CHAPTER 3	**Maintenance**	29
	Cleaning	29
	Cleaning the body/finishes	29
	Cleaning the fingerboard	31
	Cleaning strings	32
	Replacing strings	32
	Classical guitars	33
	12-hole tie-blocks	35
	Acoustic guitars	38
	Storing your guitar	39
	Humidity	39
	Tuning machines	41
	Checking tuner operation	41
	Lubrication	43
CHAPTER 4	**Setup**	45
	What is setup?	45
	Fret levelling and re-crowning	45
	Initial assessment	46
	Levelling	47
	Re-crowning	48
	Polishing	49
	Relief adjustment	50
	Guitars with a truss rod	50
	Guitars with no truss rod	53
	Nut adjustment and replacement	53
	Lowering the nut height	53
	Raising the nut height	55
	Making a new nut	56
	Saddle adjustment and replacement	59
	Lowering the saddle height	60
	Raising the saddle height	61
	Making a new saddle	61
	Intonation and compensation	63
	What are intonation and compensation?	63
	Checking intonation	64
	Adjusting intonation	64
	Filling and re-routing the saddle slot	65
CHAPTER 5	**Body and plate repairs**	67
	Crack repairs	67
	Causes of cracks	67
	Repairing closed cracks	68
	Cleating	70
	Repairing open cracks	72
	Side cracks	73
	Splinting	78
	Stepped cracks	82
	Damage to laminated (plywood) plates	87
	Type of damage	87
	Laminated side repair	87
	Loose braces	90
	Dents	93
	Steaming a dent	93
	String whip repair	94
CHAPTER 6	**Neck and head repairs**	99
	Neck construction types	99
	Separate neck/body construction	99
	Spanish heel construction	99
	Neck resets and relief correction	100
	Heat resetting	100
	Fingerboard capping	102
	Full neck reset	112
	Open heel glue joint	118
	Re-gluing an open heel joint	118
	Open heel body joint	119
	Replacing tuning machines	120
	Classical/slotted head tuners	120
	Acoustic/flat head tuners	122
	Truss rod replacement	123
	Before you proceed	123

	Removing the truss rod	123
	Fitting the new truss rod	126
	Fitting the new fingerboard	127

CHAPTER 7 Fingerboard and fret work — 131
- Loose frets — 131
- Re-fretting — 134
  - To glue, or not to glue? — 134
  - Removing the old frets — 135
  - Repairing damaged fret slots — 136
  - Installing the new frets — 137
  - Bevelling and smoothing the fret ends — 140
- Worn fingerboards — 142
- Bound fingerboards — 142

CHAPTER 8 Finish repairs — 145
- Types of finish — 145
- Oil finishes — 146
  - Repairing or renovating oil finishes — 146
  - Removing the finish — 147
  - Refinishing with oil — 151
  - Dents in oil finishes — 152
- Shellac finishes — 152
  - Repairing or renovating a shellac finish — 152
  - French polishing — 155
  - Dents in shellac finishes — 157
- Poly finishes — 161
  - Repairing or renovating poly finishes — 161
  - Refinishing — 165
  - Scratch removing — 165
  - Dents in poly finishes — 165
- Nitrocellulose finishes — 167
  - Repairing and renovating nitro finishes — 167
- Colour matching — 167
  - Natural wood colours — 168
  - Stains vs. coloured finishes — 168
  - Basic method and colour theory — 168
  - Colour matching repair patches — 168

CHAPTER 9 Bridge repairs — 171
- Bridge rotation — 172
  - Measuring bridge rotation — 172
  - Correcting bridge rotation — 173
  - Adding bracing — 173
  - Preparing the braces — 176
  - Gluing the new braces — 177
- Lifting bridge – removal and replacement — 178
  - Bridge removal — 179
  - Surface clean-up and repair — 180
  - Preparation for re-gluing — 182
  - Re-gluing the bridge — 184
- Re-gluing a detached bridge — 187
- Lifting bridge – simple glue down — 189
- Fitting bridge pins — 190
- Worn tie-blocks — 192
- Remedying low break angles — 193
  - Classical 12-hole tie-block conversion — 194
  - Bridge string ties — 198
  - Steel-string pin bridge — 199
- Saddle replacement — 199

CHAPTER 10 Inlay and binding repairs — 201
- Types of inlay — 201
- Rosette inlay replacement — 201
  - Making the replacement inlay — 202
  - Gluing the replacement inlay — 203
- Fret marker replacement — 204
  - Cutting the cavities for the inlays — 205
  - Gluing and levelling the inlays — 208
  - Replacing the side fret marker dots — 209
- Binding repairs — 210
  - Binding damage — 210
  - Binding removal and replacement — 215

CHAPTER 11 Wolf notes and resonances — 219
- What are wolf notes? — 219
  - Can wolf notes be eliminated? — 219
- Measuring resonances — 219
  - Chladni patterns — 220
  - Frequency response curves — 224
- Adjusting resonances — 226
  - Adding weight/mass — 226
  - Adding or reducing bracing/stiffness — 229

CHAPTER 12 Catastrophic damage — 231
- What counts as catastrophic? — 231
- Broken neck/headstock — 232
  - Preparation — 232
  - Re-gluing the headstock — 234
  - Small patch repairs — 235
  - Refinishing — 239
- Back removal — 239
  - Removing the bindings — 239
  - Removing the back — 242
  - Repairing damage and preparation — 247
  - Re-gluing the back — 252
  - Replacing the bindings and purflings — 254
- Soundboard replacement — 256
  - Removing the damaged soundboard — 256
  - The replacement soundboard — 258
  - Preparing to glue the new soundboard — 259
  - Checking the neck angle — 261
  - Gluing the new soundboard in place — 261
  - Replacing the bindings and purflings — 262

Glossary — 265
List of suppliers — 268
Index — 269

Introduction

When I first embarked on a career in luthiery some twenty years ago, I was expecting to do 'the odd bit of repair work' to supplement the sometimes erratic income received from making guitars. In fact, I now spend about a third of my time in the workshop on repair and refinishing work. Before starting my training, my only experience in the repair and maintenance of acoustic guitars was re-stringing my own guitar, making slight adjustments to the action and very occasionally giving it a wipe down with a damp cloth. In my four years of study, first at London Guildhall University and then at Newark College, repair work was never officially covered, but during this time, a friend asked me to repair his 1930s archtop guitar. With a lot of help from the tutors and technicians, I managed to complete a respectable repair of a large, stepped crack in the soundboard. The work involved in this repair was far more challenging than most of the guitar building work I was doing at the time, and immensely satisfying.

As well as returning a damaged or neglected guitar to a playable condition, there is great pleasure to be found in saving a musical instrument from the scrap heap (or more likely the attic), particularly in today's throwaway world. Just performing a basic setup on a guitar will make the experience of playing the guitar more enjoyable. Even improving the appearance can inspire the player to pick up their guitar. Of course, many mass-produced guitars can be replaced for less than the cost of a significant repair, but often the owner has an attachment to the instrument that goes beyond mere economics.

Almost every repair job is unique, and may require some adaptation of the techniques in this book, and occasionally some creativity on the part of the repairer. The ability to handle different and unusual repair jobs can only really come with experience, but by carefully following all the techniques covered here, you will, over time, develop the ability to cope with pretty much anything that is thrown at you!

For readers working on their own guitar, you will have a good idea of what you are trying to achieve with the particular repair or maintenance tasks you are conducting. When working on someone else's instrument, it is important to have a conversation with them to be clear about what they are expecting from the work you will be doing. A good example would be a crack repair, where it is usually straightforward to carry out an effective structural repair, but if a customer is expecting cosmetic perfection as well, this will be far more challenging and time-consuming (and hence expensive).

My hope is that the following pages will be both a starting point and an ongoing guide on your journey into the world of guitar repairs and maintenance. It will help you to gain the experience needed to tackle any repair task and enable you and other players to continue to enjoy making music.

Audience

This book is aimed at both the aspiring professional repair person, and the guitarist who wishes to carry out maintenance and repair on their own instruments. It is very satisfying to complete your own basic maintenance and repair jobs, and in time you should become confident enough to carry out some of the more challenging tasks covered. As any experienced luthier knows, repairs are sometimes required during construction of an instrument, and so the book should also be a valuable resource for guitar makers. The book assumes some level of aptitude for working with your hands, and ideally a little experience in working with wood, finishes and measuring equipment. In order to help the reader assess which tasks are within their scope, each has a 'level of difficulty' indicator, ranging from 'Easy' through 'Moderate' to 'Challenging.'

Scope of the book

The book covers a wide range of repair and maintenance procedures that are likely to be encountered by anyone working on acoustic guitars. Acoustic guitars can be defined as those instruments primarily designed to be played without amplification, and will include nylon-string (classical and flamenco), and steel-string (folk, western or just acoustic). Electric guitar repairs are not included, although many of the subjects covered will also apply to solid-body guitars.

Note that the content does *not* extend to restoration of acoustic guitars. Many of the techniques described here will be used in the process of a restoration project, but the knowledge and skills required for the sympathetic restoration of historical instruments go beyond the coverage of this book.

There will usually be more than one way to successfully complete any given repair job. The methods and techniques described are all tried and tested. Although alternatives are given in some cases, it is not practical to cover every single possible method to complete every repair task.

The first chapter will introduce the reader to the anatomy of acoustic guitars, both steel-string and nylon-string, and consider the differences between these two instruments in terms of the types of maintenance and repair work required for each. The second chapter will discuss the workspace, tools and materials that will be needed to tackle most repair and maintenance jobs. The third chapter covers basic cleaning and maintenance procedures, and the fourth chapter covers setup operations, some of which are very simple, and some more complex. The remaining chapters will look in detail at the particular repair operations, each with detailed photographs showing the critical stages of each process.

Research

Before conducting any repair work on a guitar, it is advisable to carry out research into the particular instrument to identify any potential pitfalls. Differences in neck construction, type of finish, soundboard construction, bracing patterns and materials used can all influence the approach to a repair job, or even whether the job should be attempted at all. A laminated or plywood soundboard will require a very different approach to a traditional solid top. An up-bowed neck will be simple to correct if the guitar has an adjustable truss rod, but one with a fixed reinforcement (or none at all) will require much more work. The type of finish can be hard to discern just by looking. For many guitars, the amount of information available will be limited or even non-existent, but spending a relatively small amount of time on research before picking up any tools can avoid serious difficulties later.

Difficulty levels

The following indicators are used within the text to give some idea of the level of skill, experience, and equipment that might be required for each task. Terms like 'easy' and 'challenging' are of course somewhat subjective, but the aim is to give the reader some guidance as to which tasks they are likely to be able to undertake with a good level of confidence.

Easy: Tasks that should be achievable by a player working on their own instrument, with relatively little experience and only simple tools, but assuming some competence in working with their hands.

Moderate: Slightly more exacting tasks, which should be well within the capabilities of the experienced repairer, or someone who has previously carried out maintenance of their own instruments for a number of years.

Challenging: Tasks that would normally be left to a professional repairer and require higher levels of skill, along with some experience of working with hand tools and finishes. Specialist tools and materials are likely to be needed.

Health and safety

As in any workshop where sharp tools, machinery and chemicals are used, health and safety should always be a consideration. When discussing accident prevention with my students, I always stress the importance of *awareness*. Whenever using a new tool or material, or conducting an unfamiliar procedure, take some time to consider the potential hazards, and what you can do to minimise them. Whenever hazards are identified, consider whether the process can be tackled in another way to remove or reduce the risk. If this is not possible, then think about what additional safety equipment should be used – either machine guards, or personal protective equipment such as goggles, gloves, dust masks or a respirator. Always wear suitable clothing in the workshop. Sturdy shoes are essential – a sharp chisel can go straight through a pair of trainers if dropped from bench height.

Dust inhalation should always be avoided. The UK Health and Safety Executive states that risks from both hardwood and softwood dust include asthma, dermatitis and nasal cancer. Always try to minimise production of dust, and where it cannot be avoided, wear suitable respiratory protective equipment. I would also recommend a workshop air filtration system to remove airborne dust.

Terminology

Any guitar that produces an audible sound without amplification can be considered an acoustic guitar, but the term 'acoustic' is generally used to refer specifically to steel-string guitars. Almost all nylon-string guitars are in fact acoustic guitars, but they are rarely referred to as such. For simplicity, in this text I will mostly use 'classical' to refer to nylon-strung acoustic guitars (including flamenco guitars), and steel-string or just 'acoustic' to refer to acoustic guitars.

Many parts of the acoustic guitar have alternative names. For example, the sides of an acoustic guitar are also referred to as ribs. Luthiers usually talk about harmonic *bars* and fan *braces*, but fan *struts* can also be used. The same may be true for some tools, materials and processes. The labels on the diagrams in Chapter 2 will give the names used in this text for all major components of the guitar.

CHAPTER 1

Anatomy of an Acoustic Guitar

The components of an acoustic guitar

The drawings show exploded views of typical nylon-string (classical) and steel-string (acoustic) guitars. Although bracing patterns, body shapes, head design and bridge types will vary, these are the most common configurations. There are exceptions, but most differences do not affect the repair and maintenance processes significantly.

The basic structure of classical and acoustic guitars is remarkably similar. Both produce sound by vibrations of the soundboard. The body of the guitar contains a volume of air and forms a 'sound box'. When a string is plucked, the vibrations are transmitted through the saddle and bridge to the soundboard. These vibrations interact with the air inside the body, and the sides and the back, which together produce sound waves that propagate away from the guitar.

The neck of the guitar serves to hold the vibrating strings. The tuning machines are mounted on the head and allow the pitch of the strings to be adjusted (tuned). The nut defines one end of the string, and holds the strings in the correct spacing across the width of the fingerboard. Frets are mounted on the fingerboard and allow the player to select notes by pressing the string onto the fingerboard behind the relevant fret. The saddle is mounted in a slot in the bridge and defines the other end of the string.

The truss rod in the acoustic guitar (and on some classical guitars) allows the player to make adjustments to the relief of the neck. The back braces strengthen the back and define the curvature, and the centre strip reinforces the centre join between the two back plates. The linings run the whole way around the sides and strengthen the join between these and both the soundboard and back. They may be individual lining blocks, kerfed, or solid continuous linings.

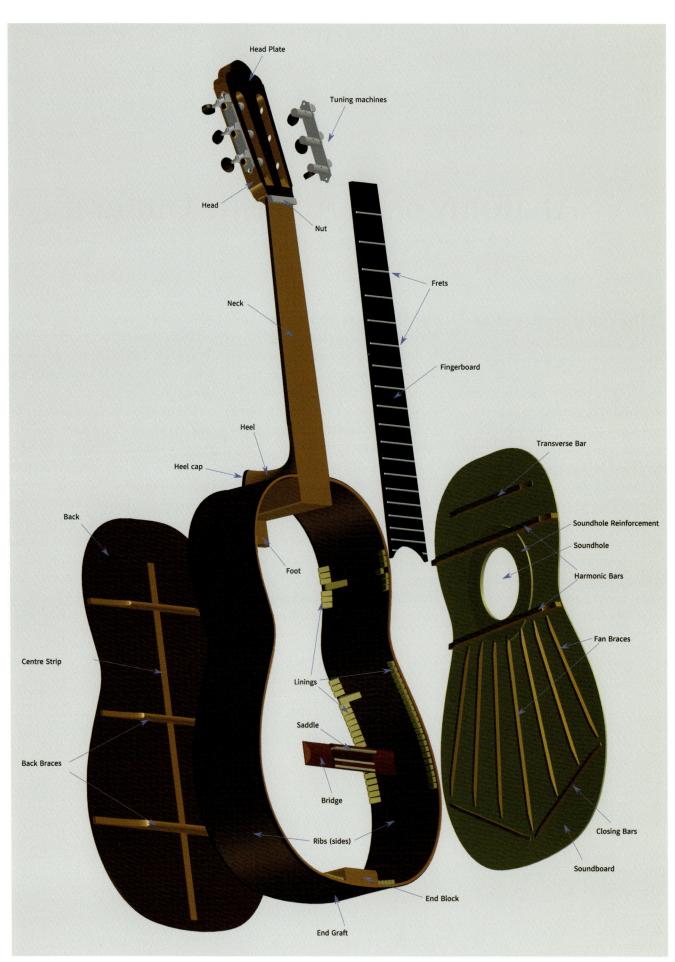

An exploded view of a typical fan-braced, nylon-string classical guitar, showing internal and external parts, labelled with the naming conventions used in this text. Although other bracing systems are now common, most forms of construction are very similar to this.

Anatomy of an Acoustic Guitar

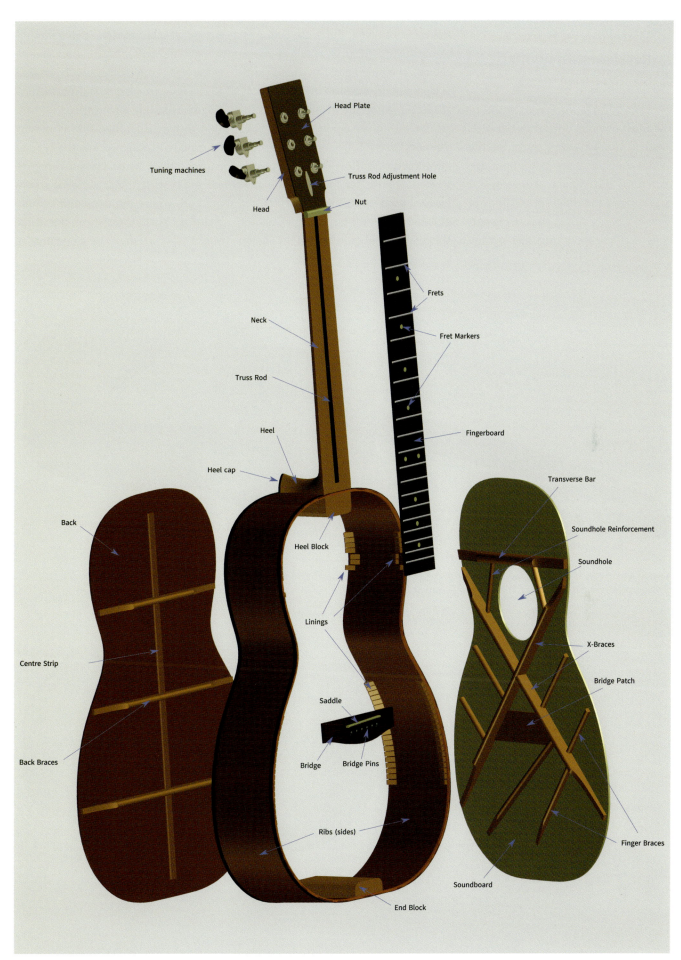

An exploded view of a typical X-braced steel-string acoustic guitar, showing internal and external parts, labelled with the naming conventions used in this text. X-bracing is by far the most common system used in acoustic guitars, although there are quite a few subtle variations.

Anatomy of an Acoustic Guitar

Differences between classical and acoustic guitars

The most obvious difference between classical and acoustic guitars are the strings, but there are also important structural differences. These result largely from the different tensions of the two types of string. Steel string tensions tend to be about twice that of nylon strings. As a result, the construction of the acoustic guitar is generally more robust. The bracing of the soundboard is significantly stronger than found in classical guitars, and the neck is usually reinforced with an adjustable truss rod. The neck/body join on classicals is almost always at the 12th fret of the fingerboard, whereas acoustic guitars most commonly have a '14-fret' neck. The body of acoustic guitars is generally larger, which allows the guitar to make the most of the higher energy available from the higher tension strings. The method of string attachment to the bridge often differs, with classical guitars using a tie-block, and most acoustic guitars having pin bridges.

Another difference that is of significance to repair work is the type of construction. Most classical guitars are built using the traditional solera method, where the neck and soundboard are glued together on the workboard (solera), then the sides/linings

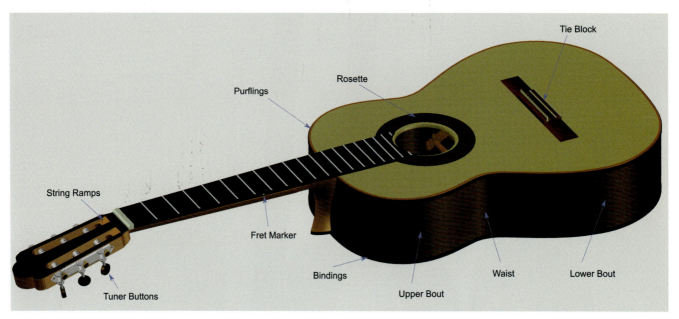

A nylon-string classical guitar. Classical guitars seldom depart from this basic external appearance. There are exceptions, but most developments have focused on the internal structure of the instrument.

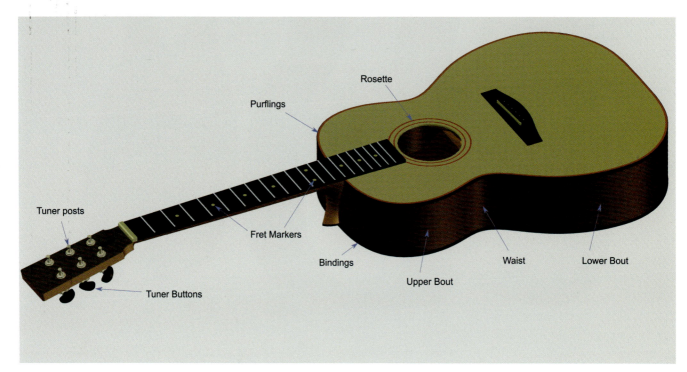

A steel-string acoustic guitar. Although sizes, shapes and other visible parts of acoustic guitars vary a lot, these differences will rarely have a significant impact on repair and maintenance processes.

are added, then the back is glued on. Most acoustic guitars are constructed in two parts – the neck/head/heel and the body, these being glued or bolted together towards the end of the build process. The solera method makes neck resetting impractical, and alternative solutions are discussed in Chapter 6. Exceptions to this rule can be found in both types of guitar.

Other less significant differences include the type of head (solid/flat or slotted), fingerboard width, fret marker positions and rosette design, but these do not have much impact on how repair and maintenance tasks are undertaken.

Modern construction methods

Alternative soundboard construction methods are becoming more common in classical guitars but are still rare in flamenco and acoustic guitars. Some makers use a composite construction for the soundboard, commonly referred to as 'double-top' guitars. These have two very thin softwood plates glued together with a honeycomb structure (most commonly Nomex) in the middle. This type of soundboard presents additional difficulties to the repairer.

Some types of lattice-braced guitars have very thin soundboards (1mm thick or less) supported by balsa wood braces, which are reinforced with carbon fibre and glued with epoxy resins. The backs and sides of these guitars are often laminated.

These modern construction methods tend to make repairs more difficult. The very thin plates used make mechanical damage more likely, and they are more challenging to repair effectively.

A few modern construction approaches actually make some repairs easier. An increasing number of acoustic guitar makers, and a few classical makers, have adopted a bolt-on neck construction. Any problems with the neck angle are relatively easy to correct, as the neck can simply be unbolted, adjusted, and bolted back on again. In some designs the neck is bolted to the body at both the heel and the fingerboard. In others, the fingerboard is still glued to the soundboard, but disassembly is still easier than with a fully glued joint.

Adjustable necks are also becoming more common, which completely remove the need for neck resets or saddle adjustments to correct the action.

ABOVE: Nomex is a synthetic material with a honeycomb structure first developed in the 1960s and widely used in the aerospace industry. It was first used in classical guitar construction in the 1990s. (Photo: Nick Pearson)

RIGHT: The bolt-on neck is a construction system that makes neck angle adjustments much easier. In designs like this one, the neck is bolted to the body at the heel and the fingerboard, making it completely detachable. (Photo: Stuart Christie)

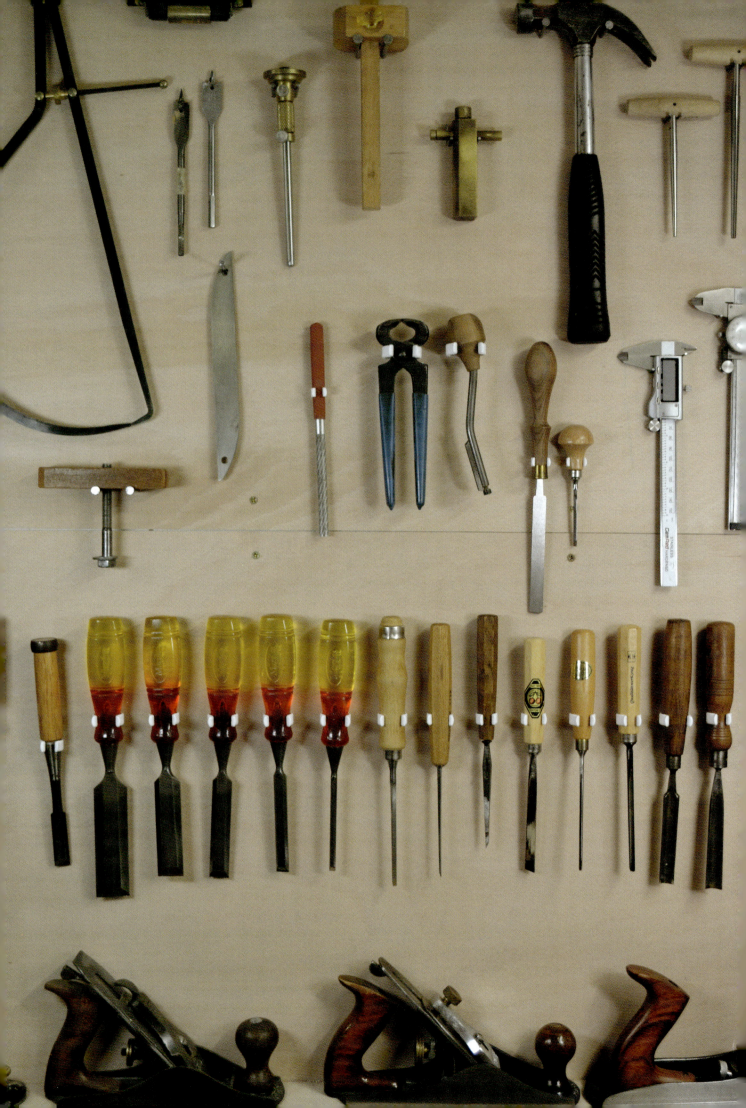

CHAPTER 2

Workshop Facilities, Tools and Materials

To successfully carry out repairs and maintenance on classical and acoustic guitars, there are certain minimum requirements in terms of tools, materials and workshop facilities. Although not all items are essential, a well set-up and equipped workshop will improve the efficiency and quality of your work.

The workbench

A solid, stable workbench is of great benefit to most repair work and is essential for some. Weight is an advantage in terms of stability, although lighter workbenches can made much more stable if they are firmly attached to a solid wall and/or the floor. The workbench should have a good-quality woodworking vice attached, and many tasks will be made easier with the addition of a pattern maker's vice. The top surface should be at a comfortable height for you to work on, and should be large enough to accommodate a guitar with plenty of space to spare.

Me at my own workbench. It's easy to make your own workbench, as I did with this one. It has a simple pine frame and an MDF top. I later added oak boards to the top, which are very tough. For added stability the workbench is screwed to the wall of the workshop.

This type of pattern-maker's vice is very useful for holding a guitar securely by the neck when working on it. The jaws are surfaced with soft plastic, and one pivots, allowing it to grip a tapered neck or head securely. I have holes in my bench allowing it to be mounted in different positions.

Good lighting is essential, and in addition to a bright overhead light, a bench mounted Anglepoise lamp is helpful. A headband magnifier with built-in light is useful for fine detail work.

Tools

Measuring and marking tools

Good-quality measuring and marking tools are essential for performing setup procedures accurately. The following are all useful and, in many cases, essential.

Steel rules: All should have metric scales, but imperial scales are occasionally useful, particularly in countries where imperial measurements are still the standard. The scales should start at the end of the rule. A small, flexible 15cm rule can be useful, a 30cm rule

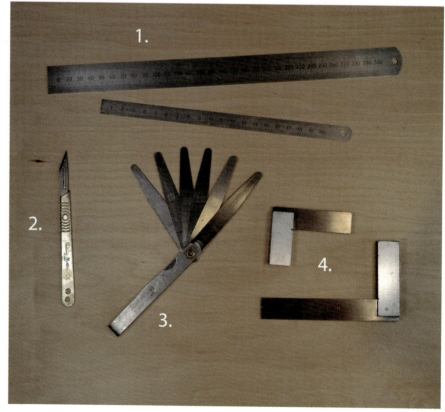

1. Steel rules   2. Scalpel   3. Feeler Gauges   4. Engineer's squares

18 Workshop Facilities, Tools and Materials

1. Dial calipers   2. Digital calipers   3. Vernier calipers   4. Action gauges

Cutting tools

Cutting tools include chisels, knives, gouges and scalpels. Sharpness is critical with these tools, and better-quality tools will be made with higher-quality steel, which will hold an edge better, and require less frequent sharpening.

Planes: Although hand planes might be considered primarily as tools for making rather than repairing, they will be required for making repair pieces and patches. A small block plane or apron plane is normally sufficient for repair work, but a larger plane might sometimes be needed, for example, when replacing, levelling or capping a worn fingerboard. As with most tools, the recommendation is to buy the best you can afford. The block plane shown is an old Stanley which works really well. At the time of writing, modern Stanley planes are fairly poor quality. The apron plane I use is a Lie-Nielson, which is one of my favourite tools.

Knives: A sharp carving knife is a useful tool for some repairs – the one shown is a Japanese double-bevel knife with a rosewood handle I made myself. Carving knives can be used for shaping and trimming repair pieces.

Chisels and gouges: One or two good-quality chisels should be all that is needed for repair work. A small V- or U-shaped gouge is very useful for cutting out small areas of damage, and for making replacement patches for these.

is essential, and a 1m rule is needed for measuring scale lengths and fret positions.

Scalpel: I use Swann-Morton scalpel handles, and prefer the 10A blades, but craft knives with replaceable blades can also be used. Used for more accurate marking than is possible with a pencil – particularly nut slot positions. Keep a supply of new blades handy.

Feeler gauges: Feeler gauges are the best way to accurately measure small clearances, which is essential when carrying out setups. Normally metric, but imperial is acceptable if preferred.

Engineer's squares: These steel engineer's squares are accurate, and can be used as fret rockers, for marking, and checking squareness of parts such as nuts and saddles. Various sizes are available, but I find a 75mm one is suitable for most tasks.

Calipers: Digital calipers are quicker to read, but vernier calipers are the most reliable if you take care when reading them. Better-quality calipers will be more expensive, but more accurate. In particular, cheap digital calipers should be avoided, as they can give unreliable readings – particularly as the battery gets towards the end of its life.

Action gauges: You can buy purpose-made action gauges from some luthier's suppliers, but these can easily be made from calibrated, tapered hardwood pieces. I have two sizes, the larger one tapering from 5.5mm down to 3mm, and the smaller one goes from 3.5mm down to 1.5mm. The thickness calibrations are measured with a vernier gauge and marked at 0.2mm intervals on the top surface with a fine pencil. The narrow edge of the gauge is simply inserted between the top of the 12th fret and the relevant string until it just touches both, and the action is read from the scale.

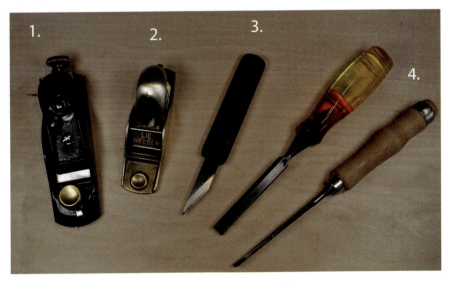

1. Block plane   2. Apron plane   3. Carving knife   4. Chisels

Workshop Facilities, Tools and Materials   **19**

1. Small scrapers 2. Large scraper 3. Gouges

of 0.6mm veneer. These are particularly useful for levelling and smoothing repairs in curved surfaces. The flexible sticks are disposable, but the solid ones can be reused by simply replacing the abrasive.

Nut files will be required for setup work. A number of different types of files are available for cutting the string slots in nuts, and all will do the job. Fine, tapered needle files have the advantage that you can select the position on the file to give exactly the right slot size for any string diameter. The finer ones are very fragile though, and great care is needed to avoid breaking them. Rigid, double-edged nut files are robust, but the size of slot is fixed for each string.

Scrapers: Cabinet scrapers are an essential tool for the luthier and are often used in repair work. The rectangular and curved ones you can buy from tool suppliers are useful, but in repair work I use small ones I've made myself more frequently. I have one with a flat edge, and one slightly curved, and both were made from an old Japanese saw blade, which is an excellent material for small scrapers. A piece of the saw blade is simply cut to the size required, and the edges filed smooth. The scraping edge can either be left flat or filed to the required curve.

1. Hand cut rasp 2. Small file 3. Solid sanding stick 4. Flexible sanding sticks

Rasps and files

The standard 'rasps' found in DIY shops are not really useful in guitar repair work. Fine, hand-cut rasps and small files can be used for making repair pieces to the required shape, and for shaping or levelling these on the instrument.

I also frequently use sanding sticks for this purpose and have both solid and flexible ones for different tasks. The solid ones are simply made from tapered hardwood pieces. The abrasive is attached to the flat surface using double-sided tape. Flexible ones are again made by using double-sided tape to fix different grades of abrasive paper to both sides of pieces

1. Fixed size nut files   2. Tapered, round nut files

Clamping

The type of dedicated repair clamps frequently used in violin family repairs are rarely needed for guitars, but they can occasionally be useful.

Rare-earth magnets are my preferred method for clamping cleats to the inside of the guitar body, as they aid alignment as well as providing good clamping pressure. It can be helpful to have a few different sizes, but I most commonly use 6mm or 10mm ones. Rectangular magnets can be useful for maintaining the correct alignment of repair cleats.

I also have some very useful clamps, which can be made from small blocks of wood and tuning pegs. These are used to hold two sides of a crack level whilst gluing a cleat.

Go-bar decks are good for some clamping operations, although care is needed not to exert too much pressure with them.

ABOVE:
1. Repair clamp
2. G-clamp
3. Peg clamp
4. Rare-earth magnets

RIGHT: I use rubber-tipped carbon fibre rods in my go-bar deck, which apply even pressure and are easy to position. Here the go-bar deck is being used to glue braces during construction, but it can also be used to hold two sides of a crack level while gluing.

Workshop Facilities, Tools and Materials

Fretting tools

A selection of fretting tools are needed for re-fretting and for setup work. Some sort of fret levelling tool is essential, and these can be made yourself very easily. I simply plane one edge of a long piece of a stable wood (plywood works well) and attach abrasive paper to this using double-sided tape. Different lengths and widths can be made to suit the particular job.

Flush-cutting fret nippers and fret crowning files are required for re-frets. Diamond crowning files are very effective for efficient workflow, and a fret mask will also speed up the work. A set of abrasive fret erasers will help achieve a high-quality finish to fretwork. A fret end dressing file is useful but not essential.

A fret rocker is a handy tool, but if you already have a couple of small engineer's squares, they will do the same job. A fret tang nipper is worth having if you are doing a lot of fret work on guitars with bound fingerboards.

A fret press or hammer will be required for re-fretting. Presses are quicker and easier over the neck, but most cannot be used over the body or the heel.

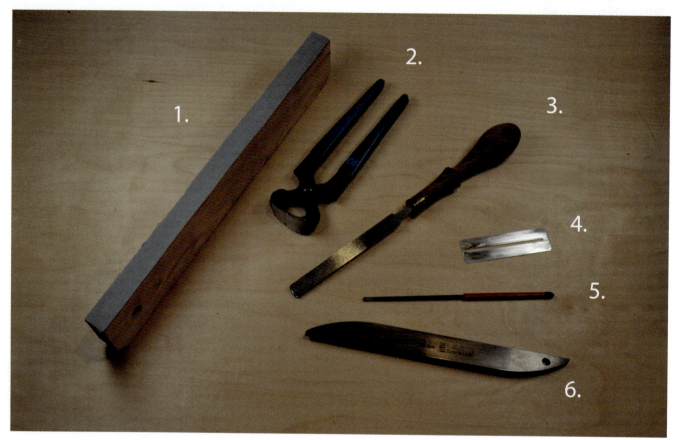

ABOVE:
1. Fret leveller
2. Flush fret end cutters
3. Fret crowning file
4. Fret mask
5. Fret end dressing file
6. Diamond fret crowning file

LEFT: This purpose-made fret hammer has a metal face on one side, and a plastic face on the other. The plastic face reduces the risk of denting the frets when hammering.

Other tools

A string winder is invaluable for anyone serious about repairing or maintaining guitars. It will save a lot of time when changing strings, or when removing and replacing them to carry out repairs. A hand crank one is fine, but battery-powered ones are also available. Attachments for power drill/drivers should only be used on low-speed settings.

For string cutters, a pair of small wire-cutters are fine for nylon strings, but heavier duty side-cutters will be needed for steel strings.

An inspection mirror is useful for inspecting the inside of the body through the soundhole.

A bridge pin reamer is used for precise fitting of new bridge pins.

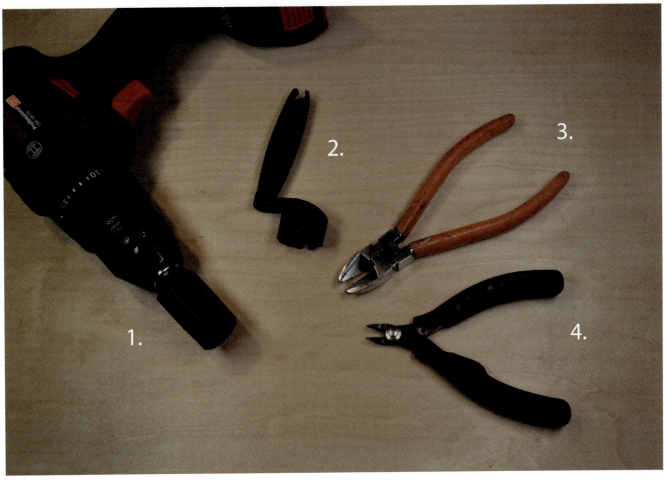

1. Power drill string winder   2. Hand crank string winder   3. Heavy duty cutters for steel strings   4. Small cutters for nylon strings

This inspection mirror has built-in LED lights, making it easier to see clearly inside the body of the guitar.

A bridge pin reamer is used for precise fitting of bridge pins and end pins. The taper angle must match that of the pins. Flamenco tuning pegs require a lower angle taper.

Materials

Glues

Various glues are required for repair work, and the specific type used will depend on the type of repair, the type of instrument and the repairer's preference.

Traditional animal glues (hot hide glue, fish glue, rabbit skin glue) are usually preferred for repair work where it is expected that future repairs might be necessary, as they are easily reversible. They are particularly appropriate for body repairs on older and more valuable instruments where this type of glue was likely to have been used in the construction of the guitar.

Modern aliphatic resin glues (for example, Titebond) are good for general wood repair work, where convenience or longer open times are desired.

Cyanoacrylate glue (superglue or CA glue) can be very effective for filling small holes and gaps, particularly in hardwoods. Some formulations can leave yellow stains in light-coloured woods (for example, spruce or maple), particularly if it gets into the end grain of the wood, so care needs to be taken and it is advisable to do tests when using a brand you are not familiar with. This staining can take days or even weeks to appear and can ruin the appearance of an otherwise good repair.

Epoxy resin glues are rarely appropriate for repair work but can be effective for filling larger gaps and dents where it will not be necessary to reverse the repair in the future, or when the instrument is of relatively low value.

1. Rabbit skin glue granules   2. Cyanoacrylate glue (Superglue)   3. Titebond original   4. Fish glue   5. Pearl glue

Workshop Facilities, Tools and Materials

Abrasives

Standard (aluminium oxide) abrasive papers in a range of grits from 120 up to 400 will be needed, along with finer finishing abrasives. Silicon carbide (wet and dry) paper is available in grits as fine as 5000 and can be used for flattening and cutting back finishes, but my preferred finish abrasive is Micro-Mesh – a cushioned abrasive in sheet or pad form that produces a very uniform scratch pattern and is available in grades from 1,500 (roughly equivalent to a standard 400 grit paper) right up to 12,000. Fine steel wool (0000 grade) is also useful for fret work.

Finishing and cleaning materials

Clean, lint-free cotton cloths and microfibre cloths are useful for both cleaning and refinishing work. A wide

1. Meguiar's swirl remover   2. Lighter fluid (Naphtha)   3. Super Nikco   4. Novus plastic polish
5. Microfibre cloth   6. Cotton cloth

1. 0000 grade wire wool   2. Abranet abrasive   3. Aluminium oxide abrasive paper   4. Micro-Mesh

Workshop Facilities, Tools and Materials

1. Danish oil   2. Gluboost Fill & Finish   3. Shellac solution   4. Nitrocellulose lacquer aerosol   5. Colour pigments   6. Shellac flakes

variety of cleaning products are available. Although most will work, some are not suitable for certain types of finish. Lighter fluid (naphtha) is a good, general-purpose cleaner. For delicate finishes, particularly French polish (shellac), my preferred burnishing cream is Super Nikco. Products from Meguiar's and Novus (amongst others) are also popular.

Acoustic guitars are finished with a wide variety of materials, and the repairer is often faced with a finish which cannot be easily identified. Steel-string guitars are more commonly finished with lacquers (nitrocellulose, polyurethane, water-based). Factory made classical and flamenco guitars might have similar finishes, but higher end instruments are more likely to be French polished (with shellac) or have a rubbed oil finish. Cyanoacrylate glues are now available in a few different colours for finish repairs, and a wide range of colours are also available in a shellac solution.

Shellac finishes should only ever be repaired with shellac, and oil finishes with oil. The same applies to nitrocellulose lacquer. These finishes will melt (burn in) when new finish is applied, which helps to give an invisible repair. Cyanoacrylate glue is often used for small repairs in lacquer finishes, particularly polyurethane.

Miscellaneous

Crack repairs will usually require reinforcement. Small offcuts of wood can be used for making cleats, but paper or linen can be used where wooden cleats are not practical.

Japanese paper is flexible, light and strong. The long fibres make it very good at reinforcing small cracks and joints.

Double-sided tape has already been mentioned for making sanding sticks, but it is also useful for holding clamping cauls and magnets temporarily in position.

Blu Tack (reusable putty adhesive) can be used as a non-permanent holder of things, but it will also be used for adding temporary mass to the soundboard in Chapter 11.

And finally, there will be a number of references in the following pages to making a record of measurements, or taking notes. I have in the past been guilty of scribbling things down on any scrap of paper that is handy, or even on a piece of spruce, or the back of some abrasive paper. I have learned to my cost that this is not a reliable way of retaining information, and in recent years I have become more disciplined, and will now (almost) always have a notebook to hand for writing anything down. Apart from recording critical measurements, a notebook is also used for taking notes when discussing a repair job with a customer, and cataloguing the time spent on repairs so that they can be invoiced accurately. Get yourself a notebook – a nice one – and make sure you use it.

1. Japanese paper   2. Wooden cleats

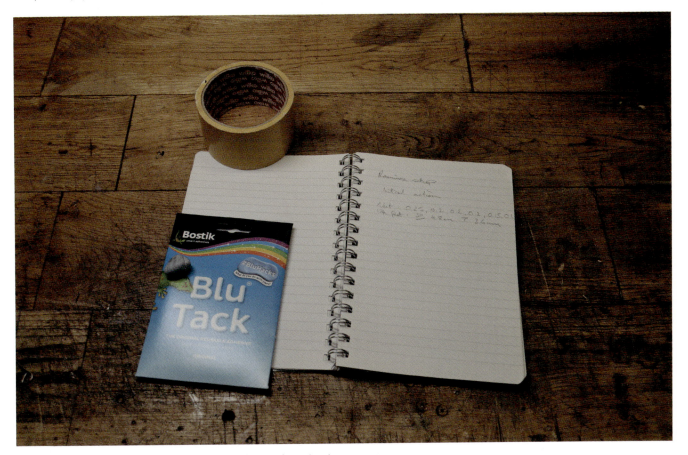

Double-sided adhesive tape, Blu Tack and a spiral-bound notebook.

Workshop Facilities, Tools and Materials

CHAPTER 3

Maintenance

Cleaning

Keeping your guitar clean is unlikely to significantly affect either how it plays or how it sounds, but it is good practice to regularly remove the grime that tends to build up. There are 'guitar cleaning kits' available on the market, but these are not necessary, and tend to be overpriced.

The most important factor when choosing a product to clean your guitar is compatibility with the finish. Shellac (French polish) is an alcohol solvent finish, so avoid alcohol-based cleaners, which will soften and damage the finish. Identifying the finish can be difficult, but there can be clues. Cheaper, factory instruments will not be French polished, simply because the process is too time-consuming and expensive. Classical guitars are more likely to be French polished than acoustic guitars, as thicker finishes tend to have a greater impact on the tone of nylon-string instruments. Sprayed lacquers were first used around the 1930s, with modern polyurethane and catalysed lacquers appearing later in the twentieth century. Rubbed oil finishes will generally be matt in appearance, and any open grain in the wood will usually be visible. A matt appearance can be achieved with all types of finish, however, so this test is not conclusive.

Cleaning the body/finishes

Use a soft brush or air blower to remove any loose particles of grit or dirt that might scratch the finish before attempting to clean surfaces. Start with as mild a cleaner as possible and use products that are known to be safe on most finishes.

You will need a clean, soft, cotton cloth. Old cotton T-shirts can be used (but avoid any printed areas) or brushed/flannel cotton. Microfibre cloths can be used, but take care with these, as they are very good at picking up small particles of dirt, which can then scratch the finish. Use a reasonably large piece of cloth to minimise the risk of your fingernails marking a delicate finish. This applies particularly to classical or flamenco players with long nails! Fold the cloth a few times and dampen it with warm water – it should not be dripping. Rub gently in circular motions and then if necessary dry with a clean, dry cloth. If this doesn't do the trick, try adding a little mild soap, then clean this off immediately with a cloth dampened with clean water, and then dry. Work in small areas at a time, frequently changing to a fresh, clean part of the cloth. If the guitar is cleaned regularly, this should be all that is needed.

Always be sure your cloth is clean – fold the cloth frequently to expose a clean section.

Lighter fluid (naphtha) can be effective for removing greasy marks both on the finish and fingerboards. It should be safe on all types of finish provided they are fully cured. Again, the cloth need only be slightly dampened. Regularly re-folding the cloth will help to lift the grime from the surface, rather than just moving it around. You can follow this up with either a water-dampened cloth, or with a guitar polish as described below.

Specialist guitar cleaners and polishes are available online and from instrument

As well as being a good general cleaner, naphtha is also effective for removing sticky residue from masking tape. The cloth was used with naphtha to clean an acoustic guitar that didn't look particularly dirty!

> ### Safety note
>
> Naphtha is a highly flammable liquid and is irritating to both the eyes and the respiratory system. Use with care, wearing gloves and eye protection, and in a well-ventilated area away from any naked flames or other potential ignition sources. Store safely in a sealed container away from heat and ignition sources.

suppliers, and these should be safe on most finishes. These usually contain a very fine abrasive to help remove dirt, and they can also remove very fine scratches. Always check the instructions provided. I would recommend avoiding these products for shellac (French polish) finishes unless they specifically say they are suitable. Do not use any products that contain silicone, as it can make subsequent repairs and refinishing work difficult.

Take extra care with any finishes that are damaged or crazed (cracked), as any cleaning product can get under the finish and be impossible to remove. Apart from

Super Nikco is a cleaner with a very fine abrasive, and is very effective at bringing most finishes up to a good shine. Guitar polishes are designed for use on lacquer finishes, and are not recommended for French polish or oil finishes.

being unsightly, this will make future repair work less effective.

Super Nikco is my preferred finish cleaner. It is designed specifically for polishing delicate finishes and contains a very mild abrasive which is safe to use even on shellac.

Shellac is probably the most delicate finish used on acoustic guitars. The finish is usually very thin and is particularly fragile for the first few months after it has been applied. For this reason, I recommend not using any cleaning products on shellac finishes when the instrument is new. In fact, shellac seems to continue to harden over a number of years, so the longer you can leave it before using anything more than a soft cloth and warm water, the better. Shellac is also prone to softening with prolonged exposure to heat and sweat in places where it is contact with the player's body. Once it has softened, it will mark very easily, and it is unlikely that you will be able to clean it successfully.

The good news is that unlike many modern lacquers, a shellac finish is relatively easily repaired by an experienced French polisher (*see* Chapter 8).

Cleaning the fingerboard

Most guitar fingerboards are unfinished, so require a different treatment to other parts of the instrument. Fingerboards that are finished (most often on electric guitars) should just be cleaned with naphtha and a cloth rather than using wire wool as described below.

Over time, grime will build up on the fingerboard, particularly at the edges of the frets. Keeping the fingerboard clean will help to increase the life of your strings and make playing a more enjoyable experience! I have seen guitars with so much build-up on the fingerboard that you would think they had never been cleaned.

Always remove the strings before cleaning the fingerboard – in fact, it is good practice to give it a bit of a clean every time the strings are changed. This prevents serious build-up of grime, and makes cleaning a quick, simple process. If cleaned regularly, the fingerboard should only need a good rub with a soft cloth dampened with some lemon oil. Note that the product used on guitar fingerboards is not pure lemon oil, but rather a mineral oil with a little lemon oil added, or even just some lemon scent.

If there is too much build-up of dirt and grease, then you will need something a bit more aggressive. Fine steel wool is very effective at cleaning deposits from the fingerboard, and at the same time cleaning up the frets themselves. Only use the finest grade of steel wool (0000), as anything coarser will leave scratches in the fingerboard that will be difficult to remove.

Dampen the steel wool with a little naphtha or alcohol and start by working across the fretboard and along the frets. Make sure you get right into the corners at the edges of the frets. If the neck and body finish is shellac, do not let any alcohol drip onto these surfaces, as it will soften and damage the finish. Keep a clean, dry cloth handy to immediately wipe off any drips or spills. Most of the grime is likely to be towards the nut end of the fingerboard, which gets the most use. Lightly clean the tops of the frets as

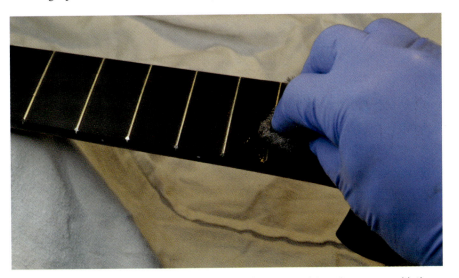

Grime tends to build up mostly at the edges of the frets, so work into the corners with the wire wool and naphtha. Finish by working along the length of the fingerboard with dry wire wool. This will bring both the frets and the fingerboard to a nice lustre.

A conditioning oil will improve the appearance of the fingerboard, and also help prevent it drying out. Work across the frets initially to get the oil right up to the fret edges.

well, but do not be too aggressive here, as you don't want to affect the levelling of the frets. Once the dirt is removed, take a fresh piece of dry 0000 grade steel wool and rub lengthwise along the length of the fingerboard and frets to give it a final clean, and to remove any light scratch marks left by working across the width.

When the fingerboard and frets are clean, work some lemon oil into the fingerboard with a fresh, clean cloth. Leave it for a few minutes, and then wipe off any residual oil with a dry cloth.

Cleaning strings

You will find many different opinions expressed on the internet about whether or not, and how, to clean guitar strings. I tend towards the view that it is worthwhile giving your strings a wipe with a dry cloth (particularly the wound strings) after each playing, to minimise any build-up of dirt. The problem with trying to clean wound strings with any solvent or other product is that you are likely to just work dirt into the windings, which is then very difficult to remove, causing these strings to lose their brightness. Probably the only way to get a deep clean of wound strings is with an ultrasonic cleaner, which is too time-consuming to be worthwhile.

Replacing strings

Every player should be confident in changing the strings on their guitar. I occasionally have customers asking me to change their strings for them, but I encourage them to do it for themselves, as it really isn't difficult. Different types of acoustic guitar have different methods of attaching the strings at both the head and the bridge.

When removing strings, always release the tension by detuning with the tuning machines. Never cut them while they are under tension. Once the strings are slack, remove the ends from the tuners, and then from the bridge. Take care with the ends of plain steel strings – it is very easy to stab your fingers with them!

The question of whether all the strings should be changed at the same time has been known to cause heated discussions on guitar forums. Some believe that removing all the strings at once (and hence all the tension) can in some way damage the guitar, but I have yet to meet a luthier who believes this to be a problem. Many repair and maintenance procedures require removal of all the strings, and at worst it might take a day or two for the guitar to settle once the tension has been restored.

Regularly wiping the strings with a dry cloth can help extend their life, particularly after playing.

Classical guitars

Most classical and flamenco guitars have a bridge with a tie-block, to which the strings are attached.

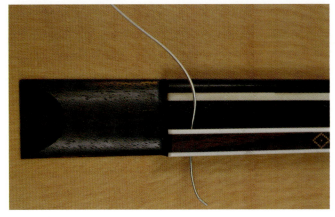

Step 1: Take the new string and pass one end through the correct hole in the tie-block, from the side nearest the saddle towards the end of the guitar. If access to the string hole is difficult, making a slight kink near the end of the string can help.

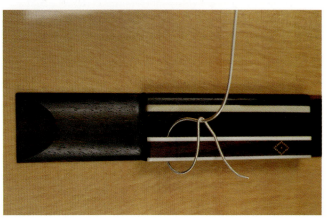

Step 2: Now pull enough string through to loop over the tie-block and around the string. Again, bending a kink in the string will help hold it in place.

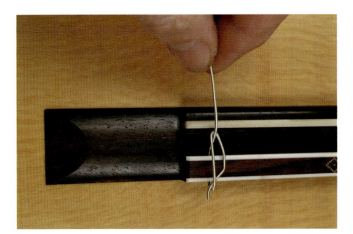

Step 3: Bass strings: Pass the end of the string through the gap between the string and the tie-block and start to pull the string through from the other end. As the loop closes over the tie-block, pull the end down so that it is caught *behind* the tie-block, not on top of it.

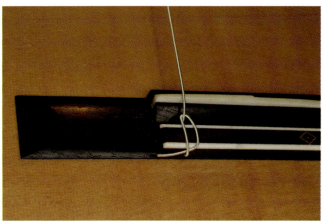

Step 4: The bass string tie should look like this once tension has been applied to the string. Trim the end of the string leaving 5–10mm protruding.

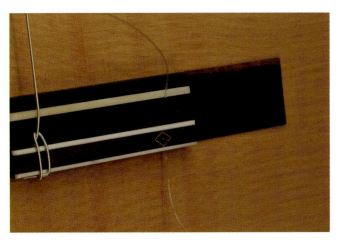

Step 5: Treble strings: Nylon treble strings have a tendency to slip. If they come loose, the tension in the string will cause it to whip out of the tie-block, and the end will make a deep dent in the soundboard. Pass the treble string through the correct hole.

Step 6: Pass the end of the string through the loop as before, leaving enough length for a second loop (plus a third loop for the first string).

Maintenance

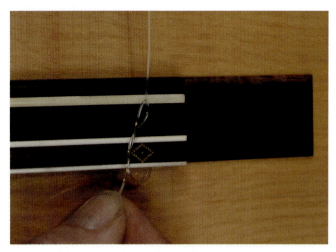

Step 7: Pass the end of the string around the loop again. For the first string, repeat this to form a third loop, as the thinner strings are more prone to slipping.

Step 8: The treble string tie should look like this once tension has been applied to the string. First string shown with three loops. Make sure that the last loop is held *behind* the tie-block, not on the top.

Step 9: Melting the end of the nylon strings to form a ball provides added insurance against strings slipping out. If this is done after the string has been tied, great care will be needed to avoid damaging the soundboard or bridge with the heat source.

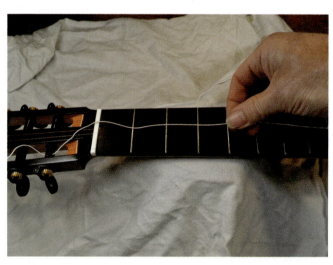

Step 10: Once the string has been secured to the bridge, pass the other end through the hole in the tuning machine roller corresponding to that string. Pull most of the excess string length through, leaving only enough length to pull the string away from the fingerboard – about 5cm.

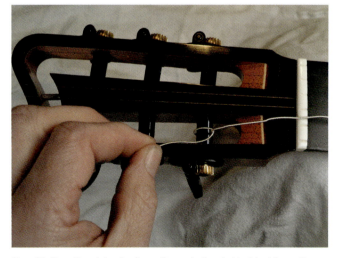

Step 11: Pass the string back up through the slot behind the roller and wrap the end back around the string to hold it in place as you start to wind the tuner.

Step 12: Now start winding the tuning machine, holding the loop with your finger until it has been gripped securely. A hand crank string winder speeds the process up a lot. Check that the string is seated in the correct slot in the nut.

Maintenance

Step 13: The string on the roller should look something like this once up to tension. There should not be too many loops around the roller, and the path to the nut should be reasonably straight.

Step 14: For the first string, it is advisable to pass the end of the string through the roller hole twice before wrapping the end around the string as above.

Repeat for all the strings, and then bring them up to tension.

12-hole tie-blocks

It has recently become common for classical type bridges to use a 12-hole tie-block system. These give a greater and more consistent break angle for the strings and look neater. It is very important to use the correct method for tying the treble strings, as it is common for the string to slip out of the tie-block and damage the soundboard. The method for the bass strings is very simple, but there are a few alternatives for the treble strings. The following is the most reliable I have found.

Step 1: Bass strings: Identify the primary string hole in the tie-block. This will usually be the lower hole of the pair, but occasionally all the holes are at the same level. Take the new string and pass one end through the correct hole, from the side nearest the saddle. If access to the string hole is difficult, create a slight kink near the end of the string.

Step 2: Now pull enough string through to loop back around the tie-block and then through the secondary hole of the pair (usually the higher of the two holes).

Step 3: Take the end of the string and pass it through the loop of string going over the tie-block. You can tell if you have used the right holes, as the strings should be equally spaced as they pass over the saddle.

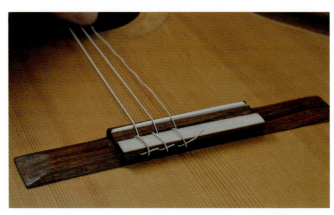

Step 4: Pull both ends of the string until the end is trapped under the loop at the back of the tie-block. Note the even spacing between strings at the saddle.

Step 5: Tie the other end of the string at the tuning machine roller, as described in the previous section, and bring the string up to tension.

Step 6: Trim the end of the string at the back of the tie-block. Trimming all the strings to the same length makes for a neater job.

Step 7: Treble strings: Pass the treble string through the correct primary hole for that string, from the side nearest the saddle towards the end of the guitar.

Step 8: Now pull enough string through to loop back around the tie-block and then through the secondary hole of the pair, the same as for the bass strings.

Step 9: Pass the end of the string through the loop of string between two holes in the tie-block, leaving enough length for a second loop.

Step 10: Now the tricky part – take the end of the string and pass it back through the loop you have just formed. Take careful note of the string path as shown on the image. If the secondary hole is on the other side of the primary hole, you will need to produce the *reverse* of the knot shown in the image.

Step 11: Take up some of the slack by pulling the string through from the soundhole end. Keep the loop positioned at the back of the tie-block, not on the top.

Step 12: Pull both ends until the knot tightens at the back of the tie-block. The end of the string should be pointing upwards.

Step 13: Tie the other end of the string at the tuning machine roller, as described in the previous section, and bring the string up to tension. This will further tighten the knot.

Step 14: Trim the end of the string at the back of the tie-block. You want the end to be level or just below the top of the tie-block, so that it will not dig in to the player's hand if they rest it on the bridge.

Step 15: Check that all the strings are tied correctly as shown in the photo. The ends could be a little shorter, but you do not want them so short that they could slip out from under the string loop.

Maintenance

Acoustic guitars

Most steel-string acoustic guitars use pin bridges, as shown in the following step-by-step sequence, but a few (for example, Ovation), have a tie-block similar to a classical guitar. As most steel strings have ball ends, the string does not need to be tied to the bridge, but simply fed through the correct hole in the tie-block and pulled through until the ball end is snug in the recess at the back of the tie-block.

Step 1: Bridge pins are tapered and should fit firmly into matching tapered holes in the bridge. The pins may be slotted to give clearance for the string or can be plain if the bridge itself is slotted.

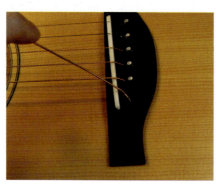

Step 2: Insert the ball end of the string into the correct hole in the bridge. If possible, locate the ball end against the underside of the soundboard.

Step 3: Now insert the pin (with the slot aligned with the string if it has one), but do not press it fully home yet. Holding the top of the pin gently with one finger, pull the string upwards until it stops.

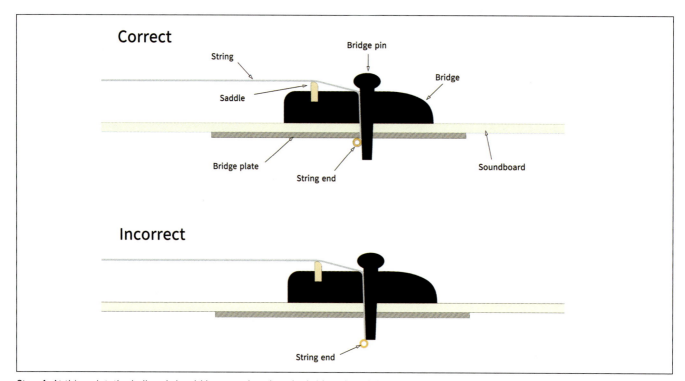

Step 4: At this point, the ball end should be seated against the bridge plate. It is important that the ball end is not caught at the bottom of the pin itself, as it will just pull the pin out when the string is tensioned.

Step 5: Pass the string over the saddle and thread the end through the hole in the correct tuning machine post. Pull enough of the string through to avoid having too much string wound onto the roller.

Step 6: Wrap the string around the roller once, and then start winding the tuning machine button until the string is tensioned. Check that the string is correctly seated in the nut. Repeat for the remaining strings, and then tune to pitch.

Storing your guitar

Acoustic guitars can be fairly fragile instruments and storing them correctly will reduce the risk of accidental damage. I recommend keeping your guitar in a good-quality case at all times when not being played. Over the years I have carried out several repairs where the guitar has been left on a stand or just propped against a wall and has been damaged by being knocked over by a pet, or having a toy thrown at it by a small child! Although the level of risk is small, the consequences can be severe – potentially requiring replacement of the entire soundboard.

Hard shell cases are only really necessary when travelling with the guitar, and they are essential for air travel. Baggage handlers are notorious for being careless with musical instruments, and although incidents are rare, that is no consolation if it happens to you. Hard foam cases are fine for keeping the guitar safe in the home, and a soft case will offer enough protection in most circumstances, provided it is well padded. Avoid fabric cases with no padding, as they offer very little protection, and can even damage delicate finishes.

If you do not want to keep your guitar in a case, then a wall hanger is the next best option, provided it is out of reach of pets and children, and away from anywhere it could get accidentally knocked off the hanger. Some types have a mechanism that automatically closes around the neck of the guitar when you put it on the hanger.

Another option is to keep your guitar in a cabinet. A well-designed cabinet will keep valuable instruments safe and if it has a glass front, allow you to show it off to visitors! It also gives the option of controlling the humidity.

Humidity

Wood is hygroscopic. A material that is hygroscopic will absorb moisture (water molecules) from the surrounding atmosphere. In the case of wood, this will lead to a change in size, and this dimensional change will vary depending on the species of wood, the direction of the grain and the amount of moisture absorbed from the air.

In general, any change in dimension *along* the grain of the wood will be relatively small. Changes *across* the grain will be greater, and more so tangentially.

As a very rough guide, for a given increase in moisture content, a particular species of wood might expand ten times as much radially across the grain as along the grain, and twice as much again tangentially across the grain.

A hard-shell case offers the best protection for your guitar. A hard case wrapped in plenty of padding and a sturdy cardboard box are essential when shipping a guitar.

Maintenance

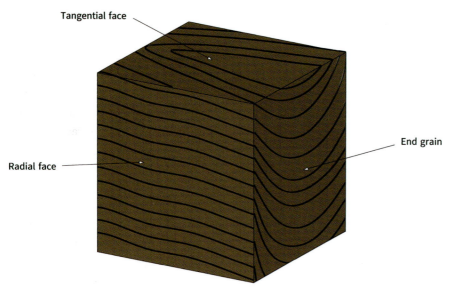

Radially cut wood is always preferred for the thin plates used on acoustic guitars due to its greater dimensional stability.

What all this means is that any part of the guitar made of wood (that is, most of it) will expand and contract as the humidity in the surrounding air changes. Most guitars these days are constructed in humidity-controlled conditions, at a relative humidity of around 45–50 per cent. The ideal is to always keep your guitar in an environment where the humidity is around this value. Changes of 15 per cent or so should not cause any problems. If the humidity reaches much higher values (greater than 70 per cent), then the soundboard and the back are likely to swell up slightly, which will raise the action and possibly cause the tone of the guitar to become dull, but it is unlikely to do any permanent damage. Low humidity values (less than 25–30 per cent) are of much greater concern, as these will cause the thin plates of a guitar to shrink, and eventually crack.

The soundboard and back plates of an acoustic guitar are usually slightly domed. This is partly to increase their rigidity, but it also helps to protect against some shrinkage. As the humidity decreases, the curvature of the top and back plates will gradually flatten out, but once completely flat, tension will build up across the grain of the wood, and at some point, it will fracture along the grain.

Some woods used in guitar making are more prone to cracking than others, and top and back plates that are cut tangentially (slab-cut or flat-sawn) are more likely to crack than radially cut (quarter-sawn) plates.

Low humidity values are often found in hot, dry climates, and in cold, dry weather in heated homes. It is worth investing in one or two hygrometers so that you know what the humidity is where the guitar is kept and can take appropriate action if it falls too low. Various types of hygrometer are available, and the more expensive ones are likely to be more accurate.

If the humidity where your guitar is kept is likely to fall below 25 per cent it is best to take measures to increase or control the humidity. Guitar accessory suppliers usually stock small humidifiers (usually just a plastic case with holes and some sort of sponge to hold water) that can be kept inside the guitar case, or even hang inside the guitar itself suspended

Digital hygrometers have the advantage that most of them have a Max/Min function that can tell you the lowest (and highest) humidity since it was last reset.

This guitar humidifier is designed to hang on the strings of the guitar when it is laid flat in its case. The sponge slowly releases moisture preventing the guitar drying out.

Checking tuner operation

Tuning machines should operate smoothly without sticking or creaking, should not slip, and should not have excessive play. Check the play by turning each tuner button back and forth. There should be very little movement of the button before the string changes pitch. If there is any sticking or creaking, this could be due to problems with the nut or with the fit of the tuners in the head, rather than the tuner itself, so check these before working on the tuner.

Tuning machines on slotted head guitars usually have posts mounted directly into the wood, although bearings are becoming more common on higher end tuners. If the tuner posts are not perfectly aligned in the holes, this can be one cause of 'creaking' as you tune. This can be alleviated by removing the tuners and working some candle wax into the inside surfaces of the tuner post holes.

Wound strings generally have ridges formed by the windings, and these are more pronounced on the lower bass strings. These can catch on any edges in the nut slot, causing the string to stick during tuning. As the string is tuned up or down, you will notice that the pitch doesn't change until the string 'clicks' onto the next winding, making fine tuning difficult. *See* Chapter 4 (Setup) sections on 'Lowering the nut height' and 'Making a new nut'.

Modern tuning machines require very little in terms of maintenance, but if they become stiff or notchy it is worth trying to clean and lubricate them before resorting to buying replacements. I would always recommend removing tuning machines from the guitar before cleaning them.

Sealed tuners are designed to never need cleaning or lubrication, so once they no longer operate smoothly, they will have to be replaced.

Closed-back or covered tuners have covers over the gears but are not sealed. These tuners can be cleaned by either

Tuning machines

Tuning machines are also referred to as machine heads, or just tuners. You will also find tuning pegs fitted to some flamenco guitars, but these are becoming rarer.

There are two main types of tuning machine used on acoustic guitars. Steel-string acoustic guitars are mostly fitted with six individual flat-head tuners mounted into holes (usually three on each side of the head), with the tuner post protruding through the top surface of the head, and the tuner buttons accessible at the side of the head. Classical guitars, and some steel-string guitars, have slotted heads with the posts accessible through the slots, and the tuner buttons at the back of the head. These can be individual tuners but are more commonly '3-on-a-plate' on each side.

These high-end classical guitar tuners by Rodgers Tuning Machines are elegant and well-engineered.

Maintenance 41

Heating a metal applicator can help when applying wax around the tuner holes, which will help the posts turn smoothly.

These Gotoh sealed tuners are designed to be maintenance-free and are good value.

Any brush with reasonably stiff bristles will work for cleaning open-geared tuners. An old toothbrush is ideal.

Once the gears are clean, leave them until any remaining solvent has evaporated, and then lubricate before re-installing them on the guitar.

Lubrication

Various lubricants are recommended for tuning machines. I prefer to avoid using any form of grease or oil, or petroleum jelly, on open tuners, as there is a risk of particles of dirt and grit being picked up by the gears, which is likely to increase wear and shorten the life of the tuners. A better option is a dry lubricant. Pencil 'lead' is actually graphite, which is a good lubricant, and can be applied directly onto the gears with the pencil. A more high-tech solution is a PTFE or Teflon dry lubricant such as Tri-Flow.

After application, turn each tuner through several rotations to distribute the lubricant. A hand or powered string winder tool will speed up this process.

squirting a solvent (naphtha or alcohol) under the casing, or by immersing the tuner in a small bath of solvent. In this case, it is best to avoid immersing the buttons in case the button material is attacked by the solvent. Open gear tuners (including most side-plate tuners) can be cleaned with an old toothbrush and a little solvent, turning the tuner button to give access to all parts of the gears.

Using a soft pencil to apply graphite to the tuning machine gears.

Maintenance 43

CHAPTER 4

Setup

What is setup?

Performing a setup on a guitar involves adjusting the string heights above the fingerboard (action), setting the relief, checking and adjusting the intonation, checking that the tuning machines operate smoothly, and that the nut slots and saddle are correctly shaped. The objective is to ensure that the guitar can be easily tuned, plays in tune over the whole fingerboard, is not too difficult to fret, and does not buzz when played hard. Every player will have a slightly different technique and strength of stroke, and hence their own idea of what is the ideal setup. This is particularly true of action, which is always a compromise between playability and avoiding fret buzzes. Fret levelling and re-crowning might not be considered a setup procedure, but it is sufficiently interconnected with the relief and action adjustments that it is best included in this section, rather than treating it as a repair job. It is important to carry out the various setup procedures in the correct order, as some adjustments will change other setup measurements and you can end up having to repeat parts of the process.

Order of setup procedures:

1. Fret levelling and crowning
2. Relief adjustment
3. Nut action adjustment
4. Saddle adjustment
5. Intonation adjustment

Fret levelling and re-crowning

Accurately levelled frets are an essential part of a good setup. If the top surfaces of the frets are not level, then it will be very difficult to set the action to a comfortable level for playing without introducing fret buzzes. In fact, we are not aiming for a perfectly flat line along the top of the frets, but rather a very slight curvature, or relief, as described below. Ideally, the tops of the frets will lie on a smooth curve, with no individual fret tops lying above or below that line.

There are two ways to approach this: we can either make the top surface of all the frets perfectly flat and then introduce a slight curvature either from the tension of the strings or by adjusting the truss rod, or we can just level the frets locally once the correct curvature is established. The first method is better, as levelling frets locally can lead to 'chasing' high or low frets up and down the fingerboard.

The fingerboard is usually very slightly curved, so when a string (or straight edge) rests on the first and 15th frets, there will be a small gap between it and the fret near the centre.

Initial assessment

There are two stages to checking how level the tops of the frets are. Some idea of the straightness of the fingerboard can be assessed by just sighting along it at a shallow angle. Any severe curvature should be visible and give an indication of what work needs to be done.

For a more accurate assessment, rest a long straightedge on the tops of the frets along the line of one of the strings. This can be done with the strings on and at tension, but it is usually easier to get an accurate idea of the overall shape of the fingerboard if the tension is removed.

If there are any gaps of greater than about 0.3mm, then the frets cannot be levelled without making them too low. In this case, all the frets will need to be removed and the fingerboard planed flat before re-fretting (*see* Chapter 7).

The straightedge should ideally rest on the tops of all the frets with no gaps. If there is some relief, then there will be a gap between the frets and the straightedge, largest near the centre of the fingerboard and getting progressively smaller towards the ends.

Now move on to checking the frets in more detail. A fret rocker is a handy tool for this, but you can do the same job with two or three different-sized engineer's squares if you have them. Place the square across the first three frets, along the line of a string. It should not rock as you transfer pressure from one end to the other of the square. If it does, then the middle of the three frets being checked is too high relative to the others. This is a very sensitive measurement, and even if you cannot feel any movement, you will hear the square tapping against the outer frets as it rocks.

At this point it is not possible to determine whether any error is due to the middle fret being too high, or one of the outer frets being too low, or a combination of the two. Continue to check the frets in this way all the way up the fingerboard.

Initial assessment of the fingerboard can be achieved by sighting along it. Any severe curvature should be immediately apparent, but more subtle problems will require accurate measurement.

When measuring relief, the straight edge needs to lie along the line of the string, otherwise any curvature across the fingerboard will affect the measurement.

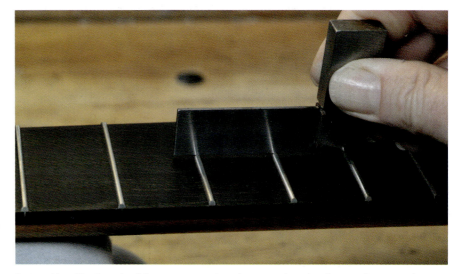

Fret rocking. The length of the square needs to be more than the distance between the outer frets. If the fingerboard has any curvature across the width, make sure the square is aligned along the line of the strings.

If *either* of these tests shows that the tops of the frets are not level, then follow the fret levelling procedure below. If the fret rocker test reveals no individual high or low frets, and there are no gaps with the straightedge test more than 0.1mm, then the frets do not need levelling and you can move on to the next part of the setup (relief adjustment).

Levelling

You will often see diamond stones used or recommended for levelling frets, but in general it's best to avoid these. A levelling beam should ideally be 18–25mm wide, and 350–400mm long, although a shorter beam can also be useful (about 250mm). The problem with wider levelling beams is that it can be difficult to use them evenly on radiused fingerboards, and they will tend to remove the twist that is built into most classical fingerboards. It is very easy to make your own levelling beam using a length of 18mm thick plywood (or any stable hardwood), with one edge planed accurately flat; 240 grit abrasive paper is stuck to this edge using double-sided tape. Try to find a tape that can be removed cleanly, as the abrasive will need to be replaced periodically.

Remove the strings and check again the flatness of the fret tops with the straightedge. If the guitar has a truss rod, first adjust this to minimise the overall curvature of the fretboard.

Before starting work, use masking tape to protect the fingerboard between the frets. Alternatively, you can use a fret mask, but taping the fingerboard gives some added security against accidentally marking it while working on the frets. Next, mark the tops of all the frets with permanent marker pen. This will make it easy to see when you have just touched the tops of all the frets with the levelling beam.

Attach a fresh strip of abrasive to the levelling beam and start working on the frets. Take care to always keep the beam

I made this levelling beam from an old piece of beech. One edge is planed accurately flat, and the abrasive is stuck to that edge with double-sided tape. The flatness is periodically checked with a straight edge.

Masking tape protects the fingerboard between the frets, and a blue permanent marker pen is used to mark all the frets before levelling. Other colours of marker pen are available.

Levelling the frets. The marker pen makes it very easy to see when the tops of all the frets have been touched.

Setup **47**

You can clearly see the flattened tops of the frets where the colour of the marker pen has been removed.

with a fret crowning file to recreate a smooth curve.

Go over the frets again with the marker pen to cover the parts exposed when levelling. Now work along the length of each fret in turn with the crowning file. If using a dual grade crowning file, or two files of different grades, start with the coarse grade.

Adjust the angle of your Anglepoise lamp until the flat area on the top of the fret can be clearly seen.

Work as evenly as possible along the length of the fret and watch carefully as the marked line on the top of the fret gets narrower. If the flat along the top of the fret varies in width, work a little more on the wider areas. This is easy to do if the fingerboard is radiused, but if

aligned with the string paths by changing the angle of the beam very slightly as you work across the tapered fingerboard.

Work slowly and methodically, working evenly across the width of the frets. Continue until the top of every fret has been touched by the leveller – this should be easy to see as a clear line where the marker pen colour has been removed.

Re-crowning

Removing material from the tops of the frets during levelling will have left a flat area, which now needs to be rounded

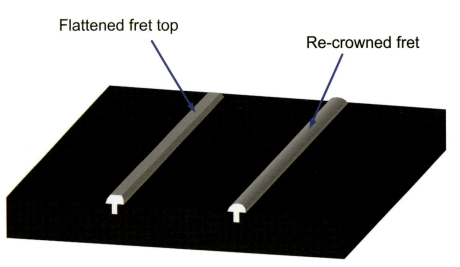

The amount of flattening resulting from levelling the frets should be minimal. If any of the frets have had much more material removed than shown in the drawing, then it may be necessary to completely re-fret the fingerboard.

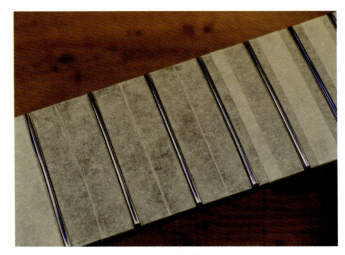

At this stage you can see that areas of some frets have only a fine line of marker pen left, whilst other areas still require more work with the crowning file.

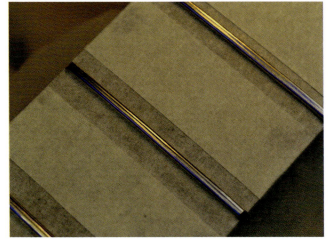

Leaving a fine line of marker remaining along the tops of the frets ensures that none of the frets have been lowered after the levelling process.

it is flat, a curved crowning file will help. Keep going until there is just a very fine, even line left along the top of the fret.

If you have to remove a lot of material from some of the frets, or if too much material was taken off any of the frets when re-crowning, you may need to repeat the process of levelling and re-crowning. This time very little material will need to be removed from the frets, and you can switch to a finer grade of crowning file if available.

Polishing

Now remove the filing marks created by the levelling beam and the crowning file. If your levelling and crowning tools are fairly coarse, start with a medium grit abrasive paper. I usually use 240 grit paper for levelling, and a 300-grade diamond crowning file, so I can start with 320 or 400 grit abrasive and be sure of removing all the filing marks quickly.

Wrap a strip of abrasive paper round your two middle fingers, gripping each end with your index and little finger.

Working along the length of the fingerboard, lightly sand all the frets just enough to remove any coarse filing marks. This action will round off the very small flat left on the top of the frets from the crowning process. Try to work evenly along all the frets. Avoid too much smoothing as this could affect the levelling. When working on new frets, use the same technique to round off any sharp edges on the bevels.

Repeat this process with a finer grade of abrasive paper, then switch to 0000 grade wire wool for final finishing. To achieve a shinier finish on the frets, use Micro-Mesh through all grades up to 12,000.

Remove the tape on the fingerboard (if used), and condition it with lemon oil as described in Chapter 3.

400 grit Abranet abrasive works well for initial cleaning up of the recrowned frets.

Working lengthwise along the fingerboard to smooth the frets, removing the filing marks, and rounding any slight flats left on the tops of the frets.

0000 grade wire wool will leave a smooth, clean finish to the frets. For a more polished look, Micro-Mesh can be used.

Relief adjustment

Relief is a measure of how much the top surface of the fingerboard (strictly speaking the top of the frets) deviates from a perfect straight line. Setting the relief correctly will allow the guitar action to be set as low as possible before any fret buzzes occur. Because of the complex way a guitar string vibrates, the amount of clearance needed between the strings and the frets to avoid buzzing will vary depending on where the string is fretted, where it is plucked, and how strongly it is plucked. Nylon strings vibrate with a greater amplitude than steel strings, so in general both the relief and the string height will be set higher on classical guitars than steel-string acoustic guitars.

Guitars with a truss rod

Most acoustic guitars have a threaded steel bar (truss rod) inserted into the neck beneath the fingerboard which allows the amount of relief to be adjusted. Most classical guitars do not have truss rods, although they are becoming more common. To adjust the relief on a guitar without a truss rod usually requires working on the fingerboard or the frets.

There are two basic types of truss rod used in acoustic guitars – one-way (single-action) and two-way (double-action).

As the name suggests, a one-way truss rod is only able to apply tension to the neck in one direction, opposing the tension of the strings. The tension of the strings will act to pull the neck upwards, creating a slightly concave curvature to the neck (positive relief). The one-way truss rod is set into the neck below the fingerboard and is firmly anchored at one end. The other end of the rod is threaded and fitted with a nut and washer. Tightening the nut increases the tension in the rod, acting to pull the neck downwards. Overtightening the truss rod will create a convex curvature to the neck (back bow), and effectively make the guitar unplayable.

A two-way truss rod can be adjusted in both directions. The most common design uses two rods (or one rod and one flat plate) connected together at both ends. One rod is threaded and has an adjustment nut at one end, which changes the length of that rod. This forces the other rod to bow forwards or backwards, causing the neck to bow in the same direction.

With both types of truss rod, the adjustment can be either at the nut end of the neck (accessible through a hole in the top of the headstock) or at the heel end (adjustable through the soundhole). Adjusters at the nut end of the neck usually have a cover plate over the adjuster hole – remove this to locate the adjuster. First determine the correct tool to adjust the truss rod. This could be a hex socket, or an Allen key, or even simply a screwdriver. Make sure you have exactly the right size tools for the job. Trying to adjust a truss rod with the wrong size hex socket, Allen key or screwdriver is likely to result in damage to the adjuster, requiring the complete truss rod to be removed from the neck. If the adjuster is at the heel end of the neck, it is sometimes difficult to find, being buried well back from the edge of the soundhole. In this case, a specialist tool designed for that particular guitar might be needed. Some electric guitars

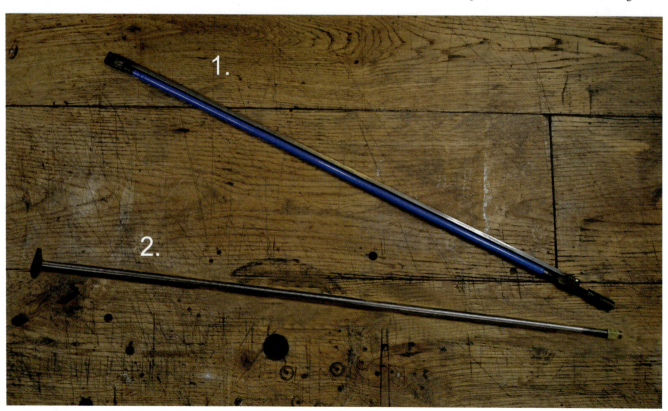

1. Two-way truss rod adjusted with an Allen key. 2. One-way truss rod adjusted with a hex socket.

than the frets, but it is actually the tops of the frets you are interested in. If the frets are so badly worn that they affect the measurement, then they need to be either levelled and re-crowned or replaced anyway. First check that the guitar is correctly tuned. If it is not, then the tension will not be correct, which will affect the relief.

To use a straightedge, place one end on the 1st fret, and the other end on whichever fret it reaches. Nearly all steel-string acoustic guitars (and an increasing number of classical guitars) have a radiused fingerboard. Make sure the straightedge is accurately aligned with one of the strings, otherwise any curvature across the fingerboard will affect the measurement. If using a string, hold it down at the 1st fret and between frets fourteen and fifteen. It is helpful to have a capo placed at the 1st fret to keep two hands free – one to hold the string down at the 14th fret, and the other to measure the relief.

Now measure the gap at around the 7th fret, or wherever the gap is largest. Measure between the top of the fret and the bottom of the string (or straightedge) using a set of feeler gauges. The correct amount of relief will depend on the type of guitar, and player preference, but for a steel-string guitar will normally be in the range 0.05mm to 0.15mm, and for a classical 0.1mm to 0.25mm.

Before making any adjustments, determine which direction you need to turn the adjuster to obtain the correct amount of relief. In the vast majority of cases, turning the adjuster clockwise will tighten the truss rod, which will in turn pull the neck down and against the string tension, and hence reduce the amount of relief. Turning it anti-clockwise will loosen the truss rod, which will allow the string tension to pull the neck upwards (one-way truss rod) or pull the neck upwards itself (two-way truss rod), which will increase the relief.

If there is no gap, or the gap is too small, then the truss rod needs to be loosened (anti-clockwise). If the gap is too

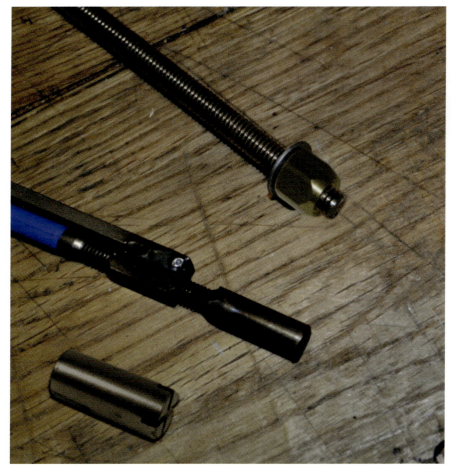

Single action truss rods are most commonly adjusted using a hex socket. Most two-way truss rods require an Allen key. The Fender type adjuster shown is normally only found on electric guitars.

One end of the straight edge is resting on the first fret, and the other at around fret 14. The relief is measured where the gap is greatest – usually between the 5th and 7th frets.

even require the neck to be removed to access the truss rod adjuster.

To measure the relief, either use a long straightedge (350–400mm long), or you can simply use the strings themselves. Notched straightedges are not really necessary. The idea is that you can measure the surface of the fingerboard itself rather

The capo holds the strings down on the first fret. One hand frets the string at the 14th fret, whilst the gap is measured with a feeler gauge.

The feeler gauge that gives a snug fit between the fret and string (or straight edge) will indicate the exact clearance.

large the truss rod should be tightened (clockwise). Make small adjustments initially (less than a quarter turn) and measure frequently to check the change in relief. The adjuster may be difficult to turn, but you should not need any more leverage than a standard size Allen key. Exerting excessive force will risk breaking the adjuster or stripping the thread, resulting in a costly repair job. There is often some slack (backlash) in the adjuster. If it feels very loose to turn, take up the slack until you feel some resistance and then make the necessary adjustment.

After setting the relief, it is worth checking it again after a day or two, as there is often some movement after the truss rod has been adjusted.

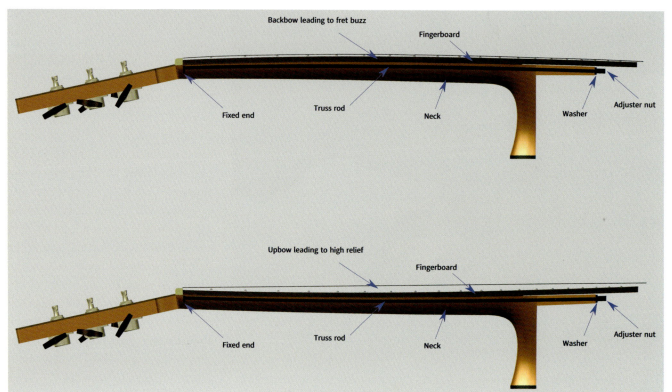

In the upper diagram, the truss rod has been over-tightened, leading to backbow (curve exaggerated). This will at best cause some fret buzzing and can make the guitar unplayable. The lower diagram shows upbow, and in this case the truss rod needs to be tightened to pull the neck down against the tension of the strings.

Guitars with no truss rod

Most classical and some steel-string acoustic guitars do not have a truss rod. They may still have some form of reinforcement, in the form of a steel or carbon-fibre bar inserted into the neck under the fingerboard, but these do not allow any adjustment.

In this case, small changes to the relief can be made by working on the frets, but if the adjustment required is more than about 0.2mm, then this would make some of the frets too low. To make larger adjustments, it is necessary to remove the frets, plane the top of the fingerboard to the correct profile, and then re-fret. Another option is to apply heat and bend the neck/fingerboard to the correct profile. Setting relief on a guitar without a truss rod is beyond the scope of 'maintenance' and will be covered in Chapter 6.

Nut adjustment and replacement

The nut on an acoustic guitar serves two purposes – to set the correct separation between the strings at the head end of the fingerboard and to set the correct height (action) at the lower fret positions.

If the string spacing is incorrect, then a new nut will have to be made (*see* below).

Adjustment of the string height at the nut can be achieved by either lowering (or raising) the whole nut, or by lowering individual string slots. Raising individual string slots is not recommended, as the materials usually suggested to 'fill' the slots tend to be too soft and will wear more quickly than the nut material itself. As with all setup procedures, the exact values used for nut action will vary depending on the type of guitar and preferences of the player.

The best way of measuring the action at the nut is to press the relevant string down between the 2nd and 3rd frets, and then measure the gap between the top of the 1st fret and the bottom of the string using feeler gauges. This method is preferred over just measuring the height of the string unfretted, as the measurement is independent of the height of the saddle and can therefore be set in isolation.

Table 1 gives the acceptable range of values for nut action for each string, for both classical and steel-string guitars. A value of 0.0mm means *just* touching.

Table 1: Typical nut clearances for nylon and steel-string guitars

String	Clearance at 1st fret Classical	Clearance at 1st fret Steel-string
E	0.15–0.25mm	0.10–0.17mm
A	0.10–0.20mm	0.07–0.14mm
D	0.05–0.15mm	0.04–0.12mm
G	0.10–0.20mm	0.03–0.10mm
B	0.05–0.15mm	0.05–0.12mm
E	0.00–0.07mm	0.00–0.04mm

Measure the clearance at the 1st fret for all the strings and compare them with the values in the table. If all the measured values are higher than those in the table, then the whole nut can be lowered by carefully removing material from the underside. If any of the measurements are too low, then either make a new nut or raise the whole nut slightly using a shim.

Lowering the nut height

Loosen the strings enough to allow the nut to be removed without over-stretching the strings. On some guitars, the nut will be glued in position, but this is usually only a small dab of glue to prevent the nut falling off and getting lost. It can usually be removed by giving the nut a light tap with a small hammer and punch, but take care not to damage either the nut or the surrounding wood.

Before starting to remove any material, measure the height of the nut accurately on both the bass side and the treble side and make a note of the measurements.

When removing material from the bottom of the nut, it is important to do so evenly, and to keep the bottom face flat and square to the sides. If you have a jig for sanding the bottom of the nut, use this, but with care the same result

This method of measuring the nut action is preferred over simply measuring the height of the string above the fingerboard, as it is independent of the fret height, and also the height of the saddle.

A small length of hardwood is ideal for gently tapping out nuts that have been glued in. No more than a small dot of glue should be used, making it easy to release.

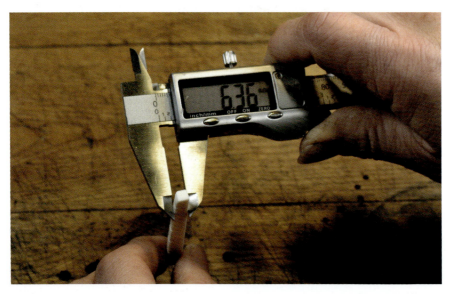

Accurately measure the height of the nut before making any adjustments. This makes it easier and quicker to achieve the correct height, and reduces the risk of overshooting, and having to make a new nut.

of 0.3mm and you wish to reduce that to 0.15mm, a reduction of 0.15mm is needed, and you would have to reduce the height of the nut by 0.3mm. As the desired measurement is approached, switch to the finer grade abrasive.

If the individual string heights need to be reduced by different amounts, then you should only remove enough from the bottom of the saddle until one string is at the correct height. The rest of the adjustments will need to be made to the individual string slots.

Reducing the height of individual string slots requires a suitable nut file. Each string will have a different diameter, and the string slot should match this diameter so that the string is neither too loose nor too tight in the slot. This can be achieved either by having a number of different size files for each string size, or by using one or two tapered round files and just using the part of the file with the correct diameter.

Another option is to cut the slots with a square file so that the string sits in the 'V' of the slot, which will give a secure anchor for any size of string. Some makers and technicians think that there is an increased risk of the string binding in this type of slot, but I haven't had any problems with it.

Loosen the string being worked on just enough to make it easy to lift it out

can be achieved with just a file or flat sanding block. It is possible to plane nuts and saddles, but if they are made from bone then they will blunt the plane blade very quickly.

Use double-sided tape to fix one sheet of coarse grade (120 grit) and one sheet of finer grade (320 grit) abrasive to a flat block of wood.

Start sanding the bottom of the nut, and regularly measure the height of the nut to see how much material has been removed. You will need to remove approximately twice as much height from the nut as you want to change the clearance at the 1st fret. So, if your initial measurement gave a clearance at the 1st fret

Resting the side of the nut against a small block with a square edge will ensure the base is kept square.

54   Setup

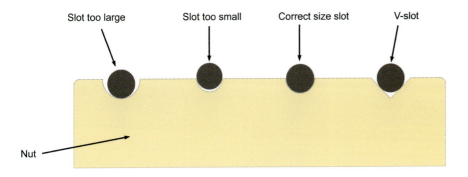

An oversized slot will allow the string to move sideways, and a slot that is too small will cause the strings to bind. A V-shaped slot will accommodate any size of string and is the best practical solution.

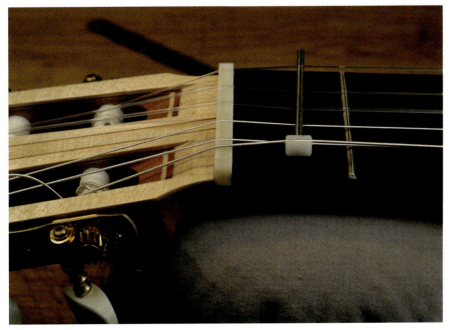

A string lifter makes easy work of holding the string out of the way whilst adjusting the slot.

The correct angle for filing the string slots – the file should be held at an angle between that of the head and that of the fingerboard. For the wound strings, lowering the angle closer to parallel with the fingerboard will reduce the risk of the string windings catching on the edge of the slot, but take great care not to go lower than this.

of the slot and rest it on the top of the nut (or in the adjacent string slot).

With the string out of the slot, start filing the base of the slot. The angle at which you hold the file (and hence the angle of the slot) is critical. Too low and the open string will buzz (this type of buzz sounds a lot like a sitar). Too high an angle and the wound strings will catch on the edge whilst tuning the string, making a clicking sound, and preventing accurate tuning. The correct angle is just slightly downwards from the plane of the fingerboard towards the head.

Return the string to its slot regularly to check progress and make very small adjustments when you are close to the required clearance. Repeat this procedure for each string using the correct size of file.

Raising the nut height

If *any* of the string clearances at the 1st fret are too low, then you will have to either make a new nut or raise the whole nut by shimming it. As when lowering the nut, first measure the height of the nut accurately on both the bass side and the treble side, and then make a note of the measurements. Various materials have been suggested for shims, but I find the best option is a piece of hardwood veneer. Although it is not strictly necessary to glue the shim to the bottom of the nut, there is a risk of it being lost when the nut is removed. Veneers of between 0.3mm and 0.6mm thickness are readily available, and maple veneer is a reasonable colour match to a bone nut.

Cut a slightly over-sized piece of the veneer and glue it to the underside of the nut using cyanoacrylate (CA) glue. Press the nut down onto the veneer on a smooth flat board, ideally with a piece of PTFE sheet on it to prevent the nut/veneer sticking to it. Once the glue has set, carefully trim the veneer up to the edges of the nut. It might take a few

Some tape on the benchtop reduces the risk of gluing the nut and veneer to the bench. Careful trimming of the veneer with a scalpel will make a neat job.

applications of CA glue to get the veneer to stick well to the nut, but a light spray of accelerant will speed up the process.

Unless the veneer was exactly the correct thickness for the adjustment needed, you will now need to reduce the height of the nut to give the correct value for each string as described in the previous section.

Making a new nut

Nuts (and saddles) can be made either from bone or from a synthetic material such as Corian or Tusq. Bone is preferred in most circumstances for nuts and saddles, but synthetic materials will generally have better uniformity, which can give a more balanced response for a saddle with an under-saddle pickup. The material used for the nut is less critical as it functions mainly to anchor the strings, whereas the saddle also has to transmit the string vibrations to the bridge, and hence to the soundboard.

Start with a suitably sized nut blank and make the bottom surface flat and square to the sides using a sanding block as described above in 'Lowering the nut height'. Next, make the front surface (adjacent to the fingerboard) flat, also keeping it square to the base.

Now reduce the thickness of the nut blank until it is a sliding fit into the nut slot. Switch to the finer grade abrasive as you approach the correct size. Once you have a good fit, reduce the length of the blank until it matches exactly the length of the slot, making sure both ends are flat and square to both the sides and base.

To mark the approximate string height, take a standard wooden pencil and plane or sand it lengthwise to create a

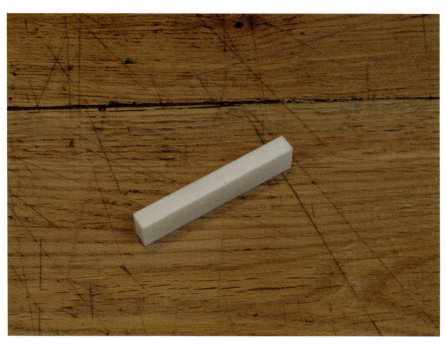

Bone nut blanks are available in different sizes from luthier suppliers, so try to obtain one that is only slightly larger than needed.

You can plane bone, but it tends to blunt the blade very quickly, so I prefer to use a sanding block.

When fitted perfectly, the nut should be easy to remove, but should not fall out of the slot when the guitar is turned upside down.

The halved pencil rests on the top of the first two frets and gives a good approximation of the correct depth for the slots.

The ends of the nut are left square at this stage, to facilitate marking of the string positions. The top surface is slightly angled back, and the front edge is left about 0.5mm above the pencil line.

flat surface level with the tip of the pencil lead. Place the nut in position and lay the pencil flat on the first two or three frets, then mark a line along the front surface of the nut.

Now remove the nut from the guitar and file the top surface of the nut down to about 0.5mm above the marked line. Do not round the top edges at this point, as they are needed for accurate referencing for the string slot marking.

Now mark the string slot positions on the top of the nut. The spacing will be determined by the width of the nut, the type of guitar, and the preferred distance of the outer strings to the edge of the fingerboard. Nut slot spacing rules are available from luthiers' suppliers, but these are not necessary, and will often employ proportional string spacing, which is not desirable in most circumstances. Strings should be equally spaced centre-to-centre, rather than having equal gaps between the edges of the strings.

On a classical guitar, the space from the 1st string to the edge of the fingerboard should be greater than from the 6th string to the edge. I normally aim for 4–4.5mm on the treble side and 3–3.5mm on the bass side (measured to the centre of the string).

Subtract the outer string spacings from the nut width and divide the result by five to give the space between each string centre. For example, given a typical classical nut width of 52mm

Setup **57**

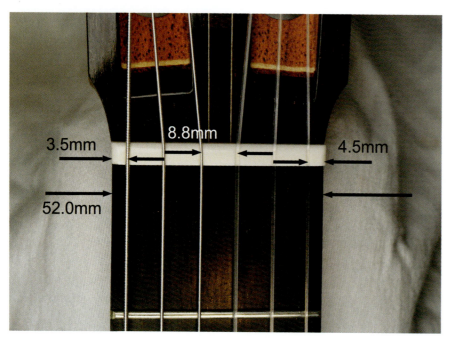

Typical string spacing for a 52mm nut width on a classical guitar. The first string is given more clearance to the edge of the fingerboard than the sixth string, as it is more prone to slipping off the edge of the fingerboard during playing.

and edge spacings of 4.5mm (treble) and 3.5mm (bass), that gives a string spacing of 8.8mm:

$$(52 - 4.5 - 3.5)/5 = 8.8$$

On a steel-string guitar, the spacing to the edge is usually the same on bass and treble sides, at about 3mm. For a nut width of 46mm and edge spacings of 3mm, that would give a string spacing of 8mm:

$$(46.0 - 3.0 - 3.0)/5 = 8.0$$

It is possible to simply measure the spacing with a rule and mark the string slot positions with a pencil, but I use a combination of digital caliper and scalpel for greater accuracy. First set and lock the caliper at the correct dimension for the space from the edge of the nut/fingerboard to the centre of the 6th string. This will be between 3–3.5mm for a classical, and between 2.5–3mm for a steel-string guitar. Locate one jaw of the caliper on the top edge of the bass side of the nut and rest the other jaw on the top. Held in this position, mark the top of the nut with the scalpel.

Now set the caliper for the 5th string, which will be the spacing from the edge to the 6th string, plus the centre-to-centre spacing (for example, 3.5mm + 8.8mm = 12.3mm for the classical). Mark the position of the 5th string with the scalpel and then repeat for the remaining string slot positions.

Whichever type of file you are using for the string slots, it is best to start with a fine square or triangular file. This will locate in the marks made with the scalpel to ensure that they are started in exactly the right position.

File just enough into the top of the nut to give a good starting cut for your chosen nut file for each string slot, and to locate the strings well enough for the final string height adjustments. Now position the nut back in its slot and place the strings in position in their slots. Tension the strings just enough to make

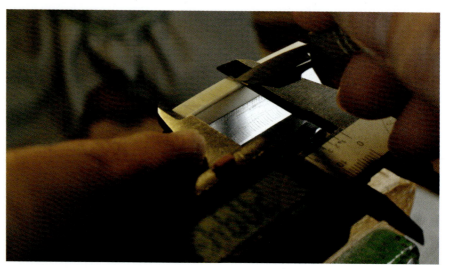

Marking the position of the 4th string slot on the nut. The combination of scalpel and vernier or digital caliper is a very accurate method for marking the positions.

A pencil has been used here to make the scalpel marks more visible. The corner of a square file will locate easily into the marks made by the scalpel.

Starting the slots with a square file will ensure that the slots follow the marked positions accurately. Once the slots have been started, you can switch to your preferred nut slot file.

This small vice was made specifically to hold nuts and saddles. A small file is used to round the back of the nut.

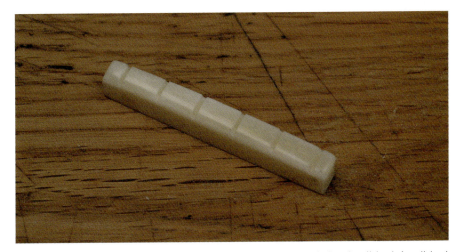

Finished nut. The ends have been rounded, and the surface sanded and polished. A polished finish isn't necessary, but looks good.

it easy to lift it out of the slot and rest it on the top of the nut.

Now continue to lower each of the string slots in the nut to the correct heights as described above in 'Lowering the nut height'. Be careful to keep the angle of the slot correct, just slightly downwards from the plane of the fingerboard towards the head. Once all the strings are set to the correct heights, loosen the strings enough to slide the nut out from its slot. Now file the top surface down to the point where the depth of each string slot is about half the diameter of the string – that is, when the strings are in position, about half of the string is above the top surface of the nut. Round the back edge of the nut to a smooth curve.

Using the correct size file for each slot, slightly round the back edge of the slot downwards so that the string will fall smoothly away towards the tuner rollers. Take care not to touch the front edge of the slots.

Now round the ends of the nut enough to make the guitar comfortable to play in the first position. Finally, go through progressively finer grades of abrasive paper to smooth the top and edges of the nut to the desired finish.

Saddle adjustment and replacement

Now that the relief and nut action are correctly set, you are ready to move on to adjusting the saddle. The saddle on an acoustic guitar transmits the vibration of the strings to the bridge, and then to the soundboard. It also sets the correct height (action) of the strings at the higher fret positions. This height should always be measured at the 12th fret. The action should be set to a height that makes the guitar comfortable to play, but without any buzzing when played hard.

Adjustment of the string height at the 12th fret is achieved by lowering or raising the height of the saddle. As with

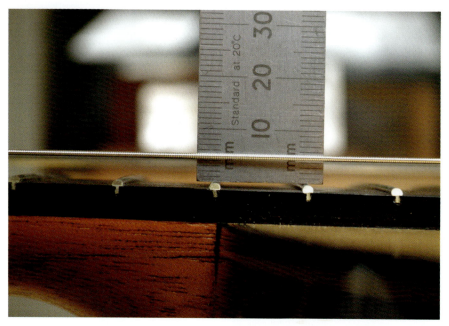

Using a steel rule to measure action. The scale must be viewed at the correct angle, with the rule just touching the string. A more accurate measurement can be obtained with a commercial action gauge, or the calibrated tapered wedge described in Chapter 2.

for classical, flamenco and steel-string guitars.

Measure the action at the 12th fret for the outer strings and compare them with the values in the table. If all the measured values are higher than those in the table, then the whole saddle can be lowered by carefully removing material from the underside. If any of the measurements are too low, then either make a new saddle, or raise the whole saddle with a shim.

Lowering the saddle height

Loosen the strings enough to allow the saddle to be removed by sliding it out sideways from under the strings. If it is too tight in the slot to slide out, remove the strings completely and lift it out.

Before starting to remove any material, measure the height of the saddle accurately at both the 1st and 6th string positions, and make a note of the measurements.

As with the nut, it is important to remove material evenly from the bottom of the saddle, and to keep the bottom face flat and square to the sides. If you have a jig for sanding the bottom of the saddle, use this, but with care the same result can be achieved with the flat sanding block previously made for lowering the nut.

the nut action, the exact values used will vary, depending on the type of guitar and preferences of the player.

Measure the action at the 12th fret for both the 1st string and the 6th string. With the string tuned to pitch, measure the gap between the top of the 12th fret and the bottom of the string using a commercial action gauge, or a homemade one as described in Chapter 2. A steel rule can be used, but will not be as accurate. Table 2 gives the acceptable range of values for action at the 12th fret for the bass and treble E strings

Start sanding the bottom of the saddle and regularly measure the height to see how much material has been removed. You will need to remove twice as much height from the saddle as the required change in action at the 12th fret. So, if your initial measurement gave an action at the 12th fret of 3.8mm, and that needs to be reduced to 3.5mm, you will need a reduction of 0.3mm and would have to reduce the height of the saddle by 0.6mm. As you approach the desired measurement, switch to the finer grade abrasive.

If the action on the bass side needs changing by a different amount to that on the treble side, then you need to remove more from one end of the saddle than the other. This is achieved by working off the end of the sanding block, starting at the

The saddle should not fall out of the slot but should be easy to remove.

Table 2: Typical 12th fret action for classical, flamenco and steel-string guitars

String	Clearance (Classical)	Clearance (Flamenco)	Clearance (Steel)
Bass E	3.5–4.3mm	2.5–3.8mm	2.2–3mm
Treble E	2.6–3mm	2–2.6mm	1.8–2.2mm

Accurately measuring the height of the saddle at marked positions on the treble and bass sides will make it easier to remove the exact amount of material needed to lower the action to the correct height.

Using a small block with a square edge to ensure the base of the saddle remains square to the sides. A plane could be used initially if a large adjustment is required.

Raising the saddle height

If the action at the 12th fret is too low, then either make a new saddle or raise the whole saddle by shimming it. Shimming the saddle is not normally recommended, as it can interfere with the transmission of vibrations to the bridge. If done correctly, any effect will be small, but it is a relatively small amount of work to make a new saddle from scratch.

As when lowering the saddle, first measure the initial height accurately, making a note of the measurements. A piece of hardwood veneer can be used as a shim, and this can be glued to the bottom of the saddle and trimmed in the same way as described for the nut. The thickness of the shim needs to be at least twice the increase in action needed at the 12th fret.

Unless the shim was exactly the correct thickness for the adjustment needed, you will have to reduce the height of the saddle to the correct value as described in the previous section.

Making a new saddle

The best material for saddles is bone, but they can be made from Corian, Tusq or other synthetic materials. Synthetic materials are sometimes preferred for guitars with under-saddle pickups.

Start with a suitably sized saddle blank and make the bottom surface flat and square to the sides using a sanding block as described previously. Next, make one side flat, keeping it square to the base. Now reduce the thickness of the saddle end that needs more material removed, and gradually working the whole saddle onto the block. Check regularly that the base of the saddle remains flat along its length and square to the sides.

When you have reached the correct height, re-fit the saddle, and bring the strings up to pitch. Repeat the action measurement at the 12th fret and make further adjustments to the saddle if necessary.

To achieve a perfect fit, the bridge blank initially needs to be thicker than the slot, particularly if it has rough-sawn surfaces like this one.

guitars tended to use a flat compensation across all the strings of about 2mm, which was a good average. Steel-string acoustics need more compensation, and there is a more significant difference between the amount needed for the 1st string and the 6th string. These therefore usually have a sloped saddle with about 2.3mm compensation for the 1st string and 5.5mm for the 6th string.

In recent years, guitar makers have attempted to improve the accuracy of intonation by calculating the compensation needed for each string individually. For steel-string acoustic guitars, this usually means the saddle has two slopes, with a step between the 2nd and 3rd strings. This step allows for the switch between the plain 2nd string and wound 3rd string. Similarly, on a classical guitar, there are two slopes with a step between the 3rd (plain) and 4th (wound) strings.

Checking intonation

The simplest way to check the intonation of a guitar is to compare the harmonic at the 12th fret with the fretted note in the same position. Play the harmonic at the 12th fret and adjust the pitch until it is exactly in tune for that string. Now play that string fretted at the 12th fret, taking great care not to pull the string sideways or exert pressure in either direction along the string (both of which will slightly shift the pitch). If the intonation is correct, then the tuner will read the same value for the note fretted at the 12th as for the harmonic. If the note fretted at the 12th fret reads sharper than the harmonic, then the string needs more compensation. If it is flatter, then the string needs less compensation.

This method does assume that a) the string is not defective, and b) that the 12th fret is accurately positioned. With modern manufacturing methods for strings, and most factories and luthiers either using machines or jigs to cut fret slots, these are rarely a problem. However, if the amount of compensation seems to be correct for the string and it is still out of tune at the 12th fret, then it is worth checking both.

You can check for a defective string in two ways. The simplest is to just replace the string with a new one, carefully checking the intonation error before and after the change. If the error remains unchanged, the string is unlikely to be the problem. Alternatively, remove the string and replace it with the ends switched round. If the string is the problem, the intonation error should change, and the string should be replaced.

Checking the accuracy of the 12th fret position is trickier. If it is incorrect, then the normal method for identifying the scale length (nut to 12th fret distance multiplied by two) will give the wrong result. If the 12th fret position is wrong, then there is a good chance that some of the other fret positions will be incorrect as well, so you cannot rely on any one fret position. The best way to accurately find the intended scale length is to measure the position of every fret as accurately as possible and plot the results on a graph against the correct fret positions for your best estimate of the actual scale length (using Microsoft Excel or similar). Find the gradient of the best fit trend line passing through the origin. Multiplying the gradient by your estimate should give the correct scale length for the guitar, or at least the nearest approximation possible.

Adjusting intonation

Small intonation errors can be improved by reshaping of the saddle. If the fretted 12th fret note for any string is sharp relative to the harmonic, then the leading edge of the saddle for that string needs to move away from the nut, increasing the string length slightly. If the fretted 12th fret note for any string is flat relative to the harmonic, then the leading edge of the saddle for that string needs to move towards the nut, decreasing the string length slightly.

If there is no room on the saddle to move the leading edge in the required direction, then the whole saddle will need to be moved. This involves filling the existing saddle slot and routing a new slot in the correct position on the bridge.

Bear in mind that any adjustment to the leading edge of the saddle may lower the height slightly, which will in turn lower the action. If the adjustment is likely to lower the action too much, then a new saddle will need to be made.

The leading edge of the saddle can be filed at the angle shown to increase the amount of compensation, either for the whole saddle, or for individual strings.

To increase the amount of compensation for an individual string, file the front edge of the saddle at about 30 degrees to the vertical until the leading edge has moved back about 0.25mm. Check the intonation again, repeating until it is correct.

Reducing the amount of compensation for an individual string is only possible if the leading edge is not already at the front surface of the saddle. File the back edge of the saddle, maintaining a smooth curve, until the leading edge has moved forward about 0.25mm. Check the intonation again, repeating until it is correct.

Repeat this procedure for all the strings and then re-check both the intonation and action at the 12th fret.

If the intonation of all the strings is incorrect in the same sense (that is, all are sharp, or all are flat), and there is insufficient room to adjust them all with the existing saddle position, then the whole saddle will need to be moved.

Filling and re-routing the saddle slot

This procedure is only likely to be needed when the bridge has been poorly positioned or when converting a guitar from right- to left-handed (or vice-versa).

First make a strip of wood to fill the original saddle slot. The wood used should match that of the bridge closely in colour and density. Adjust the width of the insert until it is a close, sliding fit into the slot. If it is too tight, it will be difficult to press into the slot once the glue has been applied. Trim the ends to the exact length of the slot. Now plane the bottom surface of the insert, making sure it is perfectly flat and square to the sides. When in place, the insert should protrude slightly above the level of the slot. Glue the insert into the slot, ensuring that it is seated firmly into the bottom. If the saddle slot is closed at the ends, use the minimum amount of glue needed, otherwise it will be difficult to press the insert fully home. Clean up any glue squeeze-out and leave to dry.

Once the glue is fully dry, plane the top of the insert down until it is exactly flush with the top of the bridge, finishing with a fine abrasive.

It is possible to make the new slot with hand tools only, but it is usually easier to get a uniform width of slot with a perfectly flat base by using a router.

Measure and mark the new slot position accurately. Ensure that the new position will allow each string to be intonated correctly within the width of the slot. You will need two boards, or one large board with a cut-out in it for the bridge, to act as a firm base for the router. Tape or glue cork or felt pads to the underside of the boards to protect the finish of the soundboard. The outer edge of one of the boards needs to be flat, as you will be using this as an edge guide for the router. Position this board so that the flat edge is accurately parallel to the new slot you will be cutting. The padded ends should rest on the edges of the guitar and be securely but carefully clamped in place. The other board should be clamped on the other side of the bridge, close enough to the first board so that the base of the router comfortably reaches across the gap. The two boards need to be level so that the base of the router does not rock – you will need to adjust the padding on the second board to achieve this.

Now set up your router with an edge guide and adjust the guide until the router bit is exactly aligned with the new slot position. Move the router along the length of the slot to check the position at both ends and adjust the angle if necessary. Fix end stops to the boards to limit the travel of the router to the correct length for the saddle. Position the router with the cutter at one end of the new slot, and clamp, screw or glue a stop positioned against the router base onto one of the boards. Repeat for the other end of the slot. It should take two or three passes to reach the correct depth for the slot. The general rule is that the depth of each cut should be no more than the diameter of the cutter. Smaller cutters tend to clog very easily, particularly in rosewood, so check and if necessary clean the cutter after each pass.

Once you have reached the required depth, check the slot carefully before removing the clamps and boards, as it will be very difficult to align them accurately enough if any more routing is needed.

Make a new saddle and fit as described earlier in this chapter.

Setup for routing a new saddle slot. This wooden base is in two parts but could be made from a single piece. It has cork glued to the underside to protect the soundboard finish and is clamped in position. It is better to have the clamps positioned at the edges of the guitar to avoid putting pressure on the soundboard.

CHAPTER 5

Body and Plate Repairs

Body and plate work comprises repairs to cracks, dents, separated joints, and loose/detached braces and linings in the main plates of the soundbox, that is, the top, back and sides. Cracks are one of the more common issues faced by the repairer, and the different types of crack and repair methods will be dealt with in some detail.

Crack repairs

Causes of cracks

There are three main causes of cracks in a guitar body:

1. Impact damage
2. Low humidity
3. Poor construction

Impact damage is usually the most difficult to repair effectively, as there will often be breaks across the grain of the wood. An impact will also frequently result in a combination of cracks, dents and tears in the wood fibres. Cracks due to low humidity or poor construction will normally be along the grain. This type of crack can often be repaired invisibly.

Impact damage can be caused in a number of ways, and I always advise customers to keep their guitars in a case whenever they are not being played. This is particularly important in households

This crack was caused by an impact – probably to the bridge. Low humidity may have been a contributing factor, causing stresses in the wood that allow the fibres to pull apart when further stressed by an impact.

The area adjacent to an ebony fingerboard is the most common place to find cracks caused by low humidity. Ebony shrinks more than most other woods as it dries out, and this puts stress on the soundboard, causing it to crack in a line along the edge of the fingerboard.

with small children and pets! Players will often say that they like to keep their guitars to hand, but it only takes seconds to remove a guitar from its case, and the consequences of a guitar being knocked off its stand can be severe. Some years ago, I had to replace the entire soundboard on one of my guitars that had been knocked from its stand by the owner's dog.

The effect of low humidity is covered in some detail in Chapter 3, but essentially these cracks are the result of shrinkage across the grain of the wood as it loses moisture to the surrounding atmosphere. Such cracks are mostly quite narrow, but in older instruments, or instruments constructed in too high a humidity, they can be wider and require splinting.

Poor construction methods are unlikely to cause cracks themselves but can do so in combination with other factors. For example, construction at too high a humidity will make low-humidity cracks more likely. Braces or bridge patches glued across the grain of the soundboard can concentrate stress at their ends, increasing the risk of cracks developing at these points – particularly in the event of an impact.

Repairing closed cracks

Closed cracks are those where there is no perceptible gap between the two sides of the crack. These are often difficult to see and can only be identified by pressing down on one side of the crack to create a slight step between the two sides. Because they are difficult to spot, they are often only noticed when repairing other damage in the same area.

Because of the closed nature of the crack, it can be difficult to get enough glue penetration to effectively repair it. CA glue is often recommended for this type of crack, as it is available in very low viscosity (thin) formulations which will wick into the crack. This can be effective on dense, dark-coloured hardwoods, but I do not recommend it for softwoods or light-coloured hardwoods. The problem with light-coloured woods is that some formulations of CA glue will leave a yellow stain where it soaks into the wood. This stain can take weeks or even months to appear, and there is nothing you can do to remove it. CA glue is also not particularly effective when gluing softwoods, as it tends to wick into the wood itself leaving little or no glue in the crack. It is also not reversible, and although one might think that you would never want to re-open a repaired crack, the general rule with repair work is that it is better not to do anything that cannot be undone in the future.

Thinned Titebond (a specialist wood glue) can be effective, but the best choice for this type of crack (and most others) is hot hide glue. Hide glue can be thinned a little more than usual to help penetration into the crack, but if too much water is added the glue will lose strength. If the crack can be reached through the soundhole, then applying some gentle pressure with a finger can help to open the crack very slightly. Repeatedly opening and closing the crack slightly whilst working the glue in to the crack with your other hand will allow the glue to penetrate further into the crack. Care is needed not to press too hard and risk opening the crack further.

In the case described here, the wood on one side of the crack has become lodged underneath the wood on the other side. Although not strictly a closed crack, this is just a slight complication, in that the wood needs to be manipulated to get the two sides level before gluing. From this point on the repair is the same as for a closed crack.

Prepare the hide glue, making it a little thinner than normal. Have the glue pot

Various types of hot hide glue are available, and most can be used for repairs. This glue comes in granular form, which is soaked in water for a few hours before being heated.

A crack along the grain of the wood will sometimes be level, but in this case the broken fibres on one side of the crack have been caught under the other side, leaving it stepped. This is not the same as the stepped cracks dealt with later in this chapter, as simply manipulating the wood on either side of the crack will be enough to make it level again.

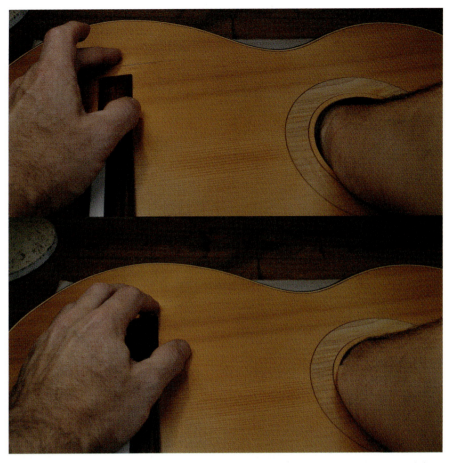

close to the guitar so that you can work quickly. If you work too slowly with hide glue, it will start to gel, and will not penetrate into the crack.

Before gluing, this particular crack needs to be levelled. This is done by reaching in through the soundhole, and gently working the wood on either side of the crack, by applying pressure both from the inside and on the outside.

Surrounding the crack with some low-tack masking tape will help you find the crack if it isn't very visible, and also reduce the amount of glue spread.

Clean the inside surface around the area of the crack by wiping with a clean cloth dampened with alcohol or naphtha.

Repeat with a fresh section of cloth until it comes out clean. The cleats will not adhere well to a dirty or oily surface. For the best results, lightly sand the area where the cleats will be glued. The best gluing surface is a fresh one.

If you can reach, position one hand inside the guitar to apply pressure to open the crack slightly. Using a brush,

This crack was just about reachable through the soundhole. If you are not able to reach it, you will have to manipulate it from the outside, but this is usually less effective.

Locking forceps are handy for holding a balled-up cloth for cleaning hard-to-reach parts inside the guitar. The cloth is dampened with alcohol.

Body and Plate Repairs

Repeatedly applying and releasing upwards pressure below the crack will open and close it, helping to work the glue into the crack.

The repaired crack is almost completely invisible in the photo, although slightly easier to see under close inspection with the naked eye.

apply a liberal amount of hide glue over the crack. Work the glue into the crack with the brush, whilst simultaneously applying and releasing pressure from the inside.

This should help to work the glue into the crack. Once you are satisfied that there is enough glue in the crack, wait for 2 minutes, and then remove the excess glue from the outside using a slightly dampened cloth. Remove any masking tape and leave for 24 hours for the glue to fully cure before proceeding.

Cleating

It is always advisable to reinforce crack repairs with two or more cleats. Cleats are small, thin pieces of wood, usually matching the wood being repaired. The cleats are glued across the crack, with the grain direction perpendicular to the line of the crack. The shape of the cleats is not critical, but I often make mine rectangular, as this aids correct alignment. For short cracks (40mm or less), one cleat at each end of the crack is normally sufficient. For longer cracks, use enough cleats so that the gap between each one does not exceed about 40mm.

There are three commonly used methods used to hold the cleats in position whilst gluing.

- *Finger pressure*
  The simplest method of gluing cleats is simply to hold them in position with a finger until the glue grabs. This is only practical when using hide glue, which has a short grab time, and it can be difficult to position the cleat accurately.
- *Threading*
  The second method involves passing a fine thread for each cleat through the crack along its length. The main advantage is that it can be used to level stepped cracks, and this method will be described later in this chapter.
- *Rare-earth magnets*
  This is my preferred clamping method, as rare-earth magnets are simple and effective, and available in a range of sizes and shapes.

Hide glue is normally the preferred adhesive, but sometimes a longer open time is needed for positions that are difficult to reach, and in these cases I will often use Titebond. If an even longer open time is needed, then Titebond Extend can be used, which has an open assembly time of up to 15 minutes.

The wood used to make the cleats should ideally match the wood being repaired (spruce in this case). Cleats should be between 1.5 and 2mm thick, or slightly thicker if the crack is stepped. Chamfering the edges will reduce the chance of creating stress points at the edges, and look neater. The size will

These cleats have been cut with the grain running diagonally across the square, and will be glued in with the grain perpendicular to that of the soundboard and the crack.

For small, square cleats I use these bar magnets. They allow you to orient the grain in the exact direction needed.

The grain direction of the cleat has been marked on the top of the outer magnets to ensure correct orientation.

depend on the crack being repaired, but generally I make mine about 7mm square or, when appropriate, rectangular (around 10 × 5mm).

Make sure that the gluing surface of the cleat is flat and clean. If cleating a crack in the sides, it may be worth shaping the gluing surface to match the curve of the sides, but this is only usually necessary on tight curves such as the waist or a cutaway.

Select appropriate magnets for the size of cleat, either rectangular ones, or alternatively use two cylindrical magnets. A second magnet (or pair of magnets) of the same size will be placed on the outside. Apply a small amount of double-sided tape to the back of the cleat and fix the magnet(s) to the tape. Do not use too much tape, as this will make it difficult to pull the magnets from the cleat when the glue has dried. Use just enough to keep the magnets fixed to the cleat until it is in position.

Check the polarity of the outer magnets so that they will attract when in position. Place the outside magnets across the crack in the position where you want the first cleat. Hold them in place with masking tape.

Before applying any glue, perform a dry run to check that the magnets hold. Look inside the guitar with an inspection mirror to make sure the cleat is correctly positioned and not fouling on a brace. It may be necessary to change the position of the cleat slightly to avoid braces or other obstructions. When the position is correct, remove the cleat and internal magnets, apply glue to the surface of the cleat, and replace the cleat.

Be sure to use enough glue. If there is a lot of squeeze-out, it will be difficult to clean up, but this is preferable to not having enough glue in the joint.

If the position needed for the cleat is too far into the body of the guitar to be reached with your hand, then use something to extend your reach. Plastic forceps can work, but alternatively you can fix the magnets to a strip of wood of suitable length using a piece of Blu

The outer magnets are taped in place over the centre of the crack, with the marks showing the grain direction perpendicular to the crack. The cleat has been fixed with double-sided tape to the inner magnets, and glue applied.

An inspection mirror with a built-in LED light is good for checking the position and orientation of the cleat. You can also use a phone camera held through the soundhole.

Second cleat after removing the magnets and tape. This guitar was built by a group of my students, who all signed the inside of the soundboard.

Tack or double-sided tape. Hold the piece of wood loosely, and when the magnets get close enough to the ones on the outside of the crack, they will be pulled into position. Once the magnets have grabbed, you should be able to pull the stick away without dislodging the magnets and cleat.

When the magnets are removed, the double-sided tape sometimes stays stuck to the cleat. This can be removed by rubbing with your fingertip.

Wait for the glue to dry before moving on to the next cleat, as the magnets from the previous cleat will pull the next ones out of position. Once the glue is dry, remove the outside magnets first, then reach in and pull the inner magnets from the cleat. If they are difficult to reach, then a steel rule can be used to remove the magnets.

Now repeat the process for the remaining cleats (in this case, just one more).

Once the glue has dried, remove the magnets, and check the position of the cleats inside the guitar using a mirror or phone camera.

It is possible to remove and reposition cleats if needed, but it can be very awkward, so it pays to take the time to ensure they are perfectly positioned before gluing.

If the crack is repaired quickly before any further damage to the exposed edges, and before any dirt can build up around the crack, the end result should be almost perfect (as in this case), and certainly acceptable without requiring any refinishing.

If the crack is not glued perfectly level, or if there is damage to the edges of the crack, then further work will be required, and also some refinishing. It is better if this can be avoided, as the aged colour of the soundboard wood will be lost when sanded level, and will then need some difficult colour matching before and during the finish touch-up.

Repairing open cracks

Open cracks need a different approach to closed cracks. If the gap is not too wide, then it should be possible to clamp the body of the guitar in such a way as to close the gap. You may also be able to close the gap by humidifying the guitar. Closing wider gaps by clamping should *not* be attempted. Firstly, there is a risk of damaging the guitar further if too much clamping pressure is used. Secondly, the glued crack will be under tension after the clamps are removed, and there will be a significant risk of the crack opening up again at some point. See the section on splinting later in this chapter for dealing with cracks that are too wide to be safely clamped.

The question arises – how wide is too wide? I will normally try to close the gap with just hand pressure, not using any clamps. If I can close the gap effectively without too much force, then there will not be too much tension in the wood after the repair. For cracks in the sides, an F-clamp can be used, or a go-bar deck. Cracks in the top and back are more difficult to clamp. Depending on the position of the crack, a sash clamp could be used, but these are quite heavy and cumbersome. Another option is to use rope or rubber straps to wrap the guitar. Many luthiers use this method of clamping to glue the bindings and the back to the guitar during assembly.

The procedure for repairing open cracks is the same as for closed cracks, with the exception that the crack needs to be closed by clamping while the glue sets. The crack should be cleated while the clamps are still in place to reduce the risk of the crack opening up again when they are removed.

On darker coloured woods like this Indian rosewood, a good aesthetic repair is generally easier to achieve. Damage like this on a maple guitar would be much more difficult to repair invisibly, particularly the fracture across the grain.

the grain. The cracks along the grain should be possible to repair invisibly, but the fracture across the grain will be more difficult.

The first job is to try to get the depressed part of the side as level as possible, without causing any further damage. If you can easily reach the damage through the soundhole with your hand, then manipulate the damaged parts to make them level. If the damage is too far inside the guitar, then a pusher stick can be used.

Reaching in through the soundhole with the pusher stick, locate the position of the depressed part, and apply gentle pressure outwards with the stick (or your fingers if you can reach). At the same time, manipulate the wood on either side of the cracks to try to level it. This

Side cracks

Cracks in the sides of the body can be difficult to repair, as there are often stresses in the sides that can cause the crack to open significantly, or to be stepped. If the crack is near the base of the guitar, access can also be a problem.

CA glue is an option with hardwoods, and thin formulations can wick into the wood very effectively. Thinned Titebond could also be used, but in the case described here, hot hide glue will be used. This can be thinned a little more than usual to help penetration into the crack.

The damage shown here was caused by an impact against a table corner. There are two cracks along the grain, joined at one end by a fracture across

This stick was made using an offcut from a bog oak fingerboard blank. The rubber tip helps provide some grip, and also conceals a magnet, which helps to locate the correct position to push.

Body and Plate Repairs

One hand manipulates and supports the damaged area whilst the other pushes with the stick from the inside.

After the first attempt, the depressed part of the crack is closer to being level with the surrounding wood, but more work is needed.

and trying to avoid lengthening the cracks or introducing further fractures across the grain. If all goes well, the wood will be completely level before gluing, but very small steps can be acceptable, and are preferable to causing further damage.

In this case just a few very slight steps could be felt in places across the cracks, but probably less than the thickness of a piece of paper.

Now prepare the hide glue, making it a little thinner than normal. Place the glue pot close to the guitar so that you can work quickly.

Apply the glue liberally with a brush, flexing the wood with your fingers as you work, to help the glue penetrate into the cracks.

When there is enough glue in the crack, wait for a few minutes, and then remove the excess glue from the outside using a slightly dampened cloth. Leave for 24 hours for the glue to fully cure before proceeding.

At this point, the appearance of the repair should already be good. The cracks along the grain are barely visible.

A photo taken with a reflection from a lamp shows that the fractures across the grain are still apparent, but further improvement should be possible.

We now need to reinforce the damaged area with cleats. In this case, the best option is to use long cleats which

is sometimes easy, but often the part of the side that has been pushed in will be wedged under the adjacent parts of the side. Keep flexing the wood and working it until a satisfactory result is achieved.

In this case, it was easy to get some improvement, but the parts were not completely level.

Continue working the wood, slowly coaxing the parts level, using the minimum amount of pressure needed

Some more gentle coaxing gives an almost perfectly level result. The better you get the parts back into position, the less work will be needed to complete the repair, and the better the final result.

Dedicated glue heaters are available, but I use an old saucepan on a hotplate. When I'm ready to glue, I place the pan on the workbench, and the hot water keeps the glue warm enough until the repair is done.

Applying the hide glue with a brush. Slightly thinner glue will help penetration into the cracks, but too thin and it will lose strength. Keeping the workshop reasonably warm will increase the time before the glue starts to gel.

span both cracks. The cracks are not very long, so two cleats should be sufficient.

The inside surface around the damage should be cleaned by wiping with a clean cloth and alcohol or by sanding the surface, as the cleats will not adhere well to a dirty surface. If you can reach, sanding with some abrasive wrapped around a flat block will also help to remove any slight steps that could reduce the strength of the cleat glue joints.

The type of wood used for the cleats for the back and sides of the guitar is not critical. In this case, cedrela (Spanish cedar) has been used. For this repair, magnets will be used to hold the cleats in place while gluing, and these will also make it easy to position the cleats correctly.

Three magnets have been taped in position over the crack. The first cleat will be positioned close to the cross-grain fracture.

The cleat has been temporarily fixed to the internal magnets using double-sided tape, and Titebond glue applied to the gluing surface. For internal repairs it is worth being generous with the amount of glue you use, as some of it can get scraped off in the process of positioning the cleat through the soundhole.

Hopefully, you will be able to reach in through the soundhole far enough to get the magnets and cleats in position. If not, use a steel rule or similar to extend your reach. Stick the magnets and cleat to the end of the ruler and move it around inside the guitar to get the cleat as close as possible to the correct position. The internal and external magnets should finish the job by pulling together and clamping the cleat in the right position.

Once the cleat is in place, carefully remove the masking tape on the outer

Once the excess glue is cleaned off, the repair looks pretty good from some angles, but the cross-grain damage is still clearly visible when viewed with a light reflection from behind. More work will be needed to give a better aesthetic result.

Body and Plate Repairs

Smaller cleats could be used for each crack, but it is more practical to use longer ones that span across both. It is also easier to make sure they are aligned correctly perpendicular to the cracks.

The glue squeeze-out will be much less visible when it dries. For these repairs, it is always better to use a little too much glue than not enough.

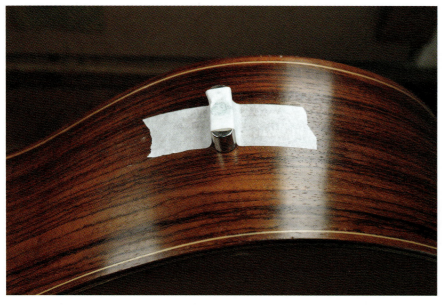

The great thing about using magnets to clamp the cleats is that it allows for perfect alignment. In this case, three magnets are used, and positioned across the cracks.

When fixing the cleat to the magnets, you need to be sure that the orientation of the magnets is correct so that they attract the outer magnets with the correct alignment.

cleats, being careful not to dislodge the magnets.

Leave the magnets in place until the glue has fully gone off. This is partly to avoid any chance of pulling the cleat off, but also because until the magnets from the first cleat have been removed, it will be very difficult to position those for the second cleat.

Once the glue has fully dried, remove the external magnets, and then reach in through the soundhole and carefully pull the internal magnets away from the cleat. The double-sided tape should come away with the magnets, but if not, peel it off with your finger.

Now repeat the process for the second cleat, which will be positioned close to the other end of the cracks.

Once both cleats have been glued, the external appearance of the damaged area can be improved if needed.

Looking again at the result of the repair, there is some evidence of the cracks along the grain, but the most obvious problem is the cross-grain fracture.

After a light sanding with 220 grit abrasive wrapped around a flat sanding block, the cracks along the grain are less visible, but the area next to the cross-grain fracture is obviously not level.

To make it easier to identify the poles of the magnets, I mark the north pole on each one with some permanent marker. Adjacent magnets have alternating pole directions, otherwise they will repel.

Both cleats are glued in place. Note the missing support blocks for the ends of the back braces – these may have been omitted during construction or may have fallen off. A repair job for another day.

At this stage, the repair is stable and effective, but needs some cosmetic improvement. The fracture across the grain is particularly noticeable.

After a light sanding with a flat block, it is clear to see that the repair was not completely level. The finish has been removed everywhere except in the depressed part of the damage.

Further sanding of the area has now levelled all of the repair, and also further improved the appearance of the cracks. If it would require removal of too much material to get the repair level, the depression should be filled with a suitable clear filler before final levelling.

There are still some lighter lines where the cross-grain cracks have been glued. These can be improved by adding some fine lines of dark colour. As there is no finish on the wood at this stage, a good option for adding colour is Van Dyck crystal solution. Van Dyck crystals are a traditional wood dye made by dissolving the crystals in water. The depth of colour can be varied by adjusting the strength of dilution, that is, adding more water to reduce the depth of colour. Here, a strong solution has been used to match the rosewood and hide the light areas of the cracks.

A wipe with a very lightly dampened cloth will help the added colour blend in with the surrounding wood.

The last job is to refinish the area that has been sanded back to bare wood. This guitar was French polished, so it is relatively easy to blend in the new finish with some fresh coats of shellac. For an oil finish, a few further applications of oil should blend in the repaired area effectively. A nitro finish may require more work, but the end result is usually acceptable, as the new finish will blend in with the old. Poly lacquer finishes will be more challenging, and it may not be possible to achieve a perfect result without completely refinishing the sides of the guitar. *See* Chapter 8 for more details on finish repairs.

Further sanding with a flat block has made the repair completely level, and after refinishing would yield a satisfactory result, but a little more work will improve things further.

A solution of Van Dyck crystals in water is applied in short strokes across the light-coloured lines left by the cross-grain fracture. A little has also been applied to the cracks along the grain.

At this stage, the repair is almost invisible, but the finish needs more work to attain a full gloss to match the surrounding area.

The only remaining evidence of the repair is the slightly darker colour compared to the surrounding wood. The outer surface of the dark rosewood has become slightly faded, and sanding the area of the repair has revealed the original darker colour. This will become less noticeable in time.

After one coat of shellac, the colour of the repaired area is already much closer to the surrounding wood. After a further two coats of shellac have been applied the repair has almost completely disappeared.

Another three or four polishing sessions builds the shellac up enough to return the damaged area to the original level of gloss.

You can see from the photo that the area that was sanded is now slightly darker than the surrounding wood. This is because over the years, the rosewood has lost some of its colour due to exposure to UV light. In this case the difference is quite small, and over time the colour difference will diminish. An alternative would be to remove all the finish from both sides of the guitar and refinish them completely.

Splinting

When a crack is too wide to close up with gentle clamping, a splint will be needed to fill the gap. Using a splint will avoid any tension being added to the plate and reduce the chance of the crack opening again in the future.

The splint should be of the same material as the wood that is cracked. Ideally, the splint would be made from a piece taken from the same piece of tonewood that is being repaired. This is rarely possible, but if you are repairing your own guitar, and kept offcuts during the build, then these can be used for the splint. Failing that, keeping a good supply of the commonly used tonewoods will increase your chances of finding a close match. The wider the crack, the more important it will be to obtain a good match. Of course, this is a purely cosmetic consideration, and any tonewood of the same or similar species can make an effective repair.

Cracks will generally have parallel sides, but the best result will be obtained by making the splint taper in thickness from top to bottom. This will allow the splint to be easily inserted into the crack, and then pressed down until the crack is completely filled on the outer surface.

This guitar has a very common open crack adjacent to the fingerboard. Ebony will shrink more than most woods as it dries out, particularly if it is not quarter sawn. The shrinking fingerboard puts a lot of tension into the adjacent softwood of the soundboard, and this can often lead to cracks forming along the edges. In this case, there are two open cracks, and it would not be possible to close the cracks with pressure applied across the body of the guitar.

Two spruce splints will be needed to repair the cracks. Once you have selected the wood for the splints, it must be shaped to fit the cracks. Measure the length of the first crack and cut the repair piece a little longer. The depth of the repair piece should be slightly greater than the thickness of the plate being repaired.

Measure the width of the crack at the widest point, and plane, scrape or sand the repair piece to slightly more than this dimension.

The splint now needs to be shaped to fit into the crack as accurately as possible. Most cracks will taper smoothly from nothing at each end to a maximum width near the centre. If (as in this case) the crack ends at an edge such as the purflings, bindings, rosette or end graft, the widest point will be at that end. Occasionally cracks will be irregular in width and require a more complex shape of splint.

I mostly use a cabinet scraper to shape splints. The splint is held on the edge of a flat board, and the scraper is held at a slight angle. This will produce a splint that slightly tapers from a little more than the crack width at the top to less than the required width at the bottom. This will make it easier to fit the splint into the crack. Start scraping at the ends of the splint (or one end if required), and gradually work back towards the point of the splint where the maximum width is needed. The aim is to produce a splint that tapers smoothly from the widest point down to nothing at the position where the crack closes. As you approach the correct width and taper, test fit the splint in the crack, checking where the fit is too tight, and where there are any gaps.

Continue removing material from the tight areas until you have a good fit along the whole length, with just a little

The most common place to find cracks caused by low humidity – adjacent to the fingerboard. Both cracks have flat ends where they meet the purflings and the rosette, but taper to nothing at the other ends.

These splints look like a poor colour match, but even if you were to use some old spruce with more colour, the splints will have to be levelled after they are glued in, which will reveal lighter coloured wood.

A cabinet scraper is the perfect tool for shaping the splint. It allows you to selectively reduce the thickness where needed to get a precise fit.

At this point, the splint fits into the crack, but only just. It needs to be worked more so that the splint can be inserted to almost flush with the soundboard. The pencil mark indicates where the splint will be trimmed to length. As this crack terminates at the purflings, it will be cut straight across with a sharp chisel.

Body and Plate Repairs

Finer adjustments can be made with a cabinet scraper, and usually give the best result, but the sanding stick is also effective, and will smooth out any marks left by the scraper.

When glued, the splint will be pressed firmly into the crack, but at this stage you are just checking that the fit is good. Pressing the fragile splint in too hard will make it difficult to remove without breaking it.

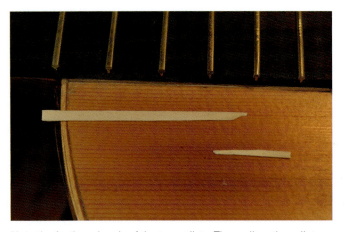

Note the feathered ends of the two splints. These allow the splints to be inserted right up to the fine end of the cracks. The larger one needs a little more trimming in depth, so that it does not protrude too far inside the body.

With hot hide glue you need to work fairly quickly, so make sure you have everything ready before you apply the glue.

of the splint sitting proud of the surface. A small sanding stick can be used for the final fine adjustments if necessary. Don't press the splint in too hard when test fitting, as it will be fragile and easy to break when removed.

When you are happy with the fit, check that the splint does not protrude at all on the inside of the plate being repaired, as this will make it difficult to glue cleats over the repair. If it does protrude, remove some material from the bottom edge of the splint.

For the repair described here, a second splint was made for the other crack in exactly the same way. Both splints are now ready to be glued in place.

Now prepare some hide glue to glue the splints into the cracks. Titebond or other glues could be used, but hide glue will generally result in the cleanest repair, and be more easily reversible if necessary.

Brush the glue generously into the crack, and quickly insert the splint, pressing down firmly, but taking care not to damage it, as it will be very fragile. If there is a second crack as in this case, try not to get any glue in the other crack unless you are planning to glue both at the same time. When the splint is fully in place, repeat for the second splint, and then clean up the excess glue with a wet brush.

Allow the glue to dry fully before continuing with the repair. The splints can then be trimmed flush with the soundboard. In this case, they were carefully pared down with a sharp chisel. This is normally preferable to sanding, which would almost certainly remove some finish, and possibly some wood from the surface of the areas surrounding the splints, which would then require further touching up.

The final part of the repair is to colour the splints to match the surrounding wood as closely as possible. This can be done with stain, or with a coloured finish, or a combination of both.

In this case I started with a weak solution of Van Dyck crystals. The solution was first applied to a test piece of spruce to check the colour match, and adjusted as necessary by adding more water until the desired shade was reached.

If a perfect colour match can be obtained with just the stain, then some clear finish is all that is needed to complete the repair. In most cases, I aim for a slightly lighter colour with the stain,

Splints glued into the cracks. Note that the splints have been pressed further in than they were in the dry test fit. This will compress the splints slightly, allowing them to fill any slight imperfections in the fit.

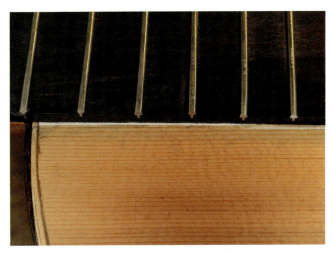

At this point, the colour mismatch is particularly apparent, but the fit is very good, which is all we need for now.

Van Dyck crystals are a natural wood dye made from the husks of walnuts. They provide a very good base for colour-matching to many wood types.

Testing is essential when applying a wood stain. When adding colour with a finish, it can always be removed if it isn't quite right, but stains penetrate into the wood. The first (lower) attempt was clearly too dark, so more water was added to the solution.

A set of high-quality sable brushes are invaluable for colour matching and touch-up work. This brush is fairly fine, but I have two sizes of brush finer than this.

The Van Dyck stain gave a good match to the surrounding wood, but the addition of some dark shellac over the repaired area helped to blend everything in.

Body and Plate Repairs

and then adjust the match with some coloured finish. The stain can be applied to the splints using a fine sable brush.

Once the stain has dried, add some coloured finish to obtain a good match with the surrounding wood. In this case I just used some dark button shellac. For darker woods, or darker coloured finishes, you may need to use a finish with some added pigment (*see* Chapter 8).

For many repairs, the amount of time that needs to be spent on colour matching and touching up of the finish will depend on the overall condition of the guitar. An instrument in pristine condition will show up any imperfections in the colour matching or the quality of finish of the repair. As a rule, it is easier to achieve a perfect colour match by starting with a stain that is a good match in tone, but too light in depth of colour. This gives a good base, and further colour can be gradually added with a coloured finish. If at any point the colour is not acceptable, or too dark, the most recent layer (or layers) of finish can be removed, and the touch up colour adjusted and built up again until a perfect colour match is obtained.

Stepped cracks

Stepped cracks are where the two sides of the crack are at different levels. Cracks where one side is wedged below the other are not treated as stepped cracks, as they will mostly return to level with some manipulation. This was the case in the 'Repairing closed cracks' example above. True stepped cracks are usually the result of tensions in the wood trying to force one side of the crack up or down relative to the other. This is sometimes caused by the bracing, but it can just be tensions in the plate itself.

One of the problems with stepped cracks is that ideally both the crack itself and the cleats should be glued at the same time. If the step is small then this may not be necessary, as the glued crack should hold until the cleats have been added. With larger steps, there is a risk that the crack will pull apart again before you can glue the cleats. If the two sides of the crack can be made level with just moderate finger pressure, then you should be safe to glue the crack and the cleats separately, in which case hide glue is appropriate. If a lot of force is required to hold the two sides level, then it is better to glue the cleats at the same time, and a glue with a longer open time should be used.

Two methods can be used for keeping the sides of a stepped crack level whilst gluing. The first is to use a go-bar deck to apply pressure to the higher side of the crack, adjusting the pressure until the crack is perfectly level. This can be quite tricky to do, particularly if you also need to apply pressure across an open crack to help close it. My preferred method is to use clamps that I have made specifically for this job. They consist of a small block of wood with a flat base, fitted with a violin peg, which is used to tension a thread that passes through a hole in the base of the wooden block, through the

These clamps are simple to make, using a piece of hardwood and an old violin or viola peg. The holes are reamed to match the taper of the peg.

Standard cotton thread is really not strong enough to exert the amount of pressure sometimes needed to pull a stepped crack flat. Polyester is stronger, but this Kevlar thread is best.

crack, and then through a cleat. The base is taped over to prevent it being glued to the repair.

A strong thread is needed, as the amount of force required to pull the two sides of the crack level is often greater than standard cotton thread can withstand.

This large, stepped crack in a spruce soundboard was caused by impact damage, combined with tensions in the wood and bracing. If the step was only due to the wood fibres of one side of the crack being caught under the other, the two sides could be levelled by careful manipulation. In this case, tensions in the wood prevented levelling with moderate finger pressure.

If the go-bar method is used, the guitar is placed in the go-bar deck on some carpet to protect the finish of the back. Flat strips of wood are used to spread the pressure from the go-bars. The length of the go-bars can be adjusted to give just enough pressure to level the crack. If more pressure is needed, more go-bars can be used, but excessive pressure could risk further damaging the soundboard. Once the correct number, length and positions of the go-bars has been determined, they must be removed so that glue can be worked into the crack. When the go-bars have been replaced, any excess glue can be cleaned up. The cleats are then glued in using magnets as described earlier in this chapter, before removing the go-bars. Great care is

For this type of repair, a go-bar deck could be used. Abrasive paper could be taped to the top surface of the blocks to ensure the go-bars do not slip off, potentially further damaging the soundboard.

This stepped crack did not require too much pressure to level. The worst stepped crack I had to deal with was the archtop guitar mentioned in the introduction. At the time I didn't have my homemade levelling clamps, so used a go-bar deck.

needed to ensure the go-bars do not slip off the strips of wood, as they will almost certainly cause further damage.

The peg-clamp method uses a thread to pull a cleat up against the underside of the crack, and at the same time the clamp body presses down on the outside of the crack, levelling the two sides. I recommend using a strong, Kevlar thread for these repairs, but here I have used a black polyester thread for better visibility in the images.

A fine needle is used to pass the thread through the crack and then out

Body and Plate Repairs

Threaded needle. It isn't essential to use a very fine needle, as most stepped cracks are fairly wide.

Be careful not to damage the edges of the cracks when feeding the needle through. If necessary, open the crack a little wider to get the needle through cleanly.

of the body of the guitar through the soundhole.

Pull plenty of length of thread through to make it easier to tie the knots.

The cleats used here are rectangular, with the long edge aligned with the grain of the cleat. This is to make it easier to align the cleat correctly by feel inside the guitar, so that the cleat grain is perpendicular to the crack. A small hole is drilled or punched through the centre of the cleat. This should be no more than 1mm diameter, or the knot can pull through the hole when tensioned.

The thread is passed through the hole in the cleat, and a knot tied in the end. The knot must be large enough to ensure it cannot be pulled through the hole. The other end of the thread (above the crack) is then threaded through the hole in the base of the clamp, and then through the hole in the peg. The peg is wound to take up the slack in the thread. Repeat for the other clamp(s).

From this point on you will need to work quickly. If you are not confident about this, use a slower grabbing glue. Apply the glue to the crack using a brush. The step helps here, making it easy to apply the glue to the edge of the higher side of the crack, but also try to work the glue into the ends, where the step reduces to nothing.

Now apply a generous amount of glue to the cleats – it is likely that some will be lost while positioning the cleat.

Pull the thread through from the outside, guiding the cleat towards the correct position with your other hand. Once the thread is pulled tight from the outside, check that the orientation of the cleat is correct, and adjust if necessary. Now take up the slack using the peg on the clamp and continue to tighten the peg as it pulls the clamp body down onto the top of the crack. Use just enough pressure to pull the crack level. Now repeat for the second clamp/cleat. Two clamps are usually enough to level the crack. More can be used if needed, but decide how many before you start gluing.

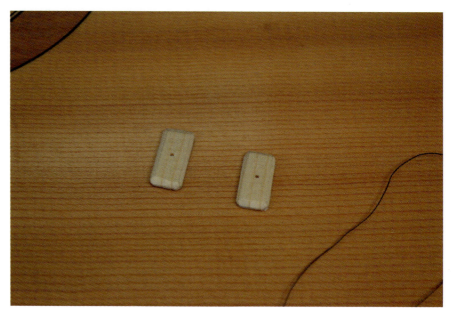

The holes in these cleats were drilled with a 1mm drill bit. It is possible to just push the needle through the wood, but you might need a thimble.

Just two clamps and cleats were used for this repair. If the crack required more pressure to pull it flat, more clamps could be used. A longer crack would not necessarily require more clamps. Provided there are enough to pull the crack level, more cleats can be added later.

Although hide glue sometimes gives a better result for crack repairs, a slower grabbing glue will give you more time to work, so here I am using Titebond, just slightly thinned.

Check inside using a mirror, or a phone camera as used here, to ensure the cleats are correctly positioned and aligned.

When the glue has dried, slacken off the peg clamps, and cut the thread. Cut as close to the surface as possible. If a suitably coloured thread has been used, the remaining end should not be visible.

If the crack pulls perfectly level, then only a minor amount of finish touch-up will be needed. Quite often, as in this repair, there is some damage to the wood fibres on either side of the crack, and it is not possible to pull it completely flat. In this case, level the crack by scraping and/or sanding with a flat block and refinish the area around the crack.

If required, and if you can reach, the cleats can be cleaned up, and the knotted end of the thread removed, by reaching in through the soundhole with some abrasive paper.

As this guitar was French polished, it was relatively easy to repair the finish to make the crack almost completely invisible. When touching up a patch of bare wood with shellac, the technique is to initially apply the shellac to just the area where the finish has been removed. It is very easy to try to apply too much shellac to a small area without giving it a chance to dry. Normally when French polishing a soundboard, you would be covering a relatively large area, so that provided you move around that area evenly, the finish has a chance to dry very slightly before it is gone over again. With a small area this doesn't happen, so just apply

Plenty of glue is applied to the cleat. If you can reach, the worst of the squeeze-out can be wiped away with your finger reaching in through the soundhole.

If the clamps do not immediately pull the crack perfectly level, applying some pressure to the high side of the crack will help.

Body and Plate Repairs

One disadvantage of this method is that you do not get the automatic cleat/grain alignment that you get with magnets. Provided you can reach the cleats through the soundhole, you should be able to adjust these rectangular ones by feel.

The thread can usually be cut so that it is almost invisible when the repair is finished, but in this case, a lighter coloured thread would help.

Some broken wood fibres on this repair meant that the glued crack was not completely invisible. Some light sanding resolved this, but has left a lighter coloured area of the soundboard, which will need to be blended in when refinishing.

Sanding off the knotted ends of the threads is not essential, but is a little neater.

Using a stain to darken the lighter patch can leave an obvious line at the edge of the sanded area. A better solution is to build up more finish in the exposed area, starting with a darker shellac, and gradually blending it in to the original finish.

the polish for a few seconds, and then stop for twenty seconds or so before repeating. This requires patience and self-control! Concentrating on the small area without pausing will just soften the finish too much and lift it off. Using some oil as a lubricant on the French polishing pad will help, but try not to use too much oil.

Once you have a reasonable build-up of finish in the repair area, continue to add shellac, but gradually widen out the area being worked on. Cover at least all the area that was touched by the abrasive when the repair was levelled. Unless there is a good reason not to, I usually continue to increase the area being covered until I am working over the whole plate. This helps to blend the finish, making the repaired area less noticeable.

Damage to laminated (plywood) plates

Type of damage

Many cheaper acoustic guitars (and increasingly some more expensive ones) are constructed with laminated backs and sides. On cheaper instruments, this is primarily to keep the cost of materials low. On more expensive instruments, laminations are used to allow thicker sides to be made, or to create a complex shape for the back, similar to that of a carved cello back.

In either case, laminated backs or sides will make repairs more difficult. When a solid-wood guitar side cracks, the split usually runs along the line of the grain, and the same is true of backs. These cracks can often be relatively easily repaired by realigning the two sides of the crack, gluing, and then cleating to reinforce the crack. Laminated plates fail rather differently. They are generally stronger than solid-wood plates, as the laminations are glued together with the grain directions of individual layers oriented at 90 degrees to the adjacent layers. The result is that although the outer lamination appears to have a grain direction, the plate as a whole doesn't, and any failure will tend to fracture the wood across the grain of the outer layers. These fractures are more difficult to repair than cracks along the grain and are particularly difficult to repair invisibly.

Repair techniques for laminated plates are therefore different, and generally less satisfactory than those used for solid-wood plates. Use of non-traditional glues (for example, cyanoacrylate) and fillers is often called for, and delicate touch-up work is often required to produce a good result.

Laminated side repair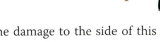

The damage to the side of this guitar was caused by an impact – presumably a fairly heavy one. Although some

Laminated backs and sides are very common on cheaper instruments like this one. Unfortunately, they are becoming more common on higher level guitars (particularly classical guitars), and are much more difficult to repair than solid plates.

of the crack runs along the grain of the outer lamination, there are several fractures across the grain, and the wood has been forced down and wedged below the surface of adjacent parts of the side. This leaves a significant indentation in the side, and making this as level as possible is the first priority.

In this case, the damage is in the lower bout of the guitar, and therefore difficult to reach internally through the soundhole. A hardwood stick as described earlier in this chapter can be used to push the recessed part of the damaged side outwards. Care needs to be taken not to make the damage worse by pushing too hard and further fracturing the laminations. Watch the outside of the damage carefully as you work and stop when the surface is almost level.

If the damage is not too deep, you may be able get the outer surface lamination back into place. In this case the damage was too severe, and there were still some indentations remaining, and some of the lighter inner lamination visible on the surface.

Once the damage has been levelled as well as possible, it needs to be stabilised

After a significant amount of time spent pushing and manipulating the wood, it is a little more level. It is rarely possible to completely level damage as bad as this on a laminated plate.

Although thin CA glue wicks well into fine cracks, it does tend to leave dark lines, which then need touching up if a good aesthetic result is required.

The process of filling indentations with CA glue can be significantly speeded up by using an accelerator spray, but care is needed. Many accelerators are quite aggressive and can cause the glue to bubble and whiten.

harden. Be careful about using accelerators, as they can often cause the glue to bubble and whiten. If you do use one, make sure it is a 'non-blushing' type such as Glu Boost.

Once this glue has gone off, start to fill the indentations with a thicker CA glue. You may need several attempts to fill deeper recesses. Allow the glue to harden fully after each application.

When the indentations are mostly filled, use a medium-grit flat sanding block to level the glue. Take care not to sand through the surrounding finish, erring on the side of caution at this stage to leave a little glue proud of the surface of the plate.

Repeat the filling process where needed, and then level again. When no further filling is required, continue sanding until the surface is completely flat, switching to finer grades of abrasive as you go, and finishing with 400 grit.

It is unlikely that a guitar with laminated back and sides will have a French polish finish (shellac), so there should not be too much risk of sanding through to the wood. Shellac finishes are very thin, however, so this type of repair will almost certainly require some refinishing work (covered in Chapter 8).

Once the damage has been levelled and fine sanded, the difficult work begins. A combination of several different colour tints will be needed to cover the areas where the light-coloured inner laminations are visible, and to disguise as well

with glue before filling the remaining indentations. Thinned hide glue could be used for this, but for laminated plates thin superglue (CA glue) is often more effective. The usual arguments for using hide glue for repairs are less convincing in cases like this, where it is unlikely that the repair will ever need to be reversed.

Apply enough thin CA glue to penetrate well into all the fractures. Leave the glue for long enough to go off fully. Although CA glue generally sets very quickly, if any pools of glue have formed, they will take significantly longer to

Levelling with a flat sanding block will make it very clear if you have any areas that need further filling, as they will not have been touched by the abrasive.

The repair is flat and structurally sound, but not very pretty. Significant improvements are possible, but a perfect result is unlikely.

These Kremer touch-up colours are shellac-based and are available in a wide range of colours. You can usually get by with just four or five different colour shades, which can be mixed to give you the exact colour you need.

A coat of clear shellac finish reveals where the touch-up work is needed. There are still a few light patches, and dark lines both along and across the grain.

as possible the cracks running across the grain of the outer lamination. Further dark shades will be used to imitate the grain pattern of the original outer lamination.

It is advisable to apply a thin coat of finish (in this case, shellac) before starting. This will give a much clearer idea of where the touch-up work is needed.

I prefer to use pigments dissolved in shellac for this process, as any mistake can very easily be removed by just wiping with a cloth dampened with alcohol. The general rule here is to use as little colour as possible. However perfectly you match the colours of the original wood, the appearance will always be different as the pigments will not reflect the light in the same way as the wood does, particularly woods like mahogany which have a 'sparkle' to them.

For the first application, it is best to use a base colour that is a close match to the lightest colour present in the wood, in this case, an orange-brown colour to match the mahogany veneer of the outer lamination. Use the minimum needed to cover any patches of the lighter inner laminations, and to break up the lines running across the grain.

The next stage is to add some grain lines using a darker shade. A very fine brush is needed for this, and again, less is more. It is easy to add more colour later if needed, but difficult to remove any excess without also removing previous applications.

After these first two applications of colour, I normally add some clear finish. The process can then be repeated if the result is unsatisfactory. Remember that adding too much colour will make the repair stand out more, giving it a more obviously 'painted' appearance. When you are happy with the appearance of the repair in terms of colour, add some clear finish over the repaired area so that when it is sanded flat none of the colours are removed. If using a spray finish, enough build-up can be achieved with just a few coats, but French polish will take some time to build up to the required thickness.

The base colour for the touch-up work should be a close match to the lightest colour of the surrounding wood. The 'patches' of light colour will become less visible after the addition of darker, finer lines.

A little too much dark colour was added at this stage. Rather than remove it all and start again, the area was very lightly sanded with a fine abrasive to take away some of the darker colour.

The final result could have been improved by adding further fine details to match the surrounding grain and wood colour. The value and general condition of this particular guitar did not warrant spending many more hours of work trying to achieve perfection.

Loose braces

Most acoustic and classical guitars use a system of braces to strengthen both the soundboard and the back of the guitar. Sufficient strength could also be attained by making the soundboard and back plates significantly thicker, but this would make them very heavy, which would increase the weight of the whole instrument, and also make the soundboard very inefficient. The bracing allows the top and back plates to be relatively thin. The bracing of the soundboard also defines the acoustic performance of the guitar.

If the braces were well glued when the guitar was made, they should never come loose, other than by mechanical damage. Occasionally, not enough care is taken with the gluing of the braces, and they can become detached, particularly at the ends. Loose braces will have an adverse effect on the sound of the guitar, and in some cases will rattle when particular notes are played.

The first task is to identify where the loose brace is. This can be quite difficult and is sometimes a process of elimination. Some form of 'hammer' will be needed to tap the top and back plates – for this I use an old piano hammer, which is firm enough to give a good impact, but the padding prevents damage to the finish.

Tap the plate with the hammer reasonably firmly and listen for a rattle. Work around the area of the plate and find the

The end result is certainly less than perfect, but the repair is stable, flat and would only be noticed on close inspection.

This piano hammer is soft enough not to damage the French polish finish of this guitar, but is very effective at revealing anything loose inside the body.

position where the rattle is loudest. This will normally be the location of the loose brace. Note that when you tap the soundboard, it will cause vibrations everywhere in the body of the guitar, and even the neck and head. Rattles often come from loose gear screws in tuning machines, and it is easy to convince yourself that the sound is coming from the soundboard when tapped. It is also likely that a loose back brace will rattle slightly when you tap the soundboard (and vice versa). Repeat the process for the back of the guitar and try to determine where the loose brace is most likely to be. This can sometimes be confirmed by reaching in through the soundhole and feeling for some movement in the brace, but it is rare to have a brace loose enough to move that easily.

Once you are reasonably confident that the loose brace has been identified, it must be securely glued. It can be challenging working through the soundhole,

Using a glue brush is not always possible. When applying glue to loose braces through the soundhole, a finger is an effective glue applicator.

as it will usually be very difficult to see what you are doing. You will need to work mostly by feel. For the same reason, it is almost impossible to photograph the procedure, so a loose soundboard has been used for the images here.

Body and Plate Repairs

Using your finger, it is easy to locate the corner between the brace and the soundboard by feel. It is also quite easy to locate the *wrong* brace when working through the soundhole, so some care is needed.

Although it is possible to apply the glue with a brush, it will be difficult to judge where to apply the glue. Provided you can reach far enough with your hand, I recommend applying the glue with a finger.

Work the glue along the corner between the loose brace and the soundboard, whilst at the same time flexing the soundboard from the outside. This will help work the glue under the brace. Repeat this on the other side of the brace, and when you have worked in as much glue as you can, run your finger along the corner to remove excess glue. This should leave a nice fillet of glue between the brace and soundboard, which will help keep them bonded if there isn't much glue under the brace.

It is also a good idea to add a blob of glue to the end of the brace (assuming the brace is not set into another brace or the linings).

Applying clamping pressure to the brace while the glue dries is best achieved with a piece of wood acting as a strut between the brace and the back of the guitar (or between a back brace and the soundboard if gluing a back brace).

The length of the stick will need to be adjusted to fit firmly between the loose brace and the facing plate. It should not exert too much force, particularly on the soundboard, as it could cause further damage. Shaping the end of the stick to fit the shape of the top of the brace will help to keep it in place.

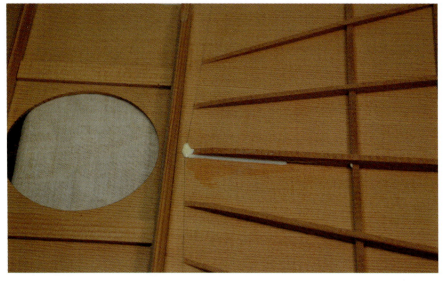

A small fillet of glue can help fix a loose brace when it is difficult to work much glue under the brace. Both the fillet and the blob of glue at the end will be far less noticeable when the glue has dried.

A small piece of wood can be used as a strut to hold the glued brace down. One clamping strut is usually enough, but if much more length of the brace is loose, two may be needed.

Struts used to apply pressure to glued braces are like mini go-bars. They either need to be adjusted in length to fit perfectly, or have some flex in them so that they can be bent to fit.

Dents

Small dents can often be steamed out, or filled, or just left. Some players like to keep their guitars looking like new, whilst others are quite happy for them to show signs of use.

Dents can simply be filled and levelled using the techniques described in Chapter 8. A better result can often be achieved by steaming the dent out of the wood. If the wood fibres have not been broken, this repair is usually very effective and can be invisible, but it is likely that some refinishing will be required.

Typically, an impact from something blunt will be more effectively steamed out than one with a sharp object. A thick, poly finish would have to be removed for the steaming method to be effective, so filling the dent is usually the best option, unless the finish is to be removed anyway.

Steaming a dent

Step 1: This dent was quite small, and no fibres appeared to be broken. This guitar has an oil finish, where steaming tends to be most effective, and requires minimal refinishing work.

Step 2: A drop of clean water is first applied to the dent and left for a few minutes to allow the water to soak into the wood a little.

Step 3: A piece of clean cloth is then dampened with more clean water, and a clothes iron is used to heat the area and create some steam, which helps to expand the compressed wood fibres. Do not let the cloth dry out.

Step 4: The result is very satisfactory, with the dent completely gone. Sometimes it takes two or three attempts, but more than that is unlikely to help further. There is a slight lightening of the wood where the finish has lifted, but this can easily be touched up with some oil.

Step 5: Here we have another small dent, but this time it appeared to be caused by a sharp edge, which has broken some wood fibres, making steaming less effective. It is still worth trying, as it should at least bring the indentation closer to level with the surrounding wood.

Step 6: Again, a drop of water is applied to the dent, and the clothes iron used with a damp cloth to heat it. The dent is reduced in depth but is still clearly visible.

Step 7: Further sanding the dent until the dent disappears would reduce the thickness of the soundboard in that area. In the upper bout this would not be a problem, but in the lower bout it is best avoided. This dent was just lightly sanded, leaving a small mark.

Step 8: Having sanded through to the wood, the finish has been touched up with a simple application of a suitable oil finish. *See* Chapter 8 for more details of refinishing methods.

Body and Plate Repairs

String whip repair

String whips are a very common repair issue on classical guitars. They occur when the string is not attached securely enough at the tie-block. When tuned to pitch, the string slips, and the end of the string whips out of the tie-block holes under high tension, embedding itself into the soft wood of the soundboard. Carbon strings are particularly prone to slipping, and the problem seems to occur more frequently with 12-hole tie-blocks, not because there is a problem with the design, but because players are not always aware of how they should be tied correctly.

Although small, these dents are difficult to repair effectively. One option is to just fill the indentation with shellac, Deft, or CA glue, but this usually leaves a darker colour where the fill is. The alternative patch repair can be more effective, but is difficult to execute well, and if executed badly can end up looking worse than the original damage. It is therefore highly recommended that the repairer conducts several test patch repairs as described below before attempting it on an actual guitar.

Note that this repair is most commonly required on guitars with a thin finish – either oil or French polish. Thick lacquer finishes are more robust and likely to suffer less from string whips, but would be very difficult to repair using this technique. In these cases, a fill is usually the best option.

This typical string whip mark was actually repaired by filling with Deft clear brushing lacquer and then polished over with shellac. The end result was reasonable, but there was an obvious darker area where the fill was. A better repair can be achieved with a patch, but this requires skill and practice to do well.

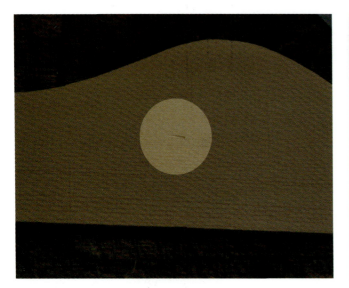

Step 1: An offcut of soundboard wood is used to practise the patch repair. Here a simulated string whip mark has been made by pressing the end of a 1mm drill bit firmly into the wood. For a more challenging repair, the mark can be angled so that it crosses a few grain lines.

Step 2: First a sharp gouge is used to remove material from around the damage. The ideal is to remove *just* enough wood to take out the damaged area and no more. Care needs to be taken with the grain direction, as working against the grain will not give as clean a cut.

Step 3: As the gouge cuts through the wood, it will initially cut deeper under the damage. The angle of the gouge is gradually lowered so that it follows a curve, and starts to cut back towards the surface when passing the midpoint.

Step 4: The end of the cut is the most difficult to get clean, as you will be cutting against the grain as the gouge exits. Here it is essential that the gouge is as sharp as you can get it.

Step 5: The damaged section has been removed, and the edges of the cut are fairly clean, giving a good chance of a successful repair.

Step 6: The repair patch has been cut from the donor wood in exactly the same way. If the same gouge is used, the shape of the underside of the patch should match the section removed around the damage.

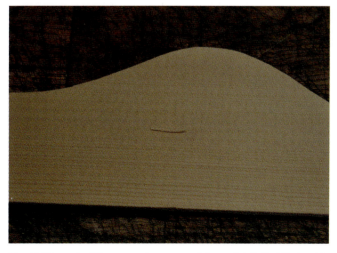

Step 7: The only difference when you cut the patch is that it should be slightly longer and deeper than the hole it needs to fill. This will allow you to press the patch firmly into the hole, compressing the fibres slightly to close any slight gaps.

Step 8: There are a few different gouge shapes you can use. For very narrow areas of damage, I use a 2mm U-shaped gouge. This makes the cuts at the sides of the repair close to vertical, and less visible. For larger areas, a V-shaped gouge is used, allowing the width of cut to be increased as you cut deeper.

Body and Plate Repairs

Step 9: Hide glue always gives the best results for this type of repair. The joins tend to be less visible, particularly at the ends of the cuts.

Step 10: Apply the hide glue generously and have the repair patch ready to place as quickly as possible. Holding it with the point of a scalpel blade works well, as tweezers are more likely to damage the fragile patch.

Step 11: Press the patch firmly into place. I find I have more control using my fingers initially, although it would be better to wear nitrile gloves to prevent getting the repair dirty. Holding the end down with the tip of the scalpel and rolling your finger off the patch minimises the risk of lifting the patch out when you remove your finger.

Step 12: Once the patch is firmly glued in place, place a weight over it, either with tape over the weight, or a sheet of plastic (Teflon is best) so that it does not stick to the repair. Never place a steel weight directly onto a softwood repair, as it will stain the wood.

Step 13: Once the glue has dried, remove the weight. As the repair has been covered with plastic, it should be left for several hours to dry thoroughly before attempting to level it.

Step 14: When the glue and surrounding wood are fully dry, you can level the repair. Start with the taped single-edge razor described in Chapter 8. Scrape gently, taking care not to tear the soft wood of the patch, working from the centre towards the ends. When almost level, switch to a sanding block and fine grade abrasive to make the repair perfectly level.

A refinement of this patch repair is to perfectly align the growth rings of the repair patch with the lines of the existing soundboard. If the growth rings of the soundboard are very fine, there will usually also be relatively low contrast between the summer and winter growth, and in these cases the alignment of the lines in the patch is less critical. Wider growth rings will have higher contrast, and if the repair crosses any winter growth lines, any misalignment will be far more obvious.

The first task is to find a donor piece of matching softwood that has growth rings of the same spacing as the area to be repaired. Start with a piece that has roughly similar spacing of the rings, and then closely inspect the line spacing to find an accurate match over the area needed for the repair. Mark the position from where the patch will be taken with a pencil.

Now cut the patch, carefully aligning the cut with the lines to match the piece removed from the soundboard. Test fit the patch in the hole to confirm the growth lines are perfectly aligned. The patch will be slightly proud of the surface, so you will need to view it looking from directly above to avoid parallax errors in the alignment. It may take several attempts to get a patch with perfectly aligned growth lines.

This practice repair should be carried out enough times to give you confidence in the process before attempting it on a guitar. The main complication with the actual repair is that the soundboard will be finished. The taped razor scraper should allow you to get the patch very close to level with the surrounding finish without damaging it, and the final light sanding should only take a small amount from the finish surface. The patch itself will need finishing, and almost certainly need some colour adding to match the aged colour of the surrounding wood and finish. *See* Chapter 8 for more on colour matching and refinishing techniques.

This damaged area that has been removed crosses two growth ring lines, and the edge is in line with a third. The growth ring spacing of the donor piece is a good match, so it should be possible to align them perfectly.

CHAPTER 6

Neck and Head Repairs

Neck construction types

There are two main classifications of construction types. Most steel-string acoustic guitars use the German construction method, where the neck and body are made separately. Spanish heel construction is used mainly on classical and flamenco guitars. For some repair tasks it is essential to know which type of construction you are dealing with. In most cases, the construction type will be determined by the type of guitar (nylon-strung or steel-strung), but this is not always the case, and needs to be checked, particularly when addressing neck angle problems.

Separate neck/body construction

Used primarily on steel-string acoustic guitars, the body and the neck are constructed separately, and then joined together by one of a variety of methods. The traditional joint is a tapered dovetail, and much has been written about the acoustic advantages of this joint. In fact, there is no evidence that the type of joint used has any significance tonally, and I have never seen any convincing argument as to why it might. The only real advantage is ease of clamping during construction, as the joint pulls itself together when clamped vertically.

Apart from the glued, tapered dovetail joint, other commonly used joints are the glued mortise/tenon, and the bolted mortise/tenon. The latter can have either a bolted or a glued fingerboard. A fully bolted construction has the advantage that it can be very easily taken apart for any necessary adjustments. Other less common joints include a screwed joint, and a simple glued butt joint.

The tapered dovetail is perhaps the most difficult to execute well during construction, although most makers use router jigs these days, significantly reducing the time needed for the task. It is also the most difficult to adjust if a neck reset is needed.

Spanish heel construction

This type of construction is used for most nylon-strung guitars. The main difference is that rather than constructing the body and neck separately before joining the two together, the neck is attached to the soundboard at an early stage of the build, and then the sides are added to the neck/soundboard assembly, and then the back attached to complete the main part of the construction. The build is carried out on a special workboard called a solera, which has an area to mount the soundboard and glue the bracing, and a neck extension which allows the angle of

Although this is a separate neck/body construction, it is slightly different to most, in that the neck will not be permanently attached to the body. The guitar has an adjustable neck, which pivots just under the fingerboard neck extension.

The Spanish build method using a solera, showing the braced soundboard glued to the neck. The lower bout section of the solera is slightly hollowed out, which creates the dome of the soundboard when the braces are glued in.

the neck to be set correctly with respect to the soundboard.

The advantages of this type of construction are that the neck angle is set during construction, rather than having to make fine adjustments to the neck/body joint, and that less material is needed for the heel/body block, keeping the guitar lighter in weight. The main disadvantage is the relative difficulty in correcting neck angle problems later in the life of the guitar, but as we will see below, these problems are not insurmountable. It has also been claimed that the Spanish heel construction is better tonally, as there is no 'joint' between the neck and the body, but as discussed above, there is no evidence to support this claim.

Neck resets and relief correction

Neck resets can be a major undertaking for the repairer. In many cases, the neck needs to be completely removed, adjusted and then reattached to the body of the guitar. There are some alternative techniques that will work in some situations, and these can often be attempted initially, and the results assessed before resorting to a full neck reset.

The first sign of a guitar needing a neck reset is usually very high string action. Excessive relief will by definition be the result of the neck bowing upwards. Although usually accompanied by high action, relief should be corrected by straightening the neck, rather than resetting the angle, as the latter will not address the real problem. If the guitar has a truss rod, then the relief can usually be corrected with a simple adjustment (*see* Chapter 4). If there is no truss rod (as is the case for most classical guitars) there are five methods that can be used to straighten a curved neck:

1. Heating the neck and forcing it back to the desired shape.
2. Removing the fingerboard, adding some reinforcement to the neck, and replacing the fingerboard.
3. Removing the frets (or some of them) and replacing them with frets with a thicker tang.
4. Removing the frets, planing the fingerboard flat (or to the desired relief), and replacing the frets.
5. Removing the frets, planing down the fingerboard to below the level of the fret slots, and gluing on a fingerboard 'cap' with matching wood.

Adding some form of reinforcement to the neck is only necessary if the neck is particularly weak. A good indicator of this will be the difference in the amount of relief measured with and without the strings up to tension. If this difference is greater than about 0.4mm, then it is likely that the neck will need strengthening. This can either be achieved by adding the reinforcement under the fingerboard (usually a carbon fibre bar), or by capping the fingerboard to increase its thickness as described in method 5. The latter method is less intrusive, although it will add some thickness to the finished neck. If the neck is too weak because it is too thin, then this is an acceptable compromise. If the neck thickness is already at or above the maximum that is acceptable for the player, then excessive bending of the neck is likely to be due to poor-quality materials, and the question should be asked as to whether the instrument is worth repairing.

Replacing frets with ones with a thicker tang has been shown to be effective, but it does rely on some trial and error, and also finding fretwire with a suitably oversized tang. It is also likely that the guitar will end up with mismatched frets, as it will be difficult to find identical fretwire with just different sized tangs.

Removing the frets and planing the fingerboard flat, and then replacing the frets, is quite effective for correcting small errors. The method for this is the same as for method 5, but in this case the fingerboard surface is planed just enough to make it flat, and the cap is not required. Using this method for larger curvatures of the neck is not recommended, as it can result in weakening an already suspect neck further by removing material from the fingerboard.

Methods 1 and 5 are generally the most efficient and effective and will be described below in detail.

Heat resetting

Heat resetting of an excessively curved neck is usually the least invasive option for correcting relief. On guitars without an adjustable truss rod it can be effective, but there is some uncertainty about whether it is a long-term solution. Before deciding on this method, you should be sure that the relief is outside acceptable limits. If the relief needs to be adjusted by less than 0.2mm, it can be corrected by just working on the frets, provided they are not already on the low side. If possible, also check for the presence of reinforcement in the neck. Many older acoustic guitars (including some Martins) had a steel bar in the neck (under the fingerboard) rather than an adjustable truss rod. More recently, the use of carbon fibre reinforcing bars has become more common. This reinforcement will make it less likely that the neck will bow under the tension of the strings, but will also make the heat resetting method less effective.

First measure the amount of relief as described in Chapter 4. It is likely that you will get a different reading with the strings up to tension than with no strings on. I usually like to take both measurements, as it can be useful to know how much difference there is between the two.

Record the measurements before moving on to making any adjustments.

Before starting to heat the neck, prepare the clamping setup. You will need a strong, flat bar that needs to be significantly stiffer than the neck itself. This could be a thick hardwood beam, or a 12mm (or thicker) square steel bar. Some spacers will be needed so that the neck can be forced into a slight back bow when clamped. Without the spacers, the most you can do is pull the neck back to flat, and this will not be enough to correct any significant curvature. Spacers of 1.5–2mm are ideal. Something to protect the back of the neck from damage by the clamp is also advisable. The clamp I use is faced with plastic, to which I've added a thick leather pad.

There are various ways to heat the fingerboard, but I find that a domestic clothes iron is perfectly adequate. Place the iron on top of the fingerboard, resting

A straight edge is positioned along the line of a string between the 1st and 13th frets. A feeler gauge is used to measure the gap between the straight edge and the top of the fret, about halfway along, or where the gap is greatest.

A steel bar is laid on spacers between the 1st and 15th frets, or anywhere above the body join, depending on the length of the bar. The spacers allow the neck to be pulled into a slight backbow.

on the frets, and positioned centred on the area of maximum relief. You may need to experiment with heat settings, but I find that the maximum setting on a domestic iron is most effective.

The time needed to heat the neck sufficiently will vary depending on the temperature of the heater used, the thickness of the neck, the contact between the heater and fingerboard, and the amount of relief correction needed. The best indicator is the temperature of the back of the neck (under the iron). There should be a noticeable rise in temperature here, but not too hot to touch, as there is a risk of damaging the finish. This usually takes about ten minutes with my setup.

Once the neck has reached the required temperature, the iron can be removed. The neck should be clamped

A hot air gun can be used to heat the neck/fingerboard, but there is a greater risk of damaging the finish. Heating the frets with an old clothes iron will transfer the heat into the fingerboard, and then the neck. As you are applying heat to the top surface, when the back of the neck becomes warm, you know the heat has gone through the glue joint.

The clamping pressure is applied somewhere between the 6th and 7th frets. If you need to apply more heat with a hot air gun, protect the finish of the soundboard, back of the neck, and the head plate.

using the bar and spacers before it cools. The spacers are placed under the ends of the bar, and on top of the frets. Use sufficient clamping pressure so that the frets touch the clamping bar, but no more. This clamping arrangement is for reducing the amount of relief, which is by far the most common adjustment necessary. In rare cases it may be necessary to correct back bow, or increase the relief, in which case the clamping should be arranged to bend the neck in the opposite direction.

You can check that the neck has been forced into a slight back bow using a straightedge whilst it is still clamped. If it has not, then it is likely that the beam is not strong enough, and it is being bent rather than the neck.

Some repairers like to heat the fingerboard and neck whilst the clamp is in place, using a hot-air gun, but I haven't found this to be necessary in most cases.

Leave the neck clamped overnight, or for at least six hours. Remove the clamp, spacers and beam, and check the relief again. Remember that this is without string tension, so compare the new measurement with the original measurement taken with the strings off. There should be some change in the amount of relief, but it is quite possible that the process will need repeating to achieve the target figure. You may need to heat the fingerboard for longer to achieve a higher temperature at the back of the neck (and hence in the glue joint), or continue to heat the neck/fingerboard once the clamp is in place. Another option is to increase the thickness of the spacers, but I would limit this to a maximum of 3mm.

Once you have reached the target relief with the strings off, replace the strings and bring them up to tension before checking the relief again.

Fingerboard capping

If heat resetting has proved ineffective, then capping the fingerboard may be required. It has the advantage that the total thickness of the neck can be increased, which will improve the stiffness and resistance to bending under the tension of the strings. The idea is to remove most of the existing fingerboard, and then glue on a cap of the same material, which is then planed down to the required thickness and flatness before re-fretting. If the fingerboard is bound, this process is more complex. Fortunately binding on fingerboards is most common on steel-string acoustic guitars, most of which have adjustable truss rods.

Before starting, take measurements of the neck thickness (including the fingerboard but not the fret) at both the 1st fret and the 9th fret (or just before the curve of the heel starts). In order to increase the stiffness of the neck, the final finished thickness after the capping will ideally be slightly greater than it was originally.

Bear in mind that the stiffness of a beam is proportional to the cube of its thickness, so a small increase in thickness can be significant. For example, increasing the thickness of a rectangular section beam from 21mm to 22mm will increase the stiffness by about 15 per cent. In general, the woods used for fingerboards are stiffer than those used for necks, so in fact the improvement gained from adding 1mm to the fingerboard thickness would be greater than this.

The first task is to remove all the frets. Opinions vary on the importance of heating the frets before removing them. The theory is that it reduces the risk of chipping the fingerboard as the tangs and barbs are pulled out. In this case, we will be planing the fingerboard down to below the bottom of the fret slots anyway, so it really isn't necessary.

Continue to remove the rest of the frets, and then proceed to planing down the fretboard. The frets can be disposed of as old frets should never be reused, partly because they will be slightly worn, but they will also be difficult to reinstall. If there are any inlaid fret markers on either the top or the side of the fingerboard, these will need to be removed and stored to be reinstated on the new fingerboard cap.

Woods used for fingerboards tend to be hard in order to minimise wear, and this is certainly the case for ebony, so a sharp and well set-up plane is essential. Using a sheet of thin plywood or similar to protect the soundboard whilst planing the fingerboard is recommended.

When you start to approach the bottom of the fret slots, start checking the flatness of the remaining fingerboard both along the length, and across the width. A flat surface is vital if you are to obtain an invisible joint between the original fingerboard and the cap.

The blade of a Japanese plane tends to keep its edge longer when planing hardwoods like ebony or rosewood. It also uses different muscles, and I sometimes alternate between this and a traditional western plane.

You can buy specialist fret pulling tools, but my old fret end cutters do the job perfectly. These were old, standard end cutters made with good-quality steel, with the face ground down to be perfectly smooth and flush.

If this were a simple re-fret, you would need to take much more care pulling the frets out, but as the fingerboard will be planed away anyway, you can just work the flush cutters under the end of the fret and pull them straight out.

Neck and Head Repairs 103

If the original fret slots were cut to an even depth, then they should all disappear at about the same time as you plane down the fingerboard. In this case, the slots were very uneven, and a few of them went most of the way through the fingerboard. With ebony it is very easy to fill any small holes in the edge of the fingerboard invisibly, so I stopped before completely planing through all the slots.

Now prepare the fingerboard cap. This should be of the same material as the original fingerboard, to maintain the original specification of the instrument, and to make it easier to hide the join between the two parts. In this case the fingerboard is ebony, making the job of hiding the join very easy. Lighter coloured woods make invisible joints far more difficult, but these are rarely used for acoustic guitar fingerboards.

The gluing surface of the cap needs to be perfectly flat to make a perfect join to the remaining part of the original fingerboard. This board came fairly flat, so no planing was necessary. There was a slight convex curvature across the width, and it is critical that this is corrected. If the surfaces aren't flat across the width, you will almost certainly end up with gaps in the join between the two plates. The best tool for removing any slight humps across the width is a cabinet scraper. Start at the centre of the fingerboard initially, gradually working out towards the edges until the surface is just slightly concave across the width.

Once you have achieved this slight concavity along the whole length of the cap, finish the flattening using a flat sanding block.

Check the finished surface for flatness along the length, but more importantly across the width.

Using a backlight to check for flatness will reveal the smallest errors, but it can suggest the gap is much bigger than it actually is. A feeler gauge will measure the exact size of any gaps.

When gluing the fingerboard cap, it is essential that the top surface of the old fingerboard, and the underside of the cap, are perfectly flat across the width. A slight curvature along the length can be tolerated, but any convex curves across the gluing surfaces will be very difficult to clamp down, leaving gaps along the edge.

The fret slots in this fingerboard were cut carelessly, and some were much deeper than necessary. The 2mm wooden alignment dowels at the 11th fret were used when the fingerboard was first glued in place.

A flexed cabinet scraper will tend to make the gluing surface slightly concave across the width. A very slight concavity is acceptable, as the fingerboard cap will be clamped along the centre line, closing up any slight gap in the centre.

If the scraper has left too much concavity, then a flat sanding block can be used to flatten it out. Keep pressure on the centre of the fingerboard to avoid rounding over any edges.

Final check of flatness using a backlight and engineer's square. The board can be very slightly concave across the width.

end of the fingerboard square to the surfaces, and perpendicular to the centre line. Next plane the edges of the board close to the final dimensions of the original fingerboard, using a shooting board if needed to keep the edges square.

Now offer the cap up to the fingerboard and check the fit. Aim for as close a fit as possible, to minimise any adjustments after the cap has been glued. Continue to plane the edges on the shooting board until you are satisfied with the fit.

The soundhole end should now be marked and cut to shape. In this case, the guitar has a fretboard that extends over the soundhole to accommodate a 20th fret.

Cut the nut end of the fingerboard cap accurately perpendicular to the centre line. At this stage, you may choose to cut the new fret slots, particularly if you have a fret slotting jig. The jig I use is designed to be used after the fingerboard has been glued to the guitar. If cutting the fret slots without a jig, they can be cut either before or after the fingerboard cap has been glued.

Plane the edges of the fingerboard cap to exactly match the taper of the original fingerboard. Start by making the nut end of the fingerboard perfectly square. Planing across the end grain of ebony or rosewood can be difficult, but can be done with a very sharp and finely set apron plane. Alternatively, use a flat sanding block, taking care to keep the

Planing the edges of the fingerboard cap to dimension on a 'shooting board'. Some makers have dedicated shooting boards, but all you really need is a flat surface for the side of the plane to rest on, and a block of wood with parallel surfaces to hold the workpiece at the correct height.

A short pencil with a sharp tip is needed to mark the underside of the fingerboard cap to match the soundhole curve, in this case including the 20th fret extension.

The closer you cut to the marked line, the less work needed to get a perfect fit, but obviously be careful not to go over the line.

The fingerboard cap is marked and drilled at the 1st and 11th frets for the 1.5mm alignment pins. The 12th fret position isn't used because there are sometimes voids in the join between the body and the neck, preventing a reliable location.

The fingerboard clamped and panel pins tapped through. Be sure to support the neck/body when hammering in the pins.

Clamp the fingerboard cap accurately in position, and then mark the underside of the cap with a short pencil following the shape of the original fingerboard.

You should end up with a clear mark of the shape required.

Cut the end of the cap close to the marked line using either a coping saw or a bandsaw with a narrow blade. Finish the fit by hand with scrapers and sanding sticks, or with a bobbin sander if you have one of the appropriate diameter.

To align the cap piece perfectly when gluing, it will need to be held in place with pins (as was the original fingerboard). I use 1.5mm diameter panel pins for this, as the holes will be covered by the frets if positioned correctly. Mark carefully the positions of the 1st and 11th frets on the cap, and drill one 1.5mm diameter hole accurately on each fret line.

Position the cap as accurately as possible over the remainder of the original fingerboard and clamp it in place. Tap two 1.5mm panel pins through the drilled holes and into the neck. Leave some of the panel pin protruding to make removal easier after gluing.

Prepare the clamps and a clamping caul before applying any glue. Notice that the clamping caul has holes drilled through it to accommodate the alignment pins. Protect the back of the neck to prevent it being damaged by the clamps – I have used a strip of thick leather for this,

This fingerboard clamping caul has holes drilled through it to clear the alignment pins. As you can see, it has been used for a number of different scale length guitars and alignment pin positions.

Applying the glue. It is becoming more common to see epoxy resin glue used for fingerboards. The argument is that water-based glues can distort the fingerboard, but I've never seen any evidence of this, and water-based glues have been used successfully for hundreds of years.

but cork-lined clamping cauls shaped to fit the neck would be better.

Apply plenty of Titebond glue to the surface of the original fingerboard and spread it evenly over the surface.

Position the cap, making sure the alignment pins fit into the holes correctly, and then the clamping caul. Apply the clamps, working from the centre outwards. In addition to the four clamps along the neck, I have used an F-clamp across the body at the 12th fret, and another clamp through the soundhole (supported by a block on the inside).

A small clamp has been used here for the 20th fret extension. Applying some masking tape along the edge of the fingerboard will make the clean-up easier.

When all the clamps have been tightened, remove the masking tape along the edge of the fingerboard and use a brush and some water to clean up all the glue squeeze-out, both along the edges, and at the nut and soundhole ends.

A small clamp used for the fretboard extension. Note the masking tape along the edges of the fingerboard, which protects the finish and makes clean-up a little easier.

LEFT: Glue squeeze-out is a good sign that enough glue has been used. If there is no squeeze out, you have either used exactly the right amount of glue, or not enough! Clean-up of the Titebond is easy with a brush and water.

A strip of thick leather was used here to protect the back of the neck from the clamps. This is adequate if not too much clamping pressure is used, but cork-lined cauls shaped to fit the back of the neck would be safer.

A cabinet scraper is the perfect tool for touching up the edges of the cap and original fingerboard to make them perfectly flush. Care is needed not to touch the finish on the neck itself. If the original fingerboard edge was finished, the new cap can be refinished to match the original, or simply apply some Danish oil.

Leave the fingerboard cap clamped overnight before removing the clamps and clamping caul. Carefully remove the alignment pins, pulling them vertically to avoid widening the holes.

Any slight imperfections in the fit of the edges of the fingerboard can be easily levelled with a cabinet scraper, taking care not to scrape any finish off the neck itself.

If the original fingerboard had finish applied to the edge, this can be carefully scraped and/or sanded back until the edges of the original fingerboard and cap are perfectly level and free from any finish. A coat of Danish oil or similar can be applied now, or once the repair is complete.

Now use a flexible sanding stick to blend the soundhole end of the fingerboard cap and original fingerboard.

You are now ready to start planing down the top surface of the fingerboard cap to the required thickness. I have applied masking tape and thin plywood to the soundboard to protect it from damage and ebony dust.

For planing ebony, I mostly use a Japanese-style plane, as the blades tend to keep their edge better than those of Western-style planes.

Try to use long, straight strokes along the whole length of the fingerboard. This will help to keep the surface flat. Most classical guitars have flat fingerboards, but an increasing number have a slight radius, as do most acoustic guitars. If the

Finished edge. The advantage of using an oil finish for the fingerboard edge is that there is no risk of the finish chipping and cracking if the fingerboard shrinks, causing the fret ends to protrude.

Sanding the end grain of the fingerboard cap should result in an invisible join between the cap and the remaining part of the original fingerboard. The flexible sanding stick helps to avoid rounding the edges.

Although functionally the same as a Japanese plane, this one is Taiwanese. Once you get the hang of using these, they are very effective, and I find the shape of this plane more comfortable than the squarer-bodied Japanese ones. Protection of the soundboard is provided by a sheet of 1.5mm plywood, cut to fit around the fingerboard.

Measuring the fingerboard thickness. Most acoustic guitars have radiused fingerboards, which should always be measured in the centre. Classical guitars will usually have a twist in the fingerboard, so the thickness should be measured at all four corners.

Measuring the 'action' with a straight edge. This will be a guide only, but it is important to get close to the desired fingerboard projection so that the string height at the bridge is kept within acceptable limits.

original was radiused, you will need to reproduce the same radius as closely as possible. Classical guitars will also usually have a twist in the fingerboard, which allows for a higher action on the bass side than on the treble side, without having a large slope on the saddle. This twist will also have to be accurately reproduced if the setup of the guitar is to be as good as possible. Acoustic guitars generally have a smaller difference between the actions on the treble side and the bass side and so there is less need for a twist.

As you progress, take frequent measurements of the thickness of the fingerboard, and the total neck thickness.

Check that the taper of the fingerboard will give the correct action at the desired string height measured at the saddle. This is done using a straightedge and some spacers, and needs to be checked on both the bass side and the treble side of the fingerboard. Place a 1.5mm thick spacer at the nut end of the fingerboard, and a 12mm spacer at the saddle position. This spacer can be placed just in front of the bridge, but for better accuracy, a dummy saddle can be made to fit in the saddle slot to represent the 12mm string height.

Place the straightedge resting on the spacers and aligned with the position of the 6th (bass E) string.

Now measure the gap between the fingerboard and the straightedge at the 12th fret. A wedged string action gauge is ideal for this. For a classical guitar, the gap should be between 4.5 and 5mm,

Neck and Head Repairs 109

This classical guitar is designed with a twist in the fingerboard. On the bass side you can see the edge tapers down towards the soundhole. On the treble side, the edge of the fingerboard is close to parallel.

which will give an action of 3.5 to 4mm when the frets are installed.

Repeat the measurement on the treble side – with the straightedge aligned along the line of the 1st (treble E) string. The gap for the treble side should be between 3.5 and 4mm for a classical guitar, to give an action of 2.5 to 3mm with the frets in place.

For a flamenco or acoustic guitar, these numbers will be lower. Refer to the action table in Chapter 4, adding 1mm to the final action height quoted to allow for the frets.

If either of the gaps is too small, then more material needs to be taken from the soundhole end of the fingerboard. If either gap is too large, more material should be taken from the nut end. In either case, care needs to be taken to keep the fingerboard flat along both its length and width (unless the fingerboard is to be radiused).

The finished fingerboard cap should be flat along the length, and across the width (unless radiused), and be tapered correctly to give the correct action. It should also be the correct thickness so that the total thickness of the neck at the 1st and 9th frets is acceptable. If the neck was originally slightly thinner than standard, then an additional 1mm or so on the fingerboard thickness will significantly

My fret slotting jig is a solid, machined aluminium block, with slots for each fret position. The jig has a fixed scale length (650mm) but saves a lot of time measuring and marking the fret slots, as most of the guitars I work on are classicals with a standard 650mm scale.

This Japanese saw has a guide and depth stop attached. When sawing slots above 12th fret the soundboard needs protection. The clamps are moved to give access to all the fret slot positions, but always keep at least one clamp in place to avoid the risk of the jig moving.

The completed fret slots after a light sanding. As this is a classical guitar, there are no fret marker inlays to worry about on the top of the fingerboard. Small dot fret markers will be inlaid into the edge of the fingerboard later.

increase the resistance of the neck to upbow under string tension.

You are now ready to cut the fret slots. If the slots were cut before gluing the cap, their depth is likely to have been reduced significantly when planing the top of the cap, and they should be cut deeper to match the tang depth of the frets being used.

Here I'm using my fret-slotting jig. If you don't have one, mark all the fret positions accurately on the fingerboard before cutting them.

I have a modified Japanese saw with guide blocks bolted to it to fit the slots of the jig. These blocks also control the depth of the cut.

The jig is clamped in place ready for the slots to be cut. If cutting the slots without a jig, it is worth clamping an alignment block in each fret position in turn (where possible) to ensure an accurate, square and clean cut. It also helps to place some masking tape on the side of the saw to mark the depth of cut required.

Now start sawing the fret slots. Be sure to use a saw which will cut the correct width of slot for the frets used. If necessary, first carry out a test on a scrap piece of hardwood.

When sawing the frets above the body join, the soundboard should be protected with a plywood sheet or similar fitted around the fingerboard.

If the fingerboard had any fret marker inlays, they should now be replaced (*see* Chapter 10). The top surface can be sanded to clean up any marks left during the slot cutting process, finishing with at least 400 grit abrasive.

You are now ready to install the new frets. These should be cut to length allowing a few millimetres overhang on each side of the fingerboard.

The remainder of the fretting procedure is covered in detail in Chapter 7.

All the frets have been cut slightly overlength, and the ends will be trimmed flush with the edge of the fingerboard after they are installed.

Neck and Head Repairs **111**

Full neck reset

If the relief is within acceptable limits, but the action is too high to be corrected by adjusting the saddle height, then it is likely that the guitar will need a full neck reset. For guitars with bolt-on necks, glued mortise/tenon joints, and tapered dovetail joints, this involves separating the neck joint, adjusting the neck part of the joint, and then reassembling.

The guitar in the case described here has a tapered dovetail joint. The procedure will be very similar for any other glued joints. If the guitar has a bolt-on neck, then adjustment is far simpler, although it is possible that the fingerboard will still be glued to the soundboard.

Although it is possible to carry out the neck removal using clamps, a purpose-built neck removal jig will make the process easier and reduce the risk of damaging the guitar. A neck removal jig is designed to clamp around the body, with a screw to apply pressure to the heel cap.

Before attempting to remove the neck, first measure the action and calculate how much you want this to change by. By the time a guitar needs a neck reset, the saddle has usually been lowered as far as it can go, so it is worthwhile returning the saddle height to the original specification to allow for some future adjustment. Make sure the neck relief is correctly set before measuring the action. When re-fitting the neck, it will not be possible to measure the action of the strings, so a quick and easy alternative measurement is obtained by placing a straightedge

The tapered dovetail joint is most commonly used in steel-string acoustics. Although there are claimed to be tonal advantages, there is no evidence for this. (Photo: Ask Eide)

You can buy neck removal jigs, but they are quite simple to make. It is possible to remove a dovetail neck without one, but it's worth the investment if you are likely to be using it more than once or twice. (Photo: Ask Eide)

along the top of the frets, and then measuring the distance between the end of the straightedge and the soundboard at the bridge.

Check that the horizontal alignment is correct by measuring the clearance between the outer strings and the edges of the fingerboard both at the nut and the 12th fret. Any difference between the treble and bass string clearance should be similar at both the nut and the 12th fret.

If the fingerboard extension is glued to the soundboard, this must be heated and carefully loosened up to the body joint. The fingerboard can be heated with a domestic clothes iron, but a purpose-made iron with slots cut to fit over the frets is perhaps easier to use. Feel under the fingerboard by reaching in through the soundhole. Continue to apply the heat until you can feel the underside of the soundboard below the fingerboard is just hot to the touch. Applying some water to the joint will also help, particularly once it starts to separate, and the water can be worked into the gap. Start to work a thin palette knife under the fingerboard. Use some card or veneer to protect the finish adjacent to the fingerboard. Work in from the corners across the soundhole, and up towards the body join. Once there is enough of a gap, switch to a sturdier knife. Once the fingerboard extension is completely free from the soundboard, inserting a thin Teflon sheet or similar between the two will prevent the glue from re-adhering until everything has cooled down.

In the case described here, the fingerboard is floating, and not glued to the soundboard.

On some Gibson guitars, the neck joint is glued before the soundboard, resulting in the soundboard covering the dovetail. In these cases, if you try to remove the neck, the soundboard will prevent the dovetail joint coming apart, and if forced the soundboard will be damaged. This can be avoided by cutting fully through the fretboard and the soundboard in the centre of a fret slot close to the end of the dovetail.

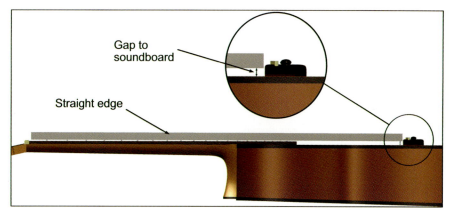

Checking the neck angle. If the neck needs resetting, the end of the straight edge will probably be much closer to the soundboard at the bridge end than shown here. The gap shown here is the neck angle you will be aiming for, with the straight edge end close to the top of the bridge.

Alternatively, the fingerboard could be completely removed from the neck to enable you to cut easily through just the soundboard at the dovetail. This will involve a lot more work, but not cutting through the fingerboard will reduce the risk of weakening the neck.

The heat should ideally be applied as close to the joint as possible, without affecting the outward appearance of the guitar. To do this, a fret is removed from the fingerboard, and two holes drilled into the neck block, into which are inserted the heating probes.

One of the best and most easily available tools to use to apply the heat are hot-wire foam cutters. These are not expensive, and the probes should be small enough to fit into a 2mm diameter hole.

First remove the appropriate fret using the method described in Chapter 7. This will be one fret up (towards the bridge) from the body join – that is, the 13th fret on a 12-fret neck guitar, or the 15th fret on a 14-fret guitar. This position should be closest to being above the end of the dovetail or tenon. If it is expected that the fingerboard will need further levelling or cleaning up, or if the frets are significantly worn, then it is worth removing all the frets at this time.

Holes drilled at the 15th fret. The size of the holes needed will depend on the diameter of the heat probes, but preferably 2mm or less. This will allow a standard fret to cover them after the reset is complete. (Photo: Ask Eide)

Neck and Head Repairs

Now drill two holes for the heat probes. The size of the holes will depend on the size of the heat probes, but if they are no more than 2mm, then the holes should be completely covered when the fret is replaced.

Try to estimate the position and the angle of the dovetail so that you can drill down at an angle to match that of the side cheeks of the dovetail. It is worth doing some research on the particular guitar to give a better understanding of the design, dimensions and angles of the dovetail. Start the holes with a short drill bit, which will be more stable and less fragile. Once the maximum depth of the shorter bit is reached, switch to a bit long enough to reach the bottom of the dovetail joint.

The neck removal jig must be mounted onto the guitar as shown in the image, and light pressure applied to the heel cap using the screw. Be careful not to apply too much pressure, as this can result in damage to the dovetail tenon.

Insert the foam cutter probes into the holes and turn on the heat. Wait for the wood to heat up before applying more pressure to the heel. This should take around 10–15 minutes.

In most cases hide glue, Titebond or PVA will have been used to glue the joint, and it should come apart fairly easily. If epoxy or another heat-resistant glue has been used, it is likely to be more difficult.

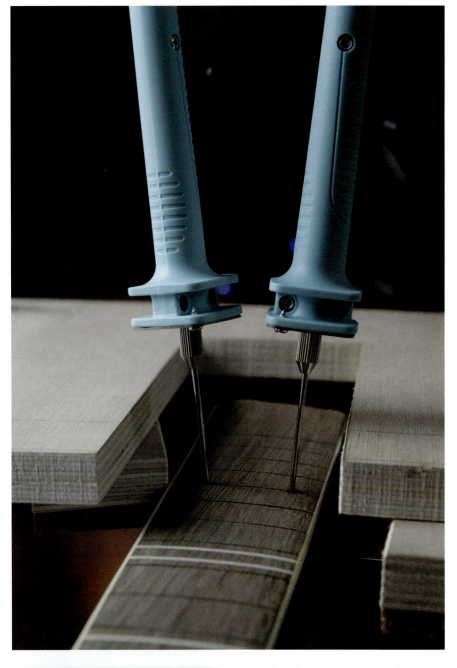

ABOVE: Note the heater probes (and hence the holes) are angled towards each other. The holes are angled to align with the edges of the dovetail. (Photo: Ask Eide)

LEFT: Here the neck removal jig is in position, and the heat probes inserted into the holes. Cork-lined blocks between the neck removal jig and the body of the guitar protect the finish. (Photo: Ask Eide)

Start wiggling the neck whilst firmly holding the body to see if it comes loose. It should separate at this point, but it might need more time for the heat to get into the joint. Water can also be injected into the holes if needed, which should help to soften the glue. You should not

The purpose of the screw is not to use excessive force to open the joint, rather to apply a reasonable amount of constant pressure while the heat does the job of loosening the joint. (Photo: Ask Eide)

On the separated joint, you can see the burn marks from the heater probes. These show that the heat was getting to the joint effectively. The position of the holes could have been improved by moving them outwards slightly so that they were closer to the edges of the joint. Unless you have detailed dimensions of the joint before you start, the position of the holes will always be an estimate. (Photo: Ask Eide)

need to add more pressure with the screw, there only needs to be enough to make the joint pop apart when the glue has softened enough.

Once the neck has come away from the body, the dovetail (or tenon) and the mortise must be cleaned up and all the old glue removed. The face of the heel can then be slightly undercut so that only the edges are in contact with the ribs, which will speed up the fitting process.

In most cases the neck will have been pulled up by the string tension over a period of years, so generally the neck will need to be angled backwards more, which will lower the action.

Now begin the process of angling the neck back. If a large angle correction is required, you will save some time by initially working with a chisel, carefully removing more material from the heel cap end of the heel contact surface than the fingerboard end. If you are not confident in working very accurately with a chisel, or if the adjustment needed is small, then go straight to using the abrasive paper method described below.

Cut strips of 120 grit abrasive paper about 20mm wide and longer than the depth of the heel. Place the neck in position with an abrasive strip between the heel and the rib, with the end tight up against the underside of the fingerboard. While exerting light pressure on the heel, pull back the abrasive through the gap between the heel and the ribs. This method ensures that the shape of the ribs will be transferred to the heel, while removing more material at the back of the heel than the front. This will have the effect of gradually angling the neck backwards.

Make sure you pull the abrasive in a straight line. If it is lifted even slightly, it will take too much material from the heel cap end of the joint. It is good practice to work equally on either side of the heel, unless the horizontal alignment also needs to be corrected. It is important to keep checking the alignment of the neck, and selecting which side of the joint you work on more to correct any errors. Unless the guitar is to be refinished anyway, it is a good idea to brush away the debris from the sanding after each pull of the abrasive strip. Also keep the abrasive clean by brushing the wood

The fingerboard and neck extension prevent the abrasive strip being pulled through the whole length of the heel. As most resets require the angle of the neck to move backwards, this works in your favour, as the abrasive strip will work more on the part of the heel nearest the cap, and progressively less towards the fingerboard, gradually tilting the neck backwards. (Photo: Ask Eide)

dust off regularly, and replace the abrasive strip when it gets worn, to ensure even removal of material.

Regularly inspect the fit between the heel and the rib on both sides of the joint. If any gaps appear, try to take more material off where the contact points are, until the gaps have gone. It may also be necessary to work into the corner of the dovetail tenon with a chisel, as working with just the abrasive paper will tend to leave a corner fillet, which will prevent a good fit.

The neck angle should be checked frequently during the process. Hold the neck in place in its pocket and use a straightedge to check the action. You will be aiming for a point where a straightedge resting on the frets is somewhere near to level with the top of the bridge, but the exact height will depend on the exact action required, and the string height at the saddle.

Keep going with the abrasive pulls until the target angle is reached.

As material is removed from the contact edges of the heel, the dovetail ends up further into the mortise, the joint will become looser. To achieve a tight fit to the joint, shims will need to be glued to the sides of the dovetail.

These can then be adjusted with chisels, files, or sanding sticks until there is a snug fit that pulls the joint together. You should be able to lift the guitar from the neck without the joint coming apart.

Precise fitting of the dovetail joint can be aided by using some form of marker to show where the contact points are. This can be strips of carbon paper, or chalk applied to one side of the joint. The neck is pressed into place, and when it is removed, there will be some carbon paper ink (or chalk) left on the other side of the joint where the contact points are. The marked positions can then be slowly

The abrasive strip tends to not remove material right into the corner of the neck part of the dovetail, so the corner needs to be cleaned up periodically with a chisel. (Photo: Ask Eide)

The material removed to correct the neck angle will have made the joint loose, so shims need to be added. These could be glued to either the neck or the body side of the joint, but the neck side is easier to access for gluing, and also easier to adjust. (Photo: Ask Eide)

If the shims used are of a uniform thickness and the same on both sides, taking material from each side fairly equally will ensure that the neck stays well centred, and the horizontal angle is maintained. (Photo: Ask Eide)

Shims adjusted for perfect fit of the dovetail. The joint should be a tight fit, but it should be possible to close it without clamping so that there are no gaps between the heel and the ribs. (Photo: Ask Eide)

With the joint complete, make a final check of the neck angles before gluing and clamping. The nature of the tapered dovetail means that you only need one clamp, and the geometry of the joint pulls everything together. (Photo: Ask Eide)

Neck and Head Repairs

chiselled or sanded back to improve the fit. Repeat the process until a tight fit is obtained, with good contact between the two parts of the dovetail.

If properly fitted, one clamp at the neck block should be enough. Either Titebond or hide glue can be used to glue the neck joint.

If the guitar has a fingerboard extension, this will need to be glued down as well. If the change in neck angle is significant, then a fine wedge will need to be made to fit between the fingerboard extension and the soundboard to adapt to the new angle. The edges of this wedge should be coloured and finished so as not to be too visible.

The 15th fret, if still usable can be re-inserted, but it is generally better to cut and fit a new one. The frets are likely to need levelling at this point, at least in the area from the body joint and to the soundhole (*see* Chapter 4 for fret levelling and subsequent setup).

Open heel glue joint

This is not a very common repair, but the tension of the strings does put a strain on the glue joints of the heel block. Some heel blocks are made using a single large block of wood, which is glued to the neck, whilst others are made by stacking three or four pieces of wood together. It might seem that multiple pieces of wood glued together is less desirable than a single piece of wood with no glue joints, but this is not generally the case. The heel is usually made from a stack of pieces because all the wood for the neck, head and heel comes from the same block of wood. This has the advantage of being perfectly matched in colour and grain, but the neck blank will not be thick enough for the heel, hence the stack. If the parts of the stack are well glued, they are very unlikely to come apart, but it does happen occasionally.

Re-gluing an open heel joint

In this example of an old classical guitar, there is a clear opening of the middle of the three glue joints in the heel. Inspecting the joint with a bright light behind shows the gap clearly.

When working on guitars, there is usually some uncertainty about the type

RIGHT: Open heel joint. The image was taken with the strings under tension to make the gap easier to see. With the tension removed, the gap was smaller.

BELOW: This looks like an excessive amount of glue, but it allows you to continue working the glue into the gap for a while without returning to the glue bottle.

An F-clamp is used to clamp up the heel, producing a reasonable amount of squeeze-out, indicating there is enough glue in the joint.

of glue that was used in construction. Without knowledge of the glue type, a choice must be made about which glue is most suitable for the repair. Although it is often said that modern aliphatic resin glues such as Titebond do not adhere well in old glue joints, I have found that they are effective in most cases. If we were certain that hide glue was originally used in the joint, then this would be the best choice for re-gluing.

I have slightly watered down the glue to help it penetrate further into the gap. Too much watering down will weaken the glue, but a small amount is acceptable. The glue is worked into the gap with a brush, whilst the joint is worked back and forth by putting tension on the neck. This will help work the glue further into the joint. When you are satisfied that the glue is in as far is it will go, closing the joint again should produce a good amount of squeeze-out.

An F-clamp is used across the heel and body, applying enough pressure to completely close the gap, but avoiding using excessive force.

The excess glue can now be cleaned up with a brush, cloth and some water. The clamp should be left in place overnight.

Open heel body joint

In addition to trying to open up any joints within the heel, the string tension will also put pressure on the joint between the heel and the body of the guitar. With the Spanish construction method used on most classicals this is very unlikely to happen, but for a separate neck/body construction type, if the joint is not perfect, then there is a chance of the heel pulling away from the body. Again, inspecting with a bright light behind the heel shows the extent of the gap.

The gap can also be assessed by inserting a strip of paper into it. This will give a

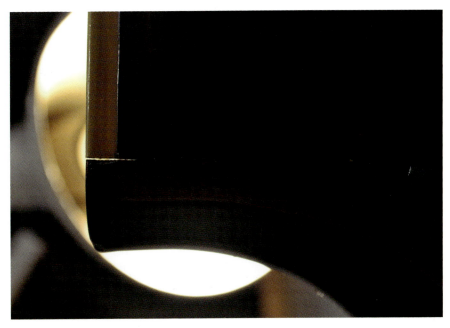

This type of gap opening is usually only seen on acoustic guitars, and it suggests an imperfect joint. Classical guitars built using the Spanish method will not suffer this problem.

An alternative method of assessing the extent of the gap. This is standard 80gsm paper, but for testing really fine gaps, cigarette paper can be used.

Working hide glue into gap. A neck support block is placed under the heel/body joint. This allows the gap to be opened and closed slightly by applying downward pressure on the back of the head, helping to work the glue into the joint. The plastic bag is to stop dripping glue soaking into the padded neck block!

Neck and Head Repairs

The neck block has been moved to the head, so that gravity (and some steel blocks) can apply closing pressure to the glued joint.

better idea of what you're dealing with if the gap does not extend right across the width of the heel, in which case no light will get through.

Work the glue into the gap with a brush, and flex the neck to help work the glue further in. For this repair I have used hide glue, and I have masked off the body where it joins the heel.

You could use a strap extending right around the body of the guitar to hold the gap closed, but here I have simply used some steel weights, with the neck supported on a neck block, and the end of the guitar on a piece of carpet to protect the finish. Clean up any glue squeeze-out.

Leave overnight and, if necessary, touch up the finish around the joint.

Replacing tuning machines

Tuning machines wear over time and can get to the stage where they no longer function correctly. In the worst cases, the gears can slip or become so tight as to make the guitar impossible to tune. It is rarely practical to repair tuners. Spare parts are not readily available, and reasonable quality tuning machines are not expensive. If tuners are tight, then it is always worth trying some lubrication first (*see* Chapter 3), but beyond that, replacement is likely to be the way to go. New factory guitars, even quite expensive ones, are still often fitted with poor-quality tuning machines. These can work adequately, but when replacing tuners, never fit cheap ones.

Classical/slotted head tuners

Classical guitars, or acoustic guitars with slotted heads, usually have '3-on-a-plate'-style tuning machines, which are mounted on the side of the head. When buying replacements, it is important that the spacing between the tuner rollers is the same as the originals. Fortunately, the vast majority of tuners have the same roller spacing of 35mm. However, some older classical guitars have a 36mm or a 39mm spacing. The 39mm ones are easy to spot, but a 36mm spacing can easily be missed. Measure the original tuners accurately using a vernier or digital caliper. If you cannot find suitable replacements of the correct size, it is usually better to use individual tuners rather than trying to adjust the hole spacing on the head.

Slotted head tuning machines are usually secured with four screws on each side. Unless identical replacements can be found, you will need to make new screw holes. It is not essential to fill the old holes, unless they are only slightly offset from the old ones, but it is good practice.

I normally use wooden cocktail sticks for filling the screw holes. I cut the points

Nearly all classical tuning machines have the roller holes spaced at 35mm, but the screw holes are seldom in the same place. Cocktail sticks and Titebond do the job of filling the old screw holes.

My fret nippers in action again – cutting the cocktail sticks flush with the side of the head. Note the cutters are used at an angle parallel to the head, so that if they did mark the finish, the marks will be covered by the new tuners.

Sticks neatly trimmed. In almost all cases the filled holes will be covered by the new tuning machines, but if not, some touch-up colour can be used to hide them.

off, leaving just a bit of taper at the end to help fit it into the old screw hole. Work a little glue into the hole and push the stick in firmly. Repeat for all the holes, and then clean up the glue.

When the glue has dried, trim the sticks flush with the side of the head. I use my flush cutting fret end trimmers for this.

Once trimmed, check whether any of the sticks will still be visible when the new tuning machines are installed. If any are, add a touch of matching colour to them to make them less visible.

Fit the tuning machines and use a bradawl to mark the centres for the new holes. In softer woods like Spanish cedar, this will be enough of a hole for the screws to cut into, but for harder woods like maple, use a 1.5mm drill but centred on the bradawl marks to drill a pilot hole, taking care not to drill through into the slots.

A new set of tuners should always come supplied with suitable screws, but I always like to keep a stock of spare screws of various types.

Screw the tuners in place, but do not over-tighten them. Repeat for the other side.

For softer head woods, a bradawl produces a satisfactory pilot hole for the screws.

Always use the correct size and type of screwdriver for the job. I once had a screwdriver slip off the screw head and scratch the plate of some fairly expensive tuners.

Neck and Head Repairs **121**

Acoustic/flat head tuners

Acoustic guitars with flat heads (not slotted) are usually fitted with individual tuning machines, mounted on the back of the head. These can be replaced individually, but they are not generally available to buy other than as complete sets. In general, if one tuner has failed, there is a good chance of others failing, so it makes more sense to replace them all anyway.

There is a bewildering array of different styles of acoustic guitar tuners available, and it may be possible to find an exact match, or a close copy, of the originals. If the originality of the instrument is important, then try to find as close a match as possible.

There are a few different ways acoustic guitar tuners are secured to the head, and various sizes of tuner holes. Most modern tuners require a 10mm hole, but older instruments often have smaller sizes, 8.7mm and 7.8mm being common. You can open out the hole to the size needed for the new tuners, but it is always better to find replacement tuners to fit the existing hole size. Tuners are mostly fixed in one of three ways:

1. A threaded bushing through the head, with one or two alignment pins at the back.
2. A threaded bushing through the head, with one securing screw at the back.
3. Two screws at the back, and a press-fit bushing on the top.

The worn tuning machines on this acoustic guitar are secured with a threaded bush on top of the head, and single screw at the back. First remove the threaded bush and washers from the top of the head.

Remove the securing screws and remove the tuners from the head. These came out very cleanly, but sometimes there is damage to the finish, which would need to be touched up.

These Gotoh tuners were close enough in size and shape to the original unbranded ones to completely cover the marks they left in the finish.

Use the correct-sized spanner for undoing the threaded bushes. An adjustable spanner can be used, but in either case take care, as the spanner can easily slip off the thin nut.

Old tuners removed, revealing an imprint in the finish. Either the finish was not fully hardened when the tuners were fitted, or they were over-tightened. This will not be a problem if the new tuners are exactly the same size and shape.

122   Neck and Head Repairs

The replacement Gotoh tuners used here were not identical to the originals, but in this case the hole size was the same (10mm) and the screw holes were in the same position. If the positions of the screw holes were different, they would need to be filled and new holes made as described for the classical tuners above. This head and neck are hard maple, so any new screw holes should be drilled using a 1.5mm bit.

Truss rod replacement

The adjustable truss rod was first introduced and patented by Gibson in the early twentieth century. Martin initially used fixed bars with a T-section or square section and didn't switch to adjustable truss rods until the 1980s. Truss rods are installed in a channel in the neck, under the fingerboard, making repair or replacement a major undertaking. Truss rods are generally very reliable, but it is possible for the threads of the adjuster to become damaged, making the adjuster difficult or impossible to turn. If this happens, it will be necessary to remove and replace the truss rod. Truss rod adjustment was covered in the setup section (Chapter 4), so here we will just be looking at replacement.

Before you proceed

Replacing a truss rod involves completely removing the frets and fingerboard, cutting out the truss rod, installing a new one, and then replacing the fingerboard and frets. This is quite a significant undertaking, so it is worth considering whether it is really necessary. Ask yourself (or the customer) how far off the ideal is the relief? If it's only a fraction off, consider leaving it as it is, or changing the gauge/tension of the strings. Lighter gauge strings will reduce the relief, heavier gauge strings will increase it. If the adjuster is very stiff, then before starting to plane off the fingerboard, you may as well exert as much force as seems reasonable without risking damage to other parts of the guitar. If the adjuster ends up damaged, you're still no worse off than before.

When you have exhausted all other options, start by sourcing a suitable replacement truss rod. It should be of the same type, and very close to the same dimensions as the original. This will mean waiting until the old truss rod has been removed before ordering a new one. Slight differences in length and width can be adjusted for by packing the existing channel or making it a little wider or longer. If the depth is greater than the original, take accurate measurements to ensure that there will be enough material left at the nut end of the bottom of the channel after it is deepened. I have seen truss rods pop out of the back of the neck when the channel was cut too deep, so it is safer to make sure the new truss rod is no deeper than the original.

Removing the truss rod

Although it is possible to remove the fingerboard intact, the heat and moisture used can distort the fingerboard too much for it to be reused anyway. The finish on both the neck and the soundboard are also likely to be damaged, which will generally cause more headaches than making a new fingerboard.

Before beginning, take careful measurements of the existing fingerboard so that the replacement can be made an exact match. Measure the thickness of the fingerboard at both the nut and soundhole ends, and also the radius (assuming it isn't flat, which will be the case for most guitars with truss rods). Just to be sure, measure the thickness both at the edges of the fingerboard and in the centre. Record all the measurements. Unless you have identified a problem with the neck angle (in addition to the truss rod problem), then you will be reproducing these measurements for the new fingerboard. A sanding block of the correct radius will be needed when finishing the new fingerboard. If the original scale length is not known, check it by measuring the distance from the nut to the centre of the 12th fret, and multiplying by two. This will give a more accurate measure of the scale length than measuring from the nut to the saddle (*see* 'Intonation and Compensation' in Chapter 4).

Begin by removing the frets and any inlays on the top of the fingerboard, and start planing down the fingerboard, as described earlier in the chapter under 'Fingerboard capping'.

Keep checking that you are removing material evenly, and not at risk of planing completely through the

At the edge of this picture you can just see where the 12th fret markers were removed from the top of the fingerboard. These were the only inlays in the top and were put aside to be reused in the new fingerboard.

Having almost planed right through the fingerboard, these two channels became visible. They are possibly there to allow some glue to squeeze into them, making the fingerboard less likely to slide when being clamped up. You can also see the remains of the side dot fret marker holes. These were dug out as soon as they were visible from the planing.

fingerboard. When there is about 1mm remaining, switch to using a cabinet scraper and/or coarse sanding block. Now concentrate on getting the surface flat, particularly across the width, to give a good gluing surface for the new fingerboard.

It is a good idea to protect the soundboard at this stage, if you haven't already done so.

Once most of the fingerboard has been removed, it should be relatively easy to cut through the remaining material in the centre of the neck to start to reveal the truss rod. In some cases, there may be a wooden cap in the truss rod slot, covering the truss rod. On this guitar, the truss rod was wrapped in plastic.

Continue to cut away the material over the truss rod, using a knife to cut clean edges, and a chisel to remove material between the cuts. Try not to blunt the chisel on the metal of the truss rod.

The adjuster on this guitar was at the soundhole end. If the adjuster is at the head end, you will only need to cut through to the end of the truss rod, which will be somewhere between the body join and the soundhole. Even with the adjuster at the soundhole end, the last bit of fingerboard can be left, as the truss rod will be lifted out from the nut end.

Now start to prise the end of the truss rod out of its slot at the nut end. If it seems tight, check that you have removed enough of the fingerboard for it to lift out. It is also possible that some glue or sealant will have been used in the slot to prevent the truss rod rattling. If so, a little more force will be needed to

With around 1mm left, some card is taped in position around the fingerboard to protect the soundboard finish.

RIGHT: Until you uncover it, you will not know how wide the truss rod is. Start cutting at the centre of the neck and work outwards until you hit the wood at the edge of the channel.

BELOW LEFT: The rosewood has been removed to reveal the steel top surface of the truss rod. The edges of the rosewood will need cleaning up before a cap can be fitted over the new truss rod.

BELOW RIGHT: The last section of fingerboard over the end of the truss rod does not need to be removed, as the rod will slide out from the recess once it has been lifted out at the nut end.

remove it, but it should still be possible to pull it out.

Once it has started to lift out, it should be fairly easy to remove the whole truss rod, taking care when it is almost out to slide it out from under the remaining piece of fingerboard at the soundhole end. If the adjuster is at the head end, it may be more difficult to pull out.

Once the truss rod is out, it can be inspected. It may be possible to repair the truss rod, but the most common problem is usually with the thread of the adjuster or the rod itself, and it is always better to replace it completely.

This truss rod was quite tight in the channel, and a screwdriver had to be used to prise it out. This has caused some damage to the end of the channel, but it is easily repaired.

Neck and Head Repairs

Fitting the new truss rod

In this case, the new truss rod had almost identical dimensions to the original. If the new truss rod is longer or wider, then you will need to take some material from the channel to allow it to fit. Increasing the length slightly is straightforward, but making the channel wider takes a lot of care. The original slot will almost certainly have been cut with a router, but setting up a router to widen the channel on a finished instrument is quite tricky, so I would recommend only working with hand tools. If the change in width is 1mm or less, then it's fine to just remove material from one side of the channel. Any more than this and the channel will have to be widened equally on both sides to keep the truss rod centred on the neck. Mark the new width on the top of the remains of the original fingerboard, and use a sharp chisel to cut back to the line. Be sure to keep the side of the channel vertical, and finish with a file or sanding stick if necessary.

Test fit the new truss rod in the channel. Although this new truss rod was the same length as the original, the adjuster ideally needed to be a little more accessible through the soundhole. Gluing a small block of ebony into the nut end of the channel extended the adjuster closer to the edge of the soundhole, and provided a cleaner end to the channel, which had been slightly damaged when prising out the old truss rod.

The new truss rod adjuster was perfectly aligned with the hole in the transverse brace. The hole may need to be opened up slightly if the adjuster nut is larger, or not perfectly aligned.

There will be a gap where the last 1mm or so of the original fingerboard was cut away to give access to the old truss rod. This gap now needs to be filled. The offcut should be adjusted to fit the width of the gap but left slightly over thickness. When gluing the piece in place, take care not to use too much glue, as you don't want any running down into the truss rod channel, and

The new truss rod is very similar in construction to the original, both being two-way adjustable. The dimensions are also almost identical, making the replacement job easier.

The new truss rod fitted, with a piece of ebony used to both repair the damage caused when prising out the old truss rod, and also to move the adjuster slightly closer to the soundhole.

New truss rod adjuster visible and easily accessible through the soundhole.

The material used for the capping strip over the new truss rod is not critical, but it should be a hardwood. In this case, I simply used an offcut from the new fingerboard blank.

soundhole. Depending on the bracing, you may need a block of wood inside the body under the fingerboard.

Once the glue has dried (at least overnight), remove the clamps, clamping caul and alignment pins. If there is any step between the new and the old fingerboard edges, use a scraper or sanding block to blend the two parts together. Try not to mark the finish on the neck itself.

Now plane the neck down to the same dimensions and radius as the original fingerboard. Aim to remove most of the material with a plane, leaving the sanding to simply perfect the radius at the end of the process.

potentially gumming up the adjuster threads. Once the glue has dried, plane, scrape and sand the insert to make it flush with the remaining surface of the old fingerboard.

Fitting the new fingerboard

Carry out a final check of the surface, making sure it is flat, particularly across the width. The new fingerboard should now be prepared. In this case, the original was rosewood, so a new rosewood blank was selected and dimensioned to exactly match the remains of the original, in the same way described under 'Fingerboard capping' earlier in this chapter.

To clamp the new fingerboard cap, you will need to make some cauls that fit to the back of the neck. Lining the cauls with cork will both protect the finish of the neck and allow them to conform to the shape.

It is important that the fingerboard cap edges are accurately aligned with the remains of the original. Use alignment pins to hold it accurately in position (see 'Fingerboard capping' earlier in this chapter). Now glue the new fingerboard in place. I have used three clamps and cauls along the length of the neck, another clamp across the body at the heel, and a final one through the

The new fingerboard has been dimensioned to fit exactly over the remains of the existing one. It will need to be pinned to ensure perfect alignment when it is glued.

These cork-lined cauls were made from softwood for ease of shaping, but have a hardwood backing so that they will not split when clamped to the neck.

Neck and Head Repairs   **127**

LEFT: Three large G-clamps along the neck, one across the body at the 14th fret, and another through the soundhole. Accurate fitting of the surfaces minimises the number of clamps needed, and also reduces the clamping pressure required, which in turn reduces the risk of damaging the back of the neck.

BELOW: A small sanding block is used to blend the new fingerboard in to the remains of the old one, and also to remove any remaining finish from the edge, without marking the finish of the neck. At the end of the process, the edge of the fingerboard will be finished with oil.

BOTTOM: Initial planing to reduce the fingerboard to the correct thickness, and to produce the radius across the width.

The sanding block can be used as a guide to where you need to take material off with the plane (or a cabinet scraper if the grain is too difficult for planing). Mark the top of the fingerboard with a white pencil, then sand along its length with the radius block and coarse grit abrasive. Sand just enough to remove a little over half of the pencil marks. Now go over the areas where the pencil marks have been removed with either a fine-set plane or cabinet scraper. Mark the fingerboard again and go back to sanding with the radius block. Repeat this process until all the marks are quickly and easily

Now proceed with cutting the fret slots, the positions being based on the scale length measured before the original frets were removed. Continue with re-fretting as described in Chapter 7, but first check the operation of the new truss rod by turning the adjuster as you check the flatness/relief of the fingerboard with a straightedge. Make sure that the straightedge is aligned along the centre line of the fingerboard, otherwise the curvature across the width will result in a false reading. The adjuster should turn without too much force, and there should be an obvious change in the relief with not much more than a quarter turn of the adjuster.

ABOVE: The radiused sanding block is slower than the plane, but will produce the correct radius and prevent any tearing of the surface, which is a common problem with rosewood and other woods with interlocked grain.

RIGHT: Measuring the fingerboard thickness at the nut end. I generally prefer to use a digital caliper, just for speed of reading.

removed using the radius block. This method is much quicker than trying to remove all the material using abrasives.

As you progress, regularly check the thickness of the fingerboard at both ends, comparing the measurements with those from the original fingerboard. As you approach the correct dimensions, work slowly and carefully to ensure you have a perfect, smooth surface with the correct radius when the target thickness is reached. If the original fingerboard thickness has been accurately reproduced, this should result in the correct neck projection, giving the same action when strung up. However, it is a good idea to double check, using the straightedge method described at the start of the 'Full neck reset' section earlier in this chapter, remembering to allow for the frets, which have not been fitted yet.

The adjuster of the new truss rod should turn smoothly, without requiring too much force. Half a turn in each direction should be plenty to see an obvious change in the curvature along the neck.

Neck and Head Repairs

CHAPTER 7

Fingerboard and Fret Work

Apart from basic setup work, fretwork is probably one of the most common repair jobs required on guitars. Fret levelling and re-frets, loose frets and protruding fret ends can keep a guitar repairer very busy. Although the work is not particularly exciting, with enough practice and the right tools it can be carried out very efficiently.

Loose frets

Modern frets have barbs on the tang, which help grip the fret into the fret slot. Some makers and manufacturers also glue the frets into the slots, but this is not normally necessary, provided the width of the slot is well matched to the size of the fret tang, and the slot is cleanly cut.

Frets will sometimes come loose and lift slightly, most commonly at the ends. This can cause strings played in lower positions to buzz, as the loose fret may be slightly raised, and can also cause the note played on the loose fret to be dull and have poor sustain, due to the fret not being seated firmly against the fingerboard. When diagnosing dead notes or fret buzz, it is always worth checking first for loose or poorly seated frets. If the guitar has a bound fingerboard, read the section at the end of this chapter.

In most cases, loose frets can be glued down, but occasionally the fretwire is too bent, and the fret needs to be removed and straightened before replacing, or better still a new fret installed. Installing new frets is covered later in this chapter.

The simplest method for gluing down loose frets is to use thin CA glue. This will wick under the fret and into the slot and is usually very effective.

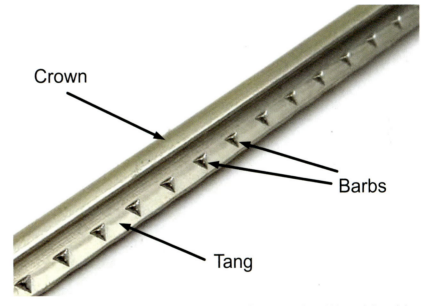

Modern fretwire comes in a variety of dimensions for the height, width, and size of the tang. The barbs on the tang are designed to hold the fret in place in its slot, but the size of the slot still needs to be matched to the size of the tang.

An obviously lifted fret end. Sometimes a fret can just be very slightly lifted, and difficult to see. Close inspection, with a magnifier if needed, whilst pressing and releasing the fret end should show any movement.

Before applying the CA glue, prepare a clamp and a block of wood as the glue will set fairly quickly. You should also use a piece of cork or leather behind the neck to protect it from the clamp. Use a very fine nozzle to apply the CA glue and take care not to let it run down the edge of the fingerboard onto the neck. Have some paper towels ready to wipe away any drips. The glue can usually be seen wicking along the edge of the fret.

Immediately clamp down the fret using a flat block of wood, using enough pressure to press the fret back down, but no more. Although CA glue generally grabs and sets very quickly, it is best to leave the clamp in place for 30 minutes or so.

When the clamp is removed, any residual glue along the edges of the fret can be easily removed with some fine (0000 grade) wire wool.

If all has gone well, the glued fret will be level with the rest of the frets, but quite often some localised levelling is needed. If necessary, the whole fret levelling and re-crowning procedure can be carried out as described in Chapter 4.

These fine-tipped nozzles for applying CA glue are invaluable for this sort of task. The excess glue seen along the edge of the fret should be wiped away before it sets, and before the fret is clamped down.

Using a hard, flat block to clamp the loose fret down will ensure that it sets level with the adjacent frets. Only moderate clamping pressure is needed, but it is still worth protecting the back of the neck.

Wire wool is good for getting into the edge between the fret and the fingerboard, but only use the finest grade 0000. Work along the fret and across the grain first, but finish by working along the grain and over the frets with the wire wool to remove any cross-grain scratches.

Fingerboard and Fret Work

Re-fretting

Frets will become worn over time, and this wear is significantly greater on steel-strung guitars. The rate of wear will also depend on the hardness of the fret material, and on how much the guitar is played. Wear will normally be most noticeable on the first few frets, which see far more use than the higher frets.

A small amount of wear can be remedied at least once by levelling and re-crowning the frets as described in Chapter 4, but if the wear is too bad, or the frets are too low due to previous levelling work, then the time has come for a complete re-fret. Occasionally, a customer will ask for a re-fret to accommodate a preference for either higher or wider frets than those fitted as standard. In either case, the new frets must have the same tang size as the old frets, unless you are planning to use a different tang size to correct some curvature in the neck (*see* Chapter 6: Neck resets and relief correction).

It will also be necessary to remove and replace the frets if they are too uneven to be levelled without removing too much material from them. If this is the case, then the frets should be removed, the fingerboard levelled and then new frets installed.

To glue, or not to glue?

Opinions differ about the necessity of gluing frets into their slots. There are some cases where glue is helpful, or even necessary. When installing frets for the first time, provided the slots are cleanly cut and of the correct width to match the tang of the fretwire, then gluing isn't required. Claims that gluing frets will improve the tone of the guitar are probably unfounded. When re-fretting, you will often find that some or all of the fret slots are in poor condition, either from being poorly cut in the first place, or from having frets removed and replaced carelessly in the past. When faced with a slot that is damaged or too wide to hold the fret securely, either fill the slot and re-cut it, or install the fret as best you can and secure it with glue.

Various glues can be used. The most efficient is CA glue – as used above for holding down frets that have lifted at the ends. CA glue can either be applied to the slot before fitting the fret, or can be wicked into the slot afterwards. Quickly wipe away any glue that runs out onto the fingerboard or down the side of the neck before it hardens.

Epoxy resin glue can be effective when the fret slot is wide, and you need something that will fill the gaps. It can get very messy and be difficult to seat the fret correctly. For this reason, I recommend filling the damaged slot completely with a mix of epoxy resin and ebony dust, waiting for it to cure, and then re-cutting a new, clean fret slot.

Water-based glues have very poor gap-filling properties, and so are only appropriate to use when the slots are in good condition. Some repairers just use them for a little extra security.

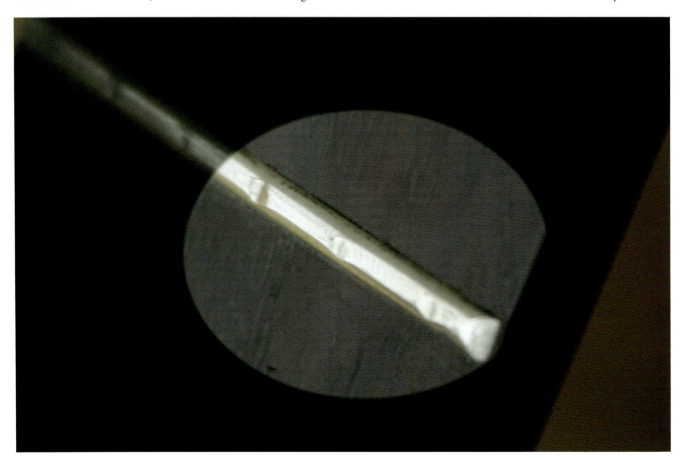

An example of bad fret wear. There are very obvious indentations below the string positions. This fret, and almost certainly the adjacent ones, will need to be replaced.

Removing the old frets

First remove the old frets. Most repairers recommend heating the frets before removing them. This can reduce the risk of chipping the fingerboard as the tangs and barbs are pulled out, and also helps loosen the glue if the frets have been glued into the slots. You can use a soldering iron to heat each fret in turn, but this is fiddly and slow. A much more efficient method is to heat the frets in batches using a domestic clothes iron.

Step 1: Place the iron over the first five or so frets and leave in place until you can feel a temperature rise in the fingerboard. Remove the iron.

Step 2: Use a pair of flush cutters to gently ease out the end of the first fret, while pressing down onto the fingerboard. The idea is to lift the fret using the chamfer on the cutters, whilst the flat side of the cutters presses down on the edges of the fret slot, minimising chipping.

Step 3: Once the cutters have closed onto the tang, move them slightly along the fret, and close them again, lifting the fret slightly further out without pulling.

Step 4: Continue working along the fret, letting the cutter lift it from the slot, rather than pulling it up. When you reach the other end of the fret, it should come away from the slot easily with minimal damage to the fingerboard.

Step 5: There is still a small amount of chipping in the ebony, where the barbs on the tangs have pulled through, but it is fairly minimal. It can either be repaired or left if it will be completely covered by the new fret.

Step 6: Now move on to the next fret, and repeat the process, remembering to keep the cutters pressed down onto the fingerboard.

Step 7: After three or four frets have been removed, you will need to heat the next group of frets again with the iron.

Step 8: Continue in this way until all the frets have been removed. When heating the frets above the body join, either protect the soundboard or use a smaller heat source such as a soldering iron.

Fingerboard and Fret Work

Repairing damaged fret slots

It is good practice to repair even small chips before re-fretting, even if they will be covered by the new frets. In any case, any larger chips should be addressed.

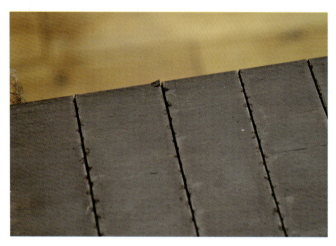

Step 1: Carefully check the edges of the fret slots for any damage that needs repairing. Note the larger chip almost detached at the end of one slot. This will need to be glued down before it detaches and is lost.

Step 2: Chips like this can be easily and quickly repaired using CA glue. Using a fine-tip nozzle, apply a small amount of CA glue to the edge of the slot needing repair.

Step 3: Any larger chips may need to be held down while the CA glue sets. The point of a scalpel blade works well for this.

Step 4: Repair all the fret slot edges in this way, and then sand the whole surface of the fingerboard to clean up the residual CA glue.

Step 5: If some of the CA glue has gone into the fret slots, this should be cleared using a saw of the correct size for the tangs of the new frets. Sand the surface of the fretboard to the required finish.

Step 6: Prepare the new frets, cutting each one to give a few millimetres overhang on each side of the fingerboard.

If the frets have been removed in order to level the fingerboard, this needs to be done now before the new frets are installed. Plane or sand the upper surface of the fingerboard, removing material from the high spots, and checking regularly with a straightedge. If planing, take care not to chip the edges of the fret slots. If sanding, always use a sanding block that is flat along its length, but radiused to match any curvature across the fingerboard.

Once the fingerboard is perfectly level, check that the depths of the fret slots have not been reduced too much to receive the fret tangs, and deepen the slots with the correct size saw if needed.

Installing the new frets

There are two options for installing the new frets – hammering and clamping. I tend to use a combination of the two. If you have a fret press, these are excellent for working along the neck but cannot be used over the body. In most cases, I hammer the frets up to about the 15th (for a 12-fret body join), and then clamp the remaining frets.

Dedicated fret hammers are available, with either a plastic or soft metal head, but the plastic ones in particular require a greater hammering force. My preference is to use a standard claw hammer, with the face smoothed and polished. Provided you are careful to hit the frets squarely, they will not be damaged.

A good support is needed behind the neck whilst hammering the frets in. This could be a purpose-made neck rest, or a shot- or sand-filled bag. Here I'm just using a steel block with a thick cork facing to prevent damage to the neck. The body is packed with spacers to ensure the neck is resting flat on the block, rather than just on one corner. The workbench should be solid and stable. Any give in the work surface will take some energy out of the hammer blow. If possible, position the neck support over or very near one of the workbench legs.

The technique for hammering in frets is important. Each strike with the hammer should make good contact with the fret, and that part of the fret should be seated with a single blow. If the hammer bounces off the fret, it will spring out of the slot, and could chip the edge on the way out. Once you start hammering frets over the body of the guitar, it is a good idea to dampen the vibrations of the soundboard by inserting some material into the body through the soundhole, which will reduce the risk of any braces being loosened.

ABOVE: My preferred fret installer is an old claw hammer. The head has been polished to prevent marking the frets when hammering. The greater weight of this hammer drives the frets home more effectively than plastic headed ones.

LEFT: The support behind the neck when hammering needs to be a compromise. You want solidity so that the energy of the hammer goes into pressing the fret home, rather than being absorbed by the support, but you also need protection to prevent damage to the finish at the back of the neck, hence the cork facing on the block.

Step 1: I recommend using fretwire supplied as a coil. The curve of the wire makes it possible to tap in both ends of the fretwire before working in towards the centre. Push the tang at both ends of the fret into the slot.

Step 2: Holding one end down with your finger to prevent it popping out, gently tap the other end into the slot with the hammer. This should take very little force.

Step 3: Now hold the seated end down and tap in the other end. Once both ends are seated, the fret will be held vertical, and there will be less chance of it tipping over when hammering in the rest of it.

Step 4: Now holding down one end, work from the other end towards the centre of the fret. Hammer firmly, making sure not to hit the fret with the edge of the hammer face.

Step 5: Now hold the other end down with your finger, and work from the other end towards the centre. If you are striking the fret firmly enough, this should take only three or four hits. Finally hold both ends of the fret down and strike the fret in the centre. Be careful not to hit your fingers!

Step 6: Inspect the fret carefully from a low angle to check that it is fully seated along the whole length. If there are any spots not fully in contact with the fingerboard, give them one or two more strikes with the hammer.

Step 7: Although it is possible to insert all the frets before trimming any of the ends, it can get quite tight around the higher frets. Cut each end as you go, pressing the cutters hard against the edge of the fingerboard, and applying a slight downward pressure on the cutters.

Step 8: When you reach the heel, the block cannot be placed directly under the fret. For the fret just before the body join and the first few after it, you can support the body of the guitar directly below the heel. Position the block directly under the fret being inserted, and adjust the angle of the body so that it rests flat against the block.

Step 9: When trimming the fret ends over the body of the guitar, be sure to protect the soundboard. As you will be applying downward pressure on the cutters, they will drop down onto the soundboard when you cut through the fret.

Step 10: You can hammer the frets over the body by holding a steel block through the soundhole up against the underside of the fingerboard, but I prefer to clamp them in. You will need a hard, flat block (or with a radius to match the fingerboard), and a block of wood on the inside of the guitar fitted between the braces.

Step 11: Gently tap the two ends of the frets in with the hammer as before. This should require minimal force, so no support is needed under the fingerboard at this stage.

Step 12: Position the block so that it is resting on the fret to be clamped, and on the frets already inserted. This will keep the clamping pressure acting vertically onto the fret. Gently tighten the clamp until it starts to press the fret home, checking that it is not tipping over. If it is, remove the clamp, push the fret vertical, and try again.

Fingerboard and Fret Work

Worn fingerboards

Fingerboards on good-quality guitars are normally made from either ebony or rosewood. Both woods are hard-wearing, and in many cases will last the lifetime of the guitar without showing any signs of excessive wear. Cheaper instruments frequently use softer woods, which are often stained to make them look like rosewood or ebony. These wear much more quickly, and if stained the wear often reveals the lighter coloured wood below the surface. Wear of this nature is primarily a cosmetic problem, as it doesn't affect the playability or structure of the guitar.

If you do need to rectify a worn fingerboard, then there are two approaches. The easiest is to just remove the frets, plane and/or sand the surface of the fingerboard until the wear marks have disappeared, making sure to keep it flat along the length, and either flat across the width, or matching the original radius. Then re-fret as described above. If the fingerboard is stained, it will need staining again before re-fretting. Depending on the depth of the wear, this method will slightly reduce the overall thickness of the neck. Also, if the wear is very deep, there is a risk of sanding through any fret marker inlays on the top of the fingerboard.

Alternatively, the fingerboard can be planed down to below the level of the fret slots, and then capped as described in Chapter 6.

Fingerboard wear is most commonly seen on the lower fret positions. In this case, the fingerboard itself was made with a cheaper, light-coloured wood, which was painted or stained black to look like ebony. This dark colour has been worn through, revealing the lighter wood below.

Bound fingerboards

A word or two about bound fingerboards. Bindings on the body of the guitar serve a purpose – they are there to protect the thin edges of the top and back plates of the guitar, particularly the end grain. The only purpose of binding on a fingerboard is to make it look pretty. I have no problem with anything that makes a guitar more aesthetically pleasing, unless it is at the expense of function.

The main problem with bound fingerboards is the risk of the ends of the frets lifting. On an unbound fingerboard, the frets are held down by the barbs on the tang of the fretwire along their whole length. On bound fingerboards the fret tang must be cut short by at least the width of the bindings, and usually a little more.

In recent years, most of the guitars I have had in my workshop with lifted fret ends had bound fingerboards. Given most of my repairs are on classical guitars, which rarely have bound fingerboards, this seems quite significant.

It is often claimed that a binding reduces the risk of fret ends sticking out from the edge of the fingerboard, but this is only the case if the ends of the frets are cut far enough short of the edge of the fingerboard to allow for any shrinkage in the wood. If the frets on a bound fingerboard *do* stick out, they are far sharper, as the tang has been cut away, just leaving the knife edge of the bevelled fret end.

Not only have the fret ends lifted from this bound fingerboard, they are also slightly protruding, leaving very sharp edges to catch the player's fingers.

Another concern with bound fingerboards is that they make repairs significantly more difficult. Any new frets to be fitted must have their tangs trimmed back, and lifted fret ends are more difficult to glue down. Cleaning out fret slots also requires a specially adapted saw. If the binding is made from a wood that matches the fingerboard, you can simply saw through the binding to allow frets with a full-length tang to be fitted. This approach is not appropriate for plastic bindings found on quite a few acoustic guitars, but for wooden bindings, it is my preferred solution, provided the customer is happy with it.

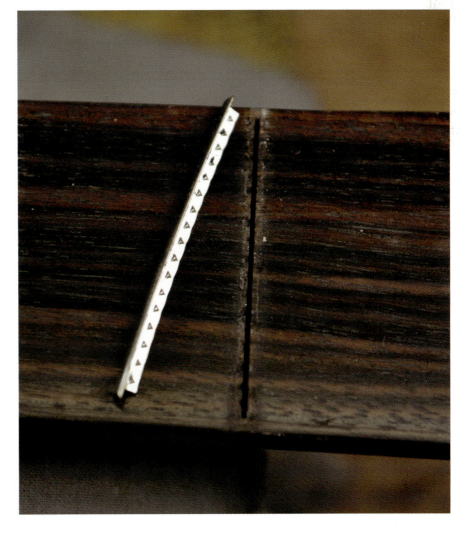

A fret removed from a bound fingerboard, showing where the tang has been cut back, leaving the ends free to lift from the fingerboard.

Fingerboard and Fret Work

CHAPTER 8

Finish Repairs

Types of finish

Over the years, many types of finish have been used for acoustic guitars. Glair (a simple mixture of egg white, sugar and honey) was used to finish lute soundboards for many years. It didn't offer much protection, but was thin and kept the top looking clean.

Rubbed oil finishes and varnishes have also been used extensively and seem to be returning to popularity, with a slight movement away from the high gloss finishes that are still used for the vast majority of guitars. These can give either a matt/satin finish, or a higher gloss if enough coats are built up.

French polish is often mistakenly thought to be a material used in finishing, but in fact it refers to the method of applying the finish, by building up a large number of very thin layers, applied with a cotton 'pad' or 'rubber'. The material used is shellac, a resin harvested from trees and secreted by the lac beetle. The resin is processed to create flakes, which are then dissolved in alcohol to form a liquid polish. It produces a high gloss finish without needing a high build-up, which has acoustic benefits, particularly for classical guitars. Although shellac can become very hard over time, it offers limited protection because it is such a thin finish.

Nitrocellulose lacquer (nitro) was developed in the 1920s and was very widely used in guitar making from around the 1950s. A combination of toxicity and flammability have made it a less desirable choice of finish, particularly for individual luthiers. The finish does not age particularly well, with a tendency to crack and yellow, but for some players the aged look is seen as a benefit. Sprayed lacquers are almost universal in a factory setting, where the fast drying time and quick build-up are a distinct advantage.

Modern polyester finishes have largely replaced nitro in factory instruments, mainly for their high level of durability, and resistance to solvent attack. The downside of these finishes is that, although they are very tough, they are much more difficult to repair if they are damaged. They also tend to be applied quite thickly, which on the soundboard is considered detrimental to the tone of the guitar.

Water-based finishes are becoming more popular, and many can be sprayed, brushed, or wiped on. They are less hazardous to use, and dry and build up quickly, but it can be difficult to achieve a clear, high-gloss finish.

When repairing finishes, it is very useful to know what you are dealing with. Unfortunately, it is not always easy to tell what the finish is just by looking at it.

One important factor is the ability of new applications of finish to blend in with the underlying coats. Many modern finishes will not 'burn in' to the existing finish, and this makes invisible finish repairs much more difficult, and any sanding back of the finish can reveal 'witness lines' between successive coats of the finish. Shellac is usually considered the easiest finish to repair successfully, as new applications of shellac will burn into the existing finish to give a seamless result (although very old shellac tends to be more resistant to this). Like shellac, nitrocellulose is a solvent release finish, curing by evaporation of the solvent. This means that the solvent present in new applications of the finish will soften the existing finish, allowing them to blend together.

Oil finishes

The term 'oil-finish' can apply to a range of finish types, from oil varnishes used traditionally in violin making, to thinned oil varnishes (often referred to as rubbed or wiped oil finishes) through to pure oil finishes. Oil varnishes of the type used on violins are rarely used for guitars, and pure oils like linseed take a long time to harden (if they do at all) and offer minimal protection. Rubbed oil finishes are actually an oil varnish that has been thinned down to make it easy to apply, usually by just wiping on with a cloth. Additives are often used to speed up the drying process. Only three or four coats need be applied to the wood, giving a matt or a satin finish. Further coats can be applied to gradually build up to a gloss finish.

Repairing or renovating oil finishes

Oil finishes that have not been built up to a high gloss are relatively easy to repair. First, the surfaces should all be thoroughly cleaned using alcohol. I have found that guitars finished with oil will sometimes have bad discolouration marks on any lighter-coloured woods, particularly the soundboard. These can be largely removed with thorough cleaning. Once the surfaces are clean, they can be assessed for condition.

A decision must be made about how far to go with renovating a finish. Generally, I try to take off as little (if any) of the original finish as possible. The problem with removing a rubbed oil finish is that it is likely to be very thin, and you will very quickly work through to the surface of the wood. If only a few coats were used, the finish may only be in the wood, with none on the surface at all. The surface of any light-coloured woods will darken over time with exposure to the air and to UV light. Removing any material from the surface will leave a lighter coloured patch.

It is possible to recover the lost colour, but very difficult to make it blend in perfectly with the original finish. Even after fresh coats of oil have been applied to the bare area, there will usually still be a very noticeable light patch.

The reverse can often be true of darker-coloured woods, and rosewood in particular tends to lighten over time. The result is that removing any wood from the surface can result in a very patchy appearance.

In order to keep a uniform colour and tone to the finish, you either need to not remove any wood at all from the surface,

This image demonstrates the problem of taking any surface material off aged finishes. The finish itself has some colour, but most of the problem is from removing the surface layer of wood, which has darkened over a number of years' exposure to UV light.

Even after adding a few coats of oil finish, the loss of colour is still very obvious. This would require some very delicate and time-consuming work to add the colour back, and the result might still not be perfect.

A similar, but opposite problem is often encountered with rosewood. Here, some repair work on the rib has necessitated sanding through the outer layer of wood that has faded over time, revealing the original darker colour below.

tonal properties of the top. As soundboards (particularly spruce) are generally light in colour, it is normally better not to remove any wood from the surface. With a thin oil finish, there may be very little finish at all on the surface, so even a very light sanding can result in some colour change.

Removing the finish

If it is necessary to remove all the finish from parts or the whole of the guitar, then I prefer to start with a cabinet scraper. It is possible to remove many finishes with solvents of various types, but this tends to be very messy, and there is a risk of staining light-coloured woods if they are close to darker woods, particularly rosewood.

The exception for me is if the finish needs to be completely removed from the soundboard, and you do not want to remove any wood. This can work

or remove wood from the whole surface evenly. The latter can often be acceptable on the head, neck, back and sides of the guitar, but it is not advisable to remove any wood from the soundboard of the guitar, as this can easily affect the

A cabinet scraper with a smooth, fine burr is very effective for removing shellac and other finishes quickly, and without creating a lot of dust. When the finish has mostly been removed it may be safer to switch to sanding, particularly if you want to minimise wood removal.

To avoid damage to the edges of the bindings, the scraper is held at an angle to the edge of the guitar, but is moved in the direction indicated by the arrow. The scraper is lifted from the surface before its end corner reaches the binding.

well with shellac, although if it is very old, it will not be as easily soluble in alcohol as you might expect. Oil finishes penetrate the wood, so removing the finish without removing any wood isn't an option. Harder finishes can be very difficult to remove with solvents, and finish strippers are often hazardous.

When scraping, take great care at the edges of the plates, as it is very easy to damage the bindings. Angle the scraper so that it doesn't catch and tear the bindings.

After scraping, sand the surface to remove any last bits of finish, and to smooth out any marks left by the scraper. Finish with a grade of abrasive that is appropriate for the type of finish being applied. For French polishing with shellac, I recommend 320 or 400 grit.

For an oil finish, the finer the abrasive used, the more sheen you will get to the finish, so I usually aim for at least 2,000 grit. Go through every grade thoroughly, making sure that the scratch

The back has been sanded with 320 grit. This level of finish is sufficient for French polishing, or lacquer spraying, provided all scratches from coarser grades have been removed.

For a rubbed oil finish, working through finer grades of abrasives will give a better result, with more of a satin look than matt. Here I've used Micro-Mesh, stopping at 3200 grade.

marks from each previous grade are completely removed. Any scratches may not be obvious until the finest grade is reached, and the oil applied. Finding coarse sanding marks at that stage can be very frustrating, as the whole process will need to be repeated, so it is worth taking your time with every grade.

On this guitar, the finish on the back was patchy and in poor condition. It could have been improved with just a further application of one or two coats

ABOVE: A patchy oil finish on a rosewood back. In this case, it was easier to remove the finish from the whole plate and start again than to try to touch it up.

LEFT: The back has been thoroughly sanded, making a much better job of preparation than was achieved when the guitar was first made.

of oil, but in this case the decision was made to sand through the oil finish, clean up the surface, and apply a new oil finish.

The surface was first scraped and sanded to remove all the original finish, and a small amount of the surface of the rosewood. This removed the patchiness and some coarse grade sanding marks which were left when the guitar was first made. A 220 grit abrasive was used first, followed by 320 grit. Further sanding with finer abrasives through to 3600 grade Micro-Mesh resulted in a clean, smooth finish, which should result in a good satin sheen after applying the oil.

Refinishing with oil

The Danish oil is simply applied with a clean cotton cloth, taking care to work it into the grain, and uniformly wet the wood.

Any excess oil is wiped off with a second clean cloth, and the finish left to dry for a minimum of 24 hours.

After the first coat has dried, a second coat is applied in the same way. The result is satisfactory, but a slightly higher level of sheen would be achieved by allowing the second coat to dry fully, and then applying a third coat, but with the oil thinned slightly with white spirit.

A rubbed oil finish is probably the simplest to master. Be sure to dispose of oil-soaked cloths safely.

> ### Safety note
>
> Rags that have been used for applying Danish (and other) oil finishes have been known to self-combust. Used rags should either be stored in an airtight metal container or soaked in a bucket of water. At the very least, lay the rag out flat on a non-combustible surface until it is completely dry before disposing of it.

RIGHT: After only one coat of Danish oil, a very respectable matt finish is achieved. This already looks much better than the original. Most of the work needed to achieve this was in the preparation.

RIGHT: After two coats of oil, there is already a very nice sheen to the surface of the rosewood. Not all tonewoods take an oil finish as well as this, and softwoods in particular can be less satisfactory.

Dents in oil finishes

Dents in a plate with an oil finish can usually be easily repaired using a combination of heat and water as described in Chapter 5, followed by a simple application of oil if needed. If any sanding is required, there is likely to be some colour change, so it is best avoided if possible.

Shellac finishes

French polishing of musical instruments is far less common than it once was, but it is still used extensively by classical guitar makers, and by a few acoustic guitar makers. As already mentioned, the very thin finish offers limited protection from mechanical damage, but is relatively easy to repair by anyone experienced in French polishing.

French polishing is often seen as a bit of a black art, and it certainly feels like that at times. Even after many years of using the process, it can still throw up unexpected (and unwanted) results. With practice, however, you should be able to achieve very good results most of the time, and there is great satisfaction in achieving a completely invisible repair, or a significant restoration of the finish without having to resort to completely stripping the original finish from the guitar.

As with oil finishes, the recommended approach is to remove as little of the original finish as possible. An old guitar with lots of dents and scratches can be given a new lease of life, and added protection, without losing the character attained from years of use. Although it may be possible to restore an instrument to 'as new' condition, this will nearly always involve removing a significant amount of wood from the surfaces of the plates, which in the case of the soundboard can have a detrimental effect on the tone, and even on the structural stability of the guitar.

Note that although shellac itself is not harmful, the solvent (alcohol) is highly flammable and exposure to the skin should be minimised.

Repairing or renovating a shellac finish

Shellac is not a particularly robust finish, and a common problem is marks and wear in the finish where the guitar is held against the player's body, or where their arm rests. This type of damage seems to be dependent on how the player holds the guitar, the temperature of the room and the player's body chemistry. Some players never leave a mark in shellac, and others can wear through it in a matter of months.

In this case, the shellac is badly worn and marked in the area that contacts the player's chest. In addition, there is some deep crazing to the finish in a few patches, that probably extends right through the finish. You might think that this would mean the finish on the back would have to be completely removed, but the beauty of shellac is that these cracks can be filled and burned into the existing finish, and should completely disappear.

The first job is to sand the damaged area. The idea is to remove some of the surface marks, but not go right through the finish. Stop when the surface is uniformly matt. The crazing will still be there, but that will be dealt with shortly. In this case, I've used 1800 grade Micro-Mesh, as I wanted to remove a reasonable amount of material from the surface, but not leave any deep scratches.

With the surface dust from the sanding wiped away, the deep crazing

An example of a French polish finish that has been badly damaged as a result of prolonged contact with the player's body. The combination of heat, along with some body chemistry, has eaten into the finish, leaving it dulled and crazed.

When sanding flat surfaces, always use a hard foam block. This will be flexible enough to follow the curve of the back, but will still flatten out any irregularities in the surface.

The dust created by the sanding has been deposited in the cracks in the shellac finish. Brush or vacuum this away before continuing with the repolishing process.

is now very apparent where it is filled with the white dust of the sanded shellac. This dust should be brushed out of the cracks before applying any fresh shellac.

I always recommend making up your own shellac solution. Shellac has a limited shelf life in liquid form, and the date of making is rarely marked on the container. It will not be apparent when it has passed its sell-by date until after you have completed the polishing, and the finish refuses to harden. Here I am using blonde, dewaxed shellac flakes. These should be dissolved in the highest purity ethanol you can get.

Rather than sanding, and then applying fresh shellac to just the damaged area, it is advisable to work on the whole area. This may seem like unnecessary work, but in fact it will take no longer (apart from the sanding bit). One of the most common mistakes when repairing French polish is to spend too long in one area, which can soften the underlying finish to the point where you can lift all the shellac from the surface of the wood. Working on the whole area of the back (or the top or sides) will allow the shellac to dry slightly as you are building up the finish. Working over the whole surface will also give a more even, professional look, usually with no evidence of the repair/refinishing work.

ABOVE: These blonde, dewaxed shellac flakes are very fine, and can dissolve fairly quickly. Stirring or agitating the jar regularly will speed up the process, and prevent a thick layer of shellac forming at the bottom of the jar.

LEFT: Sanding the whole back, rather than just the damaged area, will result in a more even, professional-looking finish.

French polishing

You are now ready to start applying the shellac to the back, using a traditional French polishing rubber. The rubber is simply made using some cotton wadding, wrapped in two layers of clean cotton cloth. I find it useful to tie the loose ends of the cloth layers with an elastic band.

Always check that you have the right amount of shellac solution in the rubber. A very common mistake is to have the rubber too wet. A good check is to dab the rubber on a paper towel – it should leave a damp mark, but not look too wet.

The number of sessions needed to renovate the finish and fill the crazing will vary depending on your level of polishing skills, how deep the crazing goes (if there is any), and on how much sanding back was done to level the damage. In this case, I did two initial polishing sessions separated by about 4 hours.

Start polishing using a circular motion, covering the whole area as evenly as possible. Vary the size of the circles, and make sure you get right up to the edges. Switch to doing straight lines along the grain from time to time, taking care to glide the rubber onto and off the surface. If you catch the edge of the plate with the rubber as you glide on to it, you are likely to get a drip of shellac running down the side. Try to avoid this, but if it happens, wipe it away immediately with the rubber. Traditionally, French polishers used a combination of circles, figures of eight, and straight lines both along and across the grain to obtain the best finish, but after many years I have found that a combination of varying sized circles and straight lines along the grain gives excellent results. Adding a drop of oil to the pad (I use walnut oil) will help it glide smoothly over the surface and reduce the risk of it sticking and leaving

Here we can still see evidence of the cracks in the finish. Over time, the fresh shellac will shrink further, making these more visible, so continue polishing until they have completely gone.

Shellac is one of the least hazardous finishes you can use on a guitar. The glove is worn to prevent a build-up of shellac on your fingers, and also reduces the risk of fingernails scratching the polish.

A very satisfactory finish, but it is likely that the cracks will reappear in the future. Other than completely stripping the finish and starting again, the only solution is to repeat the process as and when the cracks return.

a mark. Any residual oil can be removed at the end of the process.

Re-charge the rubber with shellac solution as required, always remembering to check it isn't too wet. Continue with this process until it gets difficult to move the rubber without it sticking. Remember that if things start to go wrong, *stop polishing*. If you have left a mark where the rubber has stuck, or if there is some dust on the surface, don't try to polish it away. Leave the shellac to dry completely, and once it's dry, lightly sand back any defects.

Once the session is complete, carefully hang the guitar to allow the shellac to dry fully – usually 24 hours.

Before starting the next polishing session, inspect the surface carefully. If it is not very flat or there are specs of dust in the surface, lightly sand again with Micro-Mesh 1800 grade. Inspecting this guitar after two polishing sessions, the cracks have been partly filled, but are still visible.

As the finish is built up, you will find that it doesn't take long before the pad becomes difficult to move across the surface. Either add a little more oil, or just stop and leave the finish to dry before resuming.

When you reach a point where the surface looks even and glossy, and any crazing or holes have been filled, move on to the final session of polishing, which should leave the surface perfectly flat, and very shiny.

Before starting the final session, lightly sand back the surface again using 1800 or 2400 grade Micro-Mesh – just enough to remove any imperfections in the finish.

The process for the final session is the same as before, but using a more diluted shellac mix. Pour a small amount of the original shellac solution and further dilute it by about a factor of five by adding more alcohol. The only other difference is that you don't want the rubber to be as wet as when building up the polish – just wet enough to allow the rubber to move over the surface easily. Work for just long enough to achieve a high gloss. Just one drop of oil on the rubber should be enough to prevent it sticking.

Any residual oil on the surface can be removed using a burnishing cream. There are various makes available – in the US, Maguiar's #9 car polish is often recommended. Novus plastic polish (#2) can also be used, but I prefer Super Nikco, which I find gives the best finish with least effort. Before using any burnishing creams, the shellac needs to be left to harden for at least a few days, and ideally a week.

The exact process will depend on the burnishing cream being used, but in general, apply just enough cream to a clean, soft cotton cloth to wet it, wipe off any excess and then work it gently into the finish using small circular motions. Work in small areas – about one eighth of

156 Finish Repairs

the area of the back. Clear any remaining product with a separate clean cloth.

With any deep marks or cracks in shellac, note that even if the finish looks perfectly flat after a few days of building it up, it will always shrink back, leaving depressions in the finish where the new shellac filled the cracks or depressions. To achieve a perfect finish, the guitar needs to be left for at least a week, before repeating the process of levelling and building up the finish again. In some cases, you will need to repeat this process a few more times.

Dents in shellac finishes

Dents in shellac finishes can be steamed out as described in Chapter 5, but some refinishing will be required. The alternative is to fill the dent, and then polish over with some more shellac to blend in the repair.

Small dents can be easily filled and levelled with the existing finish. In some cases, the repair can be made invisible, but even if visible, there is usually some improvement in appearance. There are a few options for filling small dents in shellac. The best chance of having the fill blend perfectly with the existing finish is to use shellac, as it will melt into the existing finish leaving no witness lines. Unfortunately, even the lightest coloured shellac will leave a darker patch where the fill is, and it is also likely that the shellac fill will shrink over time, leaving a smaller, but still visible indentation where the dent was.

A second option, and the quickest, is to fill the dent with CA glue.

It will not blend perfectly with the French polish, but a few coats of shellac over the repair and the surrounding area can usually make it close to invisible. I usually apply the CA to the dent using a cocktail stick or similar, which gives more control than even a very fine applicator nozzle.

The fill should go fully to the edges of the dent and be slightly proud of the

A very small dent in a spruce soundboard. Many players will just accept that small marks like these are inevitable with a French polished guitar. Others seem to want their guitar to always look perfect.

A cocktail stick, with the tip nipped off, is a very precise way of applying very small amounts of CA glue to a repair. Brushes cannot be used for this, as the CA glue will cure rapidly in the bristles of the brush, ruining it.

The drop of CA glue here is obviously proud of the surface, but you also need to be sure that it extends right to the edges of the dent, and preferably very slightly over.

I first learned of the taped single-edge razor blade idea from a fellow tutor, but don't know where they got it from. I believe it was originally attributed to Frank Ford.

surface. Although there will be minimal shrinkage of the CA glue when it dries, it is better to be sure the dent is fully filled in one go, rather than having to build up layers.

The best way of initially levelling the fill is to use a single-edge steel razor blade as a scraper. Wrapping a single layer of Sellotape (Scotch tape) over both edges of the blade will allow it to scrape the fill down without damaging the surrounding finish. You can use the blade as it is, but creating a slight burr on the edge will allow it to cut a little faster.

Rest the blade so that the taped areas are either side of the fill, and gently scrape across it. Repeat until the scraper no longer removes any more material from the fill.

The fill will now be barely proud of the surrounding finish – just the thickness of the tape. Switch to a fine abrasive wrapped around a plastic pencil eraser. Start gently at the centre of the fill, working slightly outwards to blend in the fill with the rest of the finish.

On a flat surface, this taped scraper will continue to remove material from the repair fill until it is almost flush with the surface. Using a flat sanding block can work, but will remove much more of the surrounding finish by the time you have it perfectly flat.

Fine abrasive wrapped around a flat, plastic eraser will finish the flattening job very quickly, with minimal impact on the surrounding finish.

French polishing for repairs can take a lot of skill and patience. The most common mistake is to have the pad too wet, particularly when working on small areas. Using a lubricating oil will help reduce the risk of the pad sticking and marking the surface.

Finish Repairs

A very faint outline of the dent can still be seen on close inspection, but the result is very satisfactory.

I have been filling small dents from this 25ml bottle of Deft brushing lacquer for a number of years, and it still isn't quite empty.

Applying Deft with a fine, synthetic brush. To keep brushes in good condition, they should be cleaned immediately after use with the appropriate cleaner or solvent.

The dent fill should be left to fully harden before levelling it with a scraper or abrasives.

At this point, you have the option of going through progressively finer grades of Micro-Mesh abrasive, and then using a burnishing cream to bring back the gloss to the area. This will give a perfectly level finish, but the fill will still be visible due to the different material used. An improved result can be obtained by French polishing over the repair and surrounding area with several more coats of shellac.

Depending on the condition of the rest of the finish on the soundboard, it might be worthwhile working over the whole surface to blend everything in and give a more professional look to the repair.

The third option is Deft clear brushing lacquer. This will not dry as quickly as CA glue, but will not shrink as much as shellac, and is clearer. As with a CA fill, it will not blend perfectly with the shellac, but is probably less visible without having to French polish over the repair and surrounding area.

The Deft is applied to the dent with a fine brush. Make sure that the fill goes all the way to the edges of the dent, and leave it so that the fill is proud of the surface to allow for some shrinkage and levelling.

The fill needs to be left to harden fully before levelling and blending in the same way described for the CA fill.

Poly finishes

Polyurethane and polyester finishes became prevalent in the 1960s and 1970s. They offer a few advantages over nitrocellulose for the manufacturer, being quick to apply and very durable. For the repairer, however, they are far more challenging. Although it is always possible to repair damaged poly finishes, the results are usually far less satisfactory than nitro or shellac finishes, where the newly applied finish blends into the existing finish. The result is that poly finish repairs are far more visible, even if the surface of the repair is perfectly flat and has been brought back to a full gloss.

Repairing or renovating poly finishes

A fairly common problem with poly (and nitrocellulose) finishes is the appearance of white spots below the finish. There are a few possible causes of these, including moisture trapped under or between the coats of finish. Whatever the cause, on poly finishes these are difficult to rectify, and usually require some or all of the finish to be removed. If the spots are confined to a relatively small area such as the head plate, it can be worth taking the finish down to bare wood and refinishing. Faced with a small patch on a much larger surface (the back, for example), you would need to consider how much work is involved in completely refinishing the back, and whether it is worthwhile. Trying to refinish just a small area is unlikely to give a satisfactory result and could end up looking worse than before.

As the head is a small area, it is not too difficult to completely refinish if necessary, and there is always a possibility that the problem is in the outer layers of finish, which turned out to be the case here.

Start removing the finish with a cabinet scraper with a smooth, fine burr. Work as evenly as possible and pay attention to the problem area. In this case, the finish was quite thick, and it soon became apparent that the white spots were only about halfway through the finish.

When the white spots were significantly reduced, but not completely removed, I switched to a sanding block for more control. Here I'm using a 240 grit open-coat abrasive wrapped around a flat, wooden sanding block.

Most of the marks disappeared quickly, but some of the spots were on the corner of the head adjacent to the sides. These were likely to be less visible, and it can be risky to sand edges, as you can very quickly go through to bare wood. In this case, the finish was sufficiently thick that I was confident of being able to remove the worst of the marks safely.

At this stage I switched to a finer abrasive (400 grit Abranet) both to further smooth the top surface, and to work more gently on the edges. Using a hard foam block keeps the flat surfaces flat, but allows you to carefully sand over the edges.

White spots like these are often seen in nitro or poly finishes and are usually attributed to moisture in the finish. For poly finishes like this one, the only option is to scrape or sand the finish until they have gone.

Finish Repairs

A cabinet scraper makes light work of removing even hard finishes and produces far less dust than sanding.

Using a flat block minimises the risk of sanding through the finish.

With a finish this thick, there is a good chance that there will be plenty of finish left on the surface once the defects have been sanded away.

Clamping the neck of the guitar securely in a vice leaves both hands free, allowing you to extract potentially harmful dust at the source when sanding.

Finish Repairs

A dense foam block is ideal when sanding finishes with Micro-Mesh. It is flexible enough to reduce clogging and follow slight contours, but firm enough not to round or sand through the finish at the edges.

The finished result after some hand burnishing. Going through all the grades of Micro-Mesh abrasive will minimise the amount of work needed with the burnishing cream.

On this repair a good result was possible without completely removing all of the finish from the head, so the next task was to use progressively finer grades of Micro-Mesh abrasive to remove the scratches from the coarser abrasives. It is essential in this process to go through *all* of the Micro-Mesh grades, making certain that at each stage you have removed the scratches from the previous (coarser) grades. It is very frustrating (and time-consuming) to reach the final grade only to realise that there are still marks from the 1500 grade (or worse the 220 grit) and then have to repeat the whole process.

The final stage is to use a burnishing cream to return the finish to close to its original level of gloss. Various products are available that can work well, but my preference is Super Nikco, which can be used on the most delicate of finishes. This final burnishing will reveal any scratches missed, which will need removing by going back through some of the coarser grades of abrasive.

Refinishing

When it is necessary to completely remove the finish down to bare wood, then a new finish will need to be applied. Ideally, you would replace the removed finish with one of the same type to match the rest of the guitar. However, without access to spray equipment, the choices are limited. It is possible to buy polyurethane and nitrocellulose aerosol spray cans, but these products are usually quite hazardous in use, and the results are not always satisfactory.

Water-based lacquers are considerably less toxic than solvent-based ones. They seldom produce quite the same level of gloss, but in smaller areas like the head, they are usually acceptable. Many can be applied with a brush, and a good level of gloss can be achieved by going through the abrasive grades and then burnishing as described above.

Another option is to French polish the area. Although it will not offer the same level of protection against mechanical damage, it is non-toxic, and requires no special equipment to apply. It does, however, take some skill and experience to achieve the best results.

Scuffs and light scratches can be seen as a sign of the instrument is being well used, but they can easily be improved, if not completely removed.

In the right light, some fine scratches are still visible, but the finish is greatly improved.

Scratch removing

Light scratch marks in poly finishes can often be removed, or at least improved, with any of the many commercially available guitar polishes or burnishing creams.

In this case, some improvement would have been possible using just a burnishing cream, but the scratches were quite deep in the finish, so it was necessary to first sand lightly using Micro-Mesh. Starting with 2400 grade and working through all the finer grades up to 12,000 effectively removed all of the scratches and scuffs.

Although I usually prefer a very delicate burnishing cream, for harder finishes a slightly more aggressive compound is called for, at least initially. Here I have used T-cut Original car paint restorer, and then finished with Super Nikco.

Dents in poly finishes

Dent repairs in poly finishes can be filled, levelled and polished to give an acceptable result, but it can be very difficult to make the repair invisible. Unless the customer wants a perfect finish, I would usually suggest accepting very small imperfections as evidence of use. Filling small dents will offer some improvement, but the nature of poly finishes makes a perfectly invisible repair difficult.

This dent in a polyurethane finish can be improved, but it is unlikely to be perfect.

A range of different coloured natural woods, all found in my workshop. There are quite a few variations of brown, but also some orange, purple and green hues.

Natural wood colours

There are a surprising variety of colours found naturally in woods. Although most softwoods and many hardwoods are a typical 'whitish cream/brown' colour, there are also woods with black, orange, purple and green hues.

Stains vs. coloured finishes

There are two basic approaches to colouring wood. Stains contain pigments that are dissolved in a solvent which is designed to penetrate into the wood. The pigments remain in the wood and cannot be removed without removing the surface layer of the wood itself. Obviously, the amount of wood you need to remove will depend on how deeply the stain penetrates. On the plus side, stains are easy to apply evenly, and the depth of colour can be adjusted by increasing or decreasing the amount of solvent. Stains cannot be used to lighten dark woods.

Coloured finishes have pigments dissolved in the finish itself. When applied to the wood, they colour it by adding a layer of colour over the surface. The colour can be removed by simply removing the finish. Often the best approach to adding some colour to a light-coloured wood is a combination of these two.

Basic method and colour theory

My preferred approach is to start with a light stain, and for this I mostly use the Van Dyck crystals discussed in Chapter 5. These are dissolved in water, and the intensity of colour can be adjusted by varying the strength of the solution. The basic colour cannot be changed, and is a sort of woody brown, which is a good base for many natural wood colours. The aim is just to slightly darken the wood to give a base for further colour that will be added with some coloured finish. For light-coloured woods, you will normally need a weak, light solution of the crystals. For darker woods, a stronger solution might be appropriate, as used when dealing with the repairs to rosewood sides in Chapter 5.

Once the stain has been applied and has dried, some coloured finish is used to match the existing wood and finish. In theory, all possible hues can be made using a combination of just three colours. Mixing green, red and blue *light* can create any colour of light. This is known as *additive* colour mixing. The situation is different when we are mixing pigments of dyes to make a particular colour. Pigments and dyes work by absorbing light of certain wavelengths, so that the colour we see is the inverse of those absorbed. For example, a pigment that absorbs blue light will appear yellow. As with additive colour mixing, we can produce any colour of pigment by mixing three different-coloured pigments. This is known as *subtractive* colour mixing, and the most effective three colours to use are magenta, cyan and yellow, just as you find in any inkjet printer. These are the complementary colours of green, red and blue. Note that strictly speaking, although we can generate any *hue* with these three bases, we cannot produce any *colour*, for which we would need to control the saturation and lightness as well as the hue.

Colour matching repair patches

In practice, it is somewhat easier to create colours to match a particular wood and finish by mixing pigments of varying shades of brown. This is because most woods (with a few exceptions) are basically variations on creamy browns, reddish browns, greenish browns and so on, so we are starting with hues that are reasonably close to what we are trying to replicate. The exception to this is guitars with brightly coloured finishes, which will not be covered here, as they are mostly found in solid body electric guitars.

When colour matching, it is important to realise that within any sample of wood there will be a range of colours, sometimes quite a wide range. A large repair patch filled with a single colour will always stand out, giving the impression of a poor colour match, even if the colour is well chosen. If the wood used for the patch is close in tone to the existing wood, this will minimise the amount of coloured finish that needs to be added. This will prevent the natural variations of tone in the patch wood being obscured by the coloured finish, and hence give a more satisfactory result.

Mixing of colours is best done on a white or transparent palette. Select the pigment that appears closest to the colour of the wood to be matched and put a small amount of this base colour on the palette. The pigments used here in shellac solution are quite concentrated, and so need diluting with more shellac before use. Add small amounts of two or three other diluted pigments to the palette and start to add small amounts of these to the base colour. Dark pigments should only be added in very small quantities, as they can change the colour dramatically. Shellac solutions will dry out quickly, so keep adding more shellac or alcohol as you work.

Keep adjusting the colour until you are close to a match, and then test it on a piece of wood matching the patch. Make further adjustments as necessary, and when you are happy with the result, add more shellac to further dilute the pigment. This will allow you to build up the finish in layers until the depth of colour is correct.

Apply the coloured shellac with a fine brush, taking great care not to get any on the surrounding wood/finish, as this will create dark areas surrounding the patch. Leave each layer of finish to dry before applying the next. If many layers are needed, each additional layer will take longer to dry. Adding more shellac too soon will risk lifting the existing layers in places, giving a patchy, uneven colour.

When you are satisfied with the colour match, leave the repair to fully dry (ideally 24 hours) before applying clear shellac over the repair and surrounding area to blend it in.

I use pigments dissolved in shellac for colour matching. These are ideal for working on French polish, but can be used on most types of finish.

A clear mixing palette on a white background helps achieve a good colour match. Once the desired hue is reached, the mix is diluted further, so that the colour can be built up in stages with successive applications.

Applying colour to a small repair patch. The inset shows the colour variation within a small area of the soundboard wood. This variation is usually most significant in softwoods, with the winter growth lines being much darker than the summer growth.

CHAPTER 9

Bridge Repairs

The majority of bridge repair work involves either bridge rotation, bridge lifting or detaching. Rotation is where the action of the string tension pulling on the top of the saddle has caused the top to deform, tilting the bridge forwards towards the soundhole. A small amount of rotation is acceptable, and indeed a guitar with no bridge rotation at all is probably overbuilt. Bridge lifting is also caused by string tension, but in this case the back edge of the bridge has started to pull away from the soundboard, leaving a gap and weakening the joint. In extreme cases, the bridge can be pulled completely from the soundboard.

This classical bridge has completely detached from the soundboard. Some of the soundboard material has come away with the bridge, and a small piece of bridge has remained attached to the soundboard.

Bridge Repairs **171**

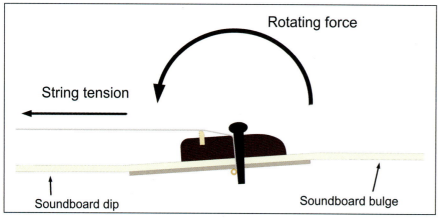

The tension of the strings act on the bridge, and this force tries to rotate the bridge in the direction shown by the arrow. The area of the soundboard behind the bridge is pushed upwards, and the area in front is pushed downwards.

Measuring bridge rotation

A visual inspection of the shape of the soundboard surface is usually enough to determine whether there is a more than acceptable amount of bridge rotation. The area between the bridge and the soundhole will become flattened or slightly concave, as the rotation of the bridge pushes down on that side. Conversely, the area below the bridge will bulge slightly upwards, often referred to as 'bridge belly'. A very slight concavity above the bridge is to be expected,

Bridge rotation

Excessive bridge rotation can be caused by the soundboard and/or bracing being too weak, or the string tension being too high. A weak soundboard/bracing system is usually due to poor quality of the materials used, or the soundboard being too thin, or the braces too small. If a guitar is built to work well with light gauge strings (referred to as low or normal tension for nylon strings), then it may not be strong enough to withstand heavier gauge (high-tension) strings for extended periods of time. Fitting steel strings to a guitar built for nylon string tensions will almost certainly cause bridge rotation, and it's surprising how often this happens. If the steel strings have been on the guitar for an extended period, the damage is likely to be permanent, but in some cases simply fitting the correct tension strings will remedy the problem. Bridge rotation only becomes an issue when it starts to affect either the action (string height) or the intonation (tuning).

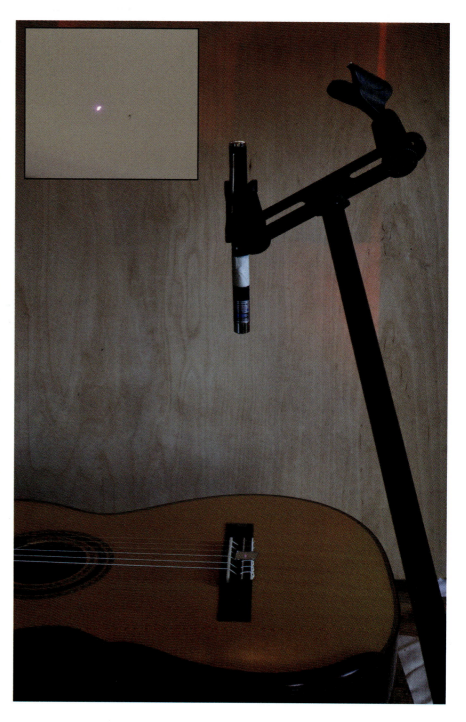

My setup for measuring bridge rotation. The laser pointer is held on a microphone stand, and a small mirror is taped to the tie-block of the bridge. The inset shows the reflected spot on a piece of paper taped to the ceiling, and the change in position of the laser spot from the pencil mark when the string tension was removed.

172   Bridge Repairs

but this area should not be depressed by more than a few millimetres. In marginal cases, check the intonation and action, and if these can be brought within acceptable limits by simply adjusting the saddle, then no further remedial work will be required.

For a more precise measurement of bridge rotation, a hand-held laser pointer can be used. The laser is clamped in position above the bridge and pointing down onto it. A small mirror is temporarily attached to the bridge and the position of the reflected laser spot is marked on a piece of paper taped to the ceiling. When the string tension is removed, the position of the reflected laser beam will move, and this new position is also marked. By measuring the distance the reflected spot moves, and the distance from the mirror to the ceiling, the angle of rotation of the bridge can be calculated. Anything more than 3-4 degrees could be considered a problem, but if the action and playability are acceptable, and the rotation isn't getting any worse, then corrective measures should not be required, other than switching to lower tension strings.

Correcting bridge rotation

Effective correction of bridge rotation is difficult. There is a device called a 'Bridge Doctor', which is fixed under the bridge of the guitar, and braced against the end block. This can be effective in terms of reducing the bridge rotation, but it will also inevitably affect the way the soundboard vibrates, having a detrimental effect on the tone of the guitar. If the aim of the repair is simply to return the guitar to a playable condition, and the tone is not critical, then this can be a viable solution.

The other way to correct bridge rotation is to add more bracing to help support the soundboard against the string tension. Although this could also have an impact on the tone of the guitar, it is preferred because the fact that the bridge has rotated suggests that the soundboard was not sufficiently braced in the first place (assuming the correct tension strings were used).

Adding bracing

Adding bracing is usually easier with the back of the guitar removed, but the additional time and cost involved in removing the back make this worthwhile only on more valuable instruments. Depending on what type of bracing the guitar has, and how good access is through the soundhole, it is often possible to add bracing without removing the back. This can be accomplished using long reach clamps or magnets. Fan braced (classical) guitars will usually be easier, as additional fan braces can be glued between the existing ones.

I will deal here only with the classical repair. A standard X-braced acoustic guitar will be more problematic because there isn't anywhere obvious to add bracing. One possible solution is to remove the diagonal braces below the bridge and replace them with braces running along the line of the string tension, parallel to the grain of the soundboard. This is unlikely to be possible working through the soundhole, so would entail removing the back, which is covered in Chapter 12.

Begin by mapping out the existing bracing. This can be done simply using two pairs of small rare-earth magnets and a sheet of plain paper. The paper should be large enough to cover most of the lower bout. With the strings removed from the guitar, cut a hole in the paper the same shape and position of the bridge, allowing the paper to sit flat on the soundboard. Fix the paper in position with masking tape. This sheet of paper should remain in place throughout the repair, to aid positioning of the additional braces, and to protect the finish from damage.

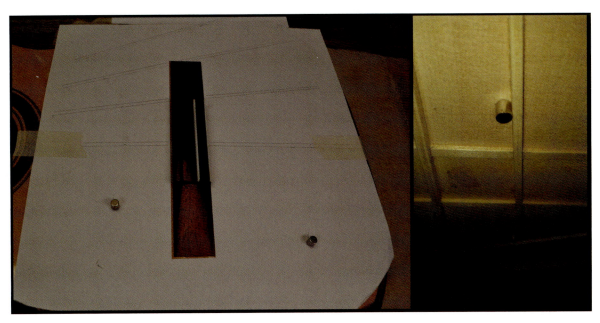

These small magnets are ideal for locating braces. The outer magnets are moved across the soundboard until they hit a brace, then the brace position is marked on the paper.

All the existing brace positions have been marked. With a fan bracing system like this, it is easy to just add a few more short fan braces. A slight complication here is the low transverse braces either side of the bridge.

The additional brace positions marked in red. These will stop just before the lower transverse brace to ease fitting. Adding them either side of the central fan brace will increase the strength along the line of the string tension, but add minimal stiffness across the soundboard.

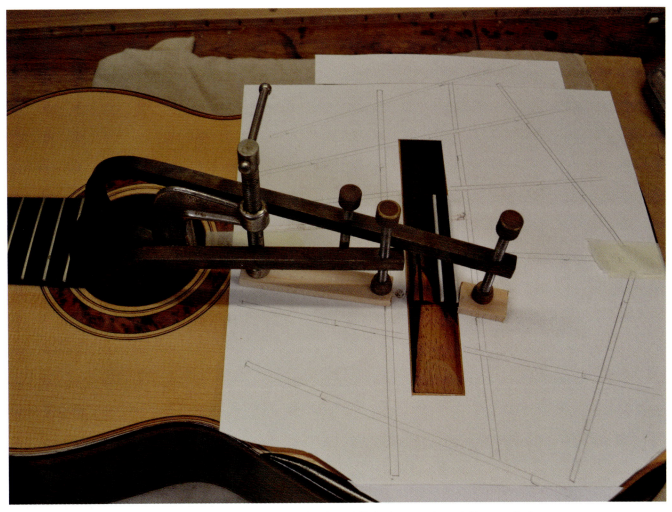

It is possible to use long-reach clamps to glue in these braces, but there is limited access through the soundhole.

You can get a rough idea of the bracing pattern by looking through the soundhole with an inspection mirror. To locate the braces precisely, place one magnet inside the guitar close to the end of a brace and locate the other magnet on the outside of the soundboard so that they hold.

By moving the outer magnet perpendicular to the brace you are trying to locate, you should be able to feel when the inner magnet contacts the side of the brace. Mark this position with a pencil on the paper sheet, and then repeat the process at each end of the brace. The furthest end of each brace does not need to be marked, as you are unlikely to need to glue the new braces much below the bridge. Repeat the process for the remaining braces.

Once the existing braces are mapped out on the paper, you need to decide where to add the new braces. The aim is to add strength to counteract the string tension, but without increasing the stiffness across the width of the soundboard. It is therefore best to add braces along the grain, and under the central part of the bridge.

Ideally, the new braces would be similar in dimension to the existing ones, but it will be easier to clamp them for gluing if they are reasonably wide. A width of about 6mm will work well, and the height should be similar to the adjacent braces. The ends of the braces can be tapered, but leave the tops of the braces flat for easy clamping. The length should be sufficient to reach from close to the lower harmonic bar to just beyond the bridge. Going far below the bridge will make clamping the far end difficult. In this particular case, rather than try to precisely fit the extra braces over both of the transverse braces, the braces will end just beyond the bridge, but just before the second transverse brace.

If enough long-reach clamps are available, and you can fit enough of them through the soundhole to clamp the brace securely, then you can use these.

Magnets are a better option in most circumstances, as positioning of the clamps through the soundhole can be difficult. Before gluing the braces, clean the inside surface of the soundboard where the braces will be glued as thoroughly as possible. A cloth dampened with alcohol is generally effective. If you cannot reach in far enough to clean to below the bridge, hold the bundled cloth in some forceps. Older guitars often have a lot of build-up of dirt, and you may need to repeat this process several times with a fresh part of the cloth, until it comes out fairly clean.

Finished inside surfaces

Some guitar makers like to finish the insides of their guitars. They will argue that this improves the 'reflection' of sound waves from the internal surfaces of the body, but there is no evidence for this that I am aware of. The main argument *against* finishing the insides of a guitar is that it makes repairs more difficult and certainly less effective if the finish is not first removed.

When carrying out repairs that will require gluing to the inside surface of the guitar (most commonly cleats), then it is always worth carefully inspecting the inside of the guitar to check that a finish has not been used. If there is a finish on the inside, then this must be sanded off before attempting to glue any cleats or additional braces.

Preparing the braces

Adjusting the height of braces through the soundhole is possible, but it is easier to make the braces the correct height before gluing them in place. It is down to the judgement of the repairer what size braces will be needed to correct (or at least reduce) the amount of bridge rotation. If the braces are made too high, then the tone of the guitar will be adversely affected – too low and the rotation will not be corrected. As a rough guide, I would suggest adding two braces of similar height to the braces either side of the central fan brace, reaching at least to the lower edge of the bridge.

Taper the ends of the braces down to 1–2mm in height, but leave most of the length at the maximum height for ease of clamping. The width of the braces is not highly critical, but very wide braces will add excess weight, and narrow braces will be more difficult to clamp. If using magnets, the braces should not be more than 1mm narrower than the magnet size.

If (as in this case) the new braces need to be fitted over existing braces, you will need a measurement of the brace height and approximate width. This can be done reasonably accurately by pressing a piece of Blu Tack over the brace and into the corners between the brace and the soundboard. Peel the Blu Tack away, work it back into shape, and measure the dimensions. The cut-out for the new brace does not have to be an exact match to the measurements, but it should not be any smaller, as this will prevent the new brace seating correctly.

The gluing surface of the braces must be flat and clean – ideally freshly planed rather than sanded. There is normally no need to shape the brace lengthwise to fit the curvature of the soundboard – classical fan braces should be flexible enough to conform to the curvature of the top when clamped.

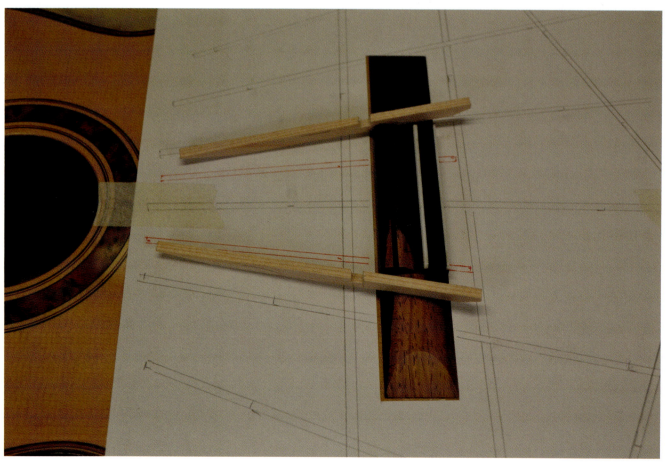

Two spruce braces prepared, with notches cut to fit over the transverse brace just above the bridge.

A piece of Blu Tack used to measure the size of a brace. After peeling it away from the brace, it needs to be worked back into shape before the brace dimensions are measured.

Gluing the new braces

Lightly mark the proposed positions of the new braces with a pencil on the sheet of paper used to map the existing braces. Lay a strip of double-sided tape along this line to hold the outer repair magnets in place. The number of magnets needed will depend on the length of the brace and the strength of the individual magnets, but they need to be spaced far enough apart that the magnetic attraction does not overcome the strength of the double-sided tape (either on the outside of the guitar, or the ones on the brace itself). I'd normally expect to use four or five. Check that the magnets have sufficient strength to pull the brace into the curvature of the soundboard. A larger, stronger magnet used at the centre of the brace can help with this.

Place the brace alongside the external magnets, and mark their position on the brace, so that the magnets will be aligned

Magnets in place on the brace and on the double-sided tape on the paper. Once the magnets are in position, keep them apart until the brace is inside the guitar.

Bridge Repairs **177**

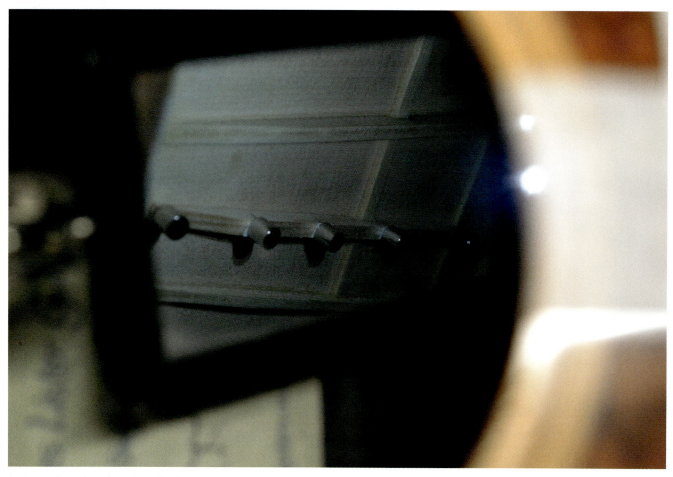

An inspection mirror is used to check that the new brace is in the correct position and firmly seated.

when the brace is positioned inside the guitar. Also check the polarity of the magnets. I mark the north pole of all the magnets with a permanent marker pen, so that I don't have to keep checking the polarity. Fix magnets to the top surface of the brace in the marked positions using double-sided tape. These magnets will have to be removed through the soundhole after the repair is complete, so be careful not to use too much tape, and check that the adhesive strength of the tape is not excessive. If the north pole of the outer magnets is facing upwards, the north pole of the inner magnets should be stuck to the tape on the brace.

Now apply glue to the bottom of the brace, and carefully insert it through the soundhole. As you approach the correct position, the magnets should pull the brace into place. If fitting over an existing brace, make sure that the new brace fits over it. Check that the brace is correctly positioned and seated using an inspection mirror.

Both braces glued in place and any remaining double-sided tape removed.

Wait for the glue to dry before moving on to the next brace. Trying to glue more than one brace at a time using magnets is not recommended, as it is easy to accidentally pull the magnets from the first brace.

When the glue for the first brace is dry, remove both the internal and external magnets, and repeat the process for the second brace (and any others needed). When all the braces are glued and the magnets have been removed, any double-sided tape left on top of the braces can be rubbed off with your fingertip.

Lifting bridge – removal and replacement

The tension of acoustic guitar strings can vary greatly, but for a 6-string guitar is typically around 40kg for nylon strings and 75kg for steel strings. In either case,

A lifted bridge on an acoustic guitar. This one has separated halfway through the joint.

there is a lot of force being exerted by the strings, and it is common for the back edge of the bridge to start to lift away from the soundboard, and eventually become completely detached.

In some instances, the bridge will start to lift along the back edge due to an area where the glue joint is poor, but then remain stable. This most commonly happens when the finish is not completely removed from the whole gluing area of the bridge during construction. Some manufacturers will leave several millimetres of finish under the bridge to ensure the finish looks good right up to the edges. Wood glues do not adhere well to finishes, so this is poor practice. It makes it far more likely that repairs will be needed, and makes the repairs more difficult.

In rare cases, it is necessary to make a completely new bridge, due to excessive distortion or damage. Making a new bridge from scratch is beyond the scope of this book, but when it is required, it is worth considering removing the bridge by planing the bulk of the bridge off, and then carefully scraping away the last 0.5mm or so. This reduces the risk of damaging the soundboard when removing the bridge using heat, moisture and a knife.

There are two approaches to repairing a lifting bridge. The simplest is to just work some glue into the gap between the bridge and the soundboard and clamp the bridge back down. This is sometimes effective but is unlikely to address the original cause of the problem. One possible exception is when higher tension strings have been used (most typically, steel strings fitted to a classical guitar). In this case, re-gluing the bridge can be effective if the correct tension strings are used in future.

Bridge removal

The repair described here was to an acoustic guitar with a pin bridge. The bridge had started to lift, but the strings had been left on the guitar at tension, and so the bridge had continued to peel away from the soundboard until less than half of the gluing area remained in contact. When a large proportion of the gluing surface has already separated, complete removal of the bridge is usually the best option, and is relatively easy to accomplish.

The gap at the back of a lifting bridge makes it easy to work the knife in to completely remove it. Care should be taken not to let the knife dig in to the soft soundboard material.

Some of the cedar soundboard material has come away with the bridge. The large clean areas left on the bridge give an indication of how poor the original joint was.

The bridge is removed using a combination of heat, moisture and a knife to separate the join. The ideal knife has a relatively thin blade to allow it to get into the joint without distorting either the bridge or the soundboard significantly. It should not be sharp, as the intention is to gently force the two pieces apart, rather than to cut through the joint. A sharp knife is also likely to further damage the soft wood of the soundboard. A thin artist's palette knife can be useful for starting to open the joint if the gap is initially very small, but these are often not strong enough to push right through.

The application of heat and water to the joint will help soften the glue, but it can be difficult to know how much will be needed, as this will depend on the type of glue used. The principle should always be to use the minimum amount needed to remove the bridge without significantly damaging the wood on either side of the joint. This is particularly true when working close to the centre joint of the soundboard, which can open very easily.

There is also a small risk of loosening the bracing glue joints.

If the bridge is unfinished, or can be easily refinished (for example, a rubbed oil finish), then heat can be directly applied to the top of the bridge. The alternative is to just heat the knife, which will take a little longer, but is generally the safer option.

In this particular case, with such a large gap at the back of the bridge, it was easy to work some water into the gap, and then insert the heated knife with little risk of damaging the finish. If the gap were smaller, it would be necessary to protect the top from the hot knife with some card cut to fit around the edge of the bridge. This card can also be a useful indicator of the temperature of the knife – if it starts to burn the card on contact, then it is too hot and will damage the finish.

Work the knife gently into the gap and start to apply pressure along the line of the joint. Try to keep the blade of the knife parallel to the surface of the top to avoid digging into the soft wood of the soundboard. Work the knife most of the way through to the front edge of the bridge, but avoid going right through. If the knife exits on the other side of the joint, then you are likely to damage the finish, or worse, the soundboard itself if the knife has cut into the soundboard at all.

Work around the edge of the bridge, being sure to keep the knife hot, and applying more water if needed. Remember that the knife is being used to gently lift the bridge from the soundboard and should not be cutting the joint. When the bridge is almost off, don't be tempted to just force the rest of the joint apart – keep working gently with the knife until the bridge is completely detached.

Surface clean-up and repair

Once the bridge is off, you will have an idea of how much damage there is to the top, and possibly some clues as to why the bridge started to lift in the first place.

In this case, looking at the image of the removed bridge and the area of soundboard where it was glued, we can see that the contact area of the bridge is slightly larger than the area where the finish was removed. This is a common practice in factory guitars, and it reduces the effective gluing area. This is particularly problematic at the back edge of the bridge, where the lifting force of the strings is greatest. It also means that the contact between the bridge and the area where the finish has been removed is not perfect.

Another thing to look for is any cutting of the fibres of the soundboard around the edge of the bridge. Some makers will cut around the bridge with a scalpel before removing the finish where the bridge is to be glued. The problem with this is that it is very difficult not to cut into the soundboard wood itself. Again, this causes problems along the back edge of the bridge, making it easier for the string tension to start lifting it, along with fibres of the soundboard.

In the case described here, some of the soundboard wood has come away with the bridge. This amount of damage is acceptable, and difficult to avoid with cedar tops. If significantly more wood than this has come away from the top, then the damaged area will need repairing before re-gluing the bridge.

ABOVE: This small scraper was made from an old Japanese saw blade and is ideal for delicate clean-up work like this.

RIGHT: Removing the last of the glue. Varying the angle of the scraper as you work will avoid the build-up of ridges on the gluing surface of the bridge.

All of the soundboard fibres left attached to the bridge should be removed, along with the residual glue. I use a small scraper for this. A small, flat sanding block will also do the job, but care is needed not to round the edges of the underside of the bridge.

Work carefully, removing just enough material to give a clean surface. Just before re-gluing the bridge, you will be giving the surface another light scrape or sand to expose fresh material, which will ensure the best possible glue joint.

Preparation for re-gluing

It is always advisable to use an internal clamping caul when gluing a bridge. This will ensure that the clamping pressure is evenly spread over the area of the bridge and give the strongest joint. For this reason, it is worth spending the time to make a caul that fits between the X-braces (or over the fan braces for a classical guitar).

Mapping the position of the braces and the bridge plate will allow an accurately sized caul to be made. This can be done using small magnets to locate the braces, and marking the positions on a sheet of paper taped to the soundboard as described earlier in the chapter under 'Adding braces'.

The finished sketch shows the positions of the braces, the bridge plate and the bridge pin holes.

On this guitar, there was some significant distortion of the soundboard around the area of the bridge. An additional bridge plate was made to recover

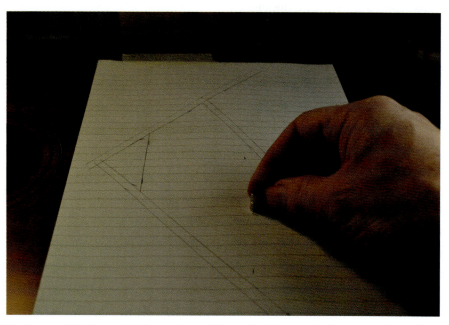

Small magnets being used to locate the positions of the braces, which are then marked out on the paper.

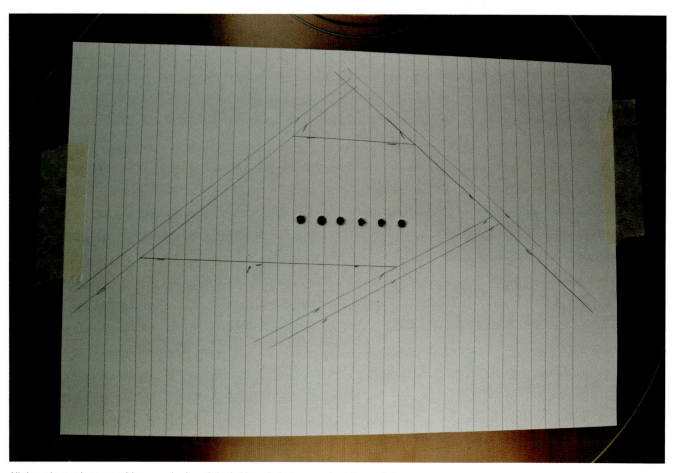

All the relevant brace positions marked, and the bridge pin holes punched through the paper.

the soundboard shape and reinforce the area. This additional step would not normally be necessary, but if there is no existing bridge plate, or it is distorted or damaged, a new plate should be added. Any hardwood can be used, but in this case a rosewood plate was cut to fit between the braces and thicknessed to 2mm.

Both inner and outer cauls were made to glue the plate in place. Both were curved slightly to match the curvature of the soundboard. The outer caul has a cork facing and is taped over in case any glue squeezes through the bridge pin holes.

Glue is applied to the surface of the new bridge plate, and it is positioned inside the guitar, followed by the internal clamping caul.

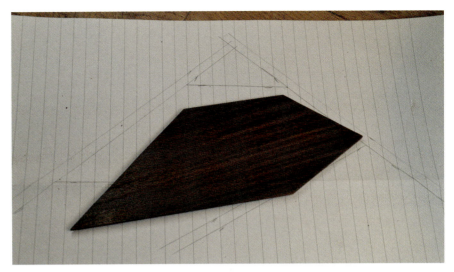

A 2mm thick rosewood bridge plate made to fit precisely between the existing braces. This patch will help stabilise the soundboard, which had deformed where the bridge was being pulled away.

RIGHT: This inner caul is shaped to fit the curvature of the underside of the bridge and will be used to glue both the additional plate, and the bridge itself.

BELOW: The outer caul for gluing the bridge plate is cork lined and taped over to prevent it being glued to the soundboard.

Bridge Repairs **183**

An inspection mirror being used to check the position of the clamps inside the guitar.

As many clamps as I could fit through the soundhole to ensure the new bridge plate is evenly and securely clamped in position.

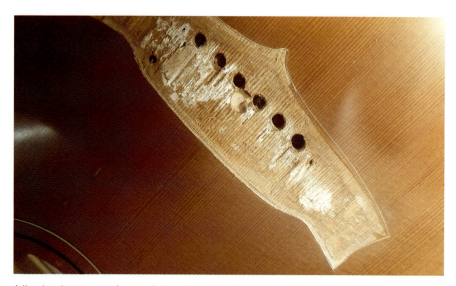

A line has been scored around the edge of the bridge. This scored line is very light and is only used as a marker – it should not go right through the finish, otherwise there is a risk of cutting into the soundboard wood. Most of the excess finish has been removed here, with one section remaining.

The outer caul is then positioned, and clamps applied. The positions of the clamps are checked with an inspection mirror.

In order to ensure a better glue joint than was originally achieved, the excess finish around the edge of the bridge contact area needs to be removed.

This can be done with either a small scraper or a small sanding block, but in either case, care is needed not to mark the finish outside the area of the bridge. Clamp the bridge precisely in the correct position and score a line around the edge, taking care to not cut right through the finish and into the soundboard wood. An alternative is to accurately tape around the bridge with masking tape. Remove the bridge, and scrape or sand away the excess finish up to the marked line (or tape). This will provide both a slightly larger gluing area, particularly at the critical back edge, and a flatter gluing surface.

Using the existing pin holes as guides, holes are now drilled through the new bridge plate. This could be done after the bridge is glued, but drilling them before allows the pins to be used to maintain correct alignment of the bridge whilst gluing.

Re-gluing the bridge

After a light sanding of both the underside of the bridge, and the corresponding surface of the soundboard, the bridge can be glued in the normal manner using the internal clamping caul, and cork-lined cauls to protect the bridge and spread the clamping pressure evenly.

The two outer bridge pins can be used to hold the bridge in position. The original pins were plastic, and one had been snapped in half by the bridge pulling away from the top. Some of the other pins were poorly fitted, so new rosewood pins were used to replace them.

Once the bridge is fully clamped, the excess glue can be cleaned up. The bridge pins should be removed as soon as the glue has grabbed enough that the bridge

The bridge pins ensure the bridge does not move when clamped. These are new pins, as the old ones were badly damaged.

ABOVE: The glue has been cleaned up, and the alignment pins removed as soon as the glue has grabbed. If left too long they would be glued in permanently!

RIGHT: With the bridge clamps removed, the bridge is secure, with no gaps at the back edge.

Bridge Repairs **185**

This guitar was fitted with an under-saddle pickup, which passes through a hole in the bottom of the saddle slot. This hole needs to be drilled through the new bridge plate, following the angle of the existing hole.

Using the bridge pin reamer to open out the holes to the correct size for the new, oversized pins.

Bridge Repairs

The finished repair, with a new set of strings fitted and brought up to tension.

cleanly along the glue line without damaging either the bridge or the soundboard, but this is rare.

In the case described here, some soundboard material was left on the bridge, and some bridge material was left on the soundboard. The central area of the bridge came away cleanly on the glue line. Simply re-gluing the bridge without doing any work to improve the glue joint is unlikely to be successful. Ideally, we would like to have both surfaces cleaned of old glue and debris, and a perfect fit between them.

If the soundboard material remaining glued to the bridge was removed, the corresponding voids in the soundboard surface would have to be filled. This would entail removing wood from the whole area of the joint, gluing in a thin patch, and then fitting and gluing the bridge to the patch.

won't move – if they are left in too long, they may be glued permanently in place!

If an under-saddle pickup is used, the existing hole in the bottom of the saddle slot can act as a guide to drill through the new bridge plate.

The bridge pin holes are now reamed out to match the new, oversized bridge pins. Work very slowly with the reamer, checking the fit of the pins frequently, until they fit perfectly, becoming tight in the hole just before they are fully seated.

After a light sanding of the bridge itself, and application of some Danish oil, the pickup and saddle are fitted, and then the guitar strung up using the new bridge pins.

Re-gluing a detached bridge

When a bridge completely detaches itself from the soundboard, it is usually an indication that it was poorly glued in the first place. It may also be the result of exposure to excessive humidity and/or temperature weakening the glue bond. In some cases, the bridge will come off

A detached classical bridge. This one came away completely with the strings at tension. Fortunately, there was no other damage to the soundboard.

Bridge Repairs **187**

As with the acoustic guitar, some cedar wood fibres have come away from the soundboard. This time they will be left in place.

The piece of rosewood left on the soundboard was smaller than the piece missing from the bridge, so this part of the bridge will be repaired before re-gluing.

The damage to the bridge has been repaired, and the gluing surface cleaned up except for the area where there is some soundboard material.

A better solution is to clean the glue from the areas where there was a clean break, and leave the detached soundboard material in place on the underside of the bridge. Provided any loose wood fibres are removed, the separated parts of the soundboard should join together perfectly. Do not remove any more material than necessary to obtain a clean surface, otherwise the fit of the bridge will be adversely affected.

The same would usually apply to any material that has detached from the bridge and remained glued to the soundboard. In this case, however, some of the material is missing, with the piece left on the soundboard being much smaller than the piece missing from the bridge. The better solution here was to remove the piece of bridge on the soundboard and repair the damage to the bridge separately before re-gluing. The glue is cleaned from the underside of the bridge, leaving a fresh surface to ensure a good glue join.

The gluing surface of the soundboard is lightly sanded using 320 grit abrasive, taking great care not to mark the surrounding finish. It is a good idea to apply low-tack masking tape up to the edge of the bridge area to protect the finish. The area where the soundboard material was left on the bridge is left unsanded, as it should be a perfect fit if no material was lost.

Always use a clamping caul when re-gluing detached bridges (and when gluing new bridges). This will spread the clamping pressure evenly, giving the best possible joint. Making a clamping caul is very simple when constructing a guitar, but more difficult when you only have access through the soundhole. Magnets are used to plot the positions of the braces, as described earlier in this chapter. The caul is placed in position on the paper, and the brace positions transferred onto the caul. Rebates can then be cut into the caul so that it sits perfectly over the braces. The rebates do not need to be the perfect depth, but must not be less than the height of the braces. The

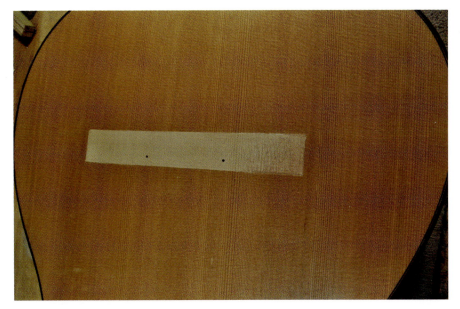
The bridge gluing area has been lightly sanded – just enough to present a fresh surface.

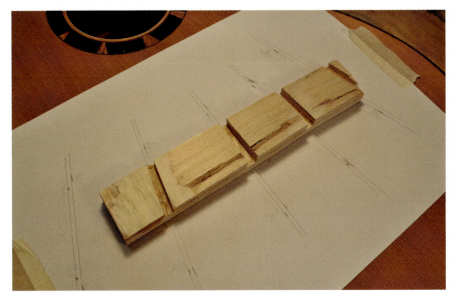
A bridge clamping caul made to fit over the fan braces, which were plotted out using magnets.

The bridge clamped in place. The cauls on the bridge wings are shaped to fit and lined with cork.

surface of the caul that will be in contact with the soundboard will also need to be curved to match the curvature of the soundboard.

The caul needs to be held in place under the bridge position until the clamps are applied. Use a small piece of double-sided tape for this, just enough to hold the caul in place until the clamps are in position. The bridge will be clamped overnight, and this can make the tape *very* difficult to release if too much is used.

Once the caul is in position, apply glue to both surfaces of the joint, and clamp the bridge in position. Three clamps should be used, and each of these should have clamping cauls shaped to fit the bridge to ensure even application of pressure. Clean up any glue squeeze-out and leave at least overnight before removing the clamps, and a further 24 hours before applying any string tension.

Lifting bridge – simple glue down

In some cases, it is possible to simply work some glue into the gap between the bridge and the soundboard and clamp the bridge down. In general, this is not the best solution, as it fails to address the reason for the bridge lifting in the first place. As mentioned above, it may be that the bridge has lifted when strings of a much higher tension are fitted. In this case, provided the correct strings are fitted in the future, a simple re-glue can be effective.

If the bridge was originally glued using hot hide glue, then gluing the bridge back down using more hide glue is often the best option. Unlike most modern adhesives, hide glue can be reactivated by applying heat and moisture. It may be enough simply to apply more hot glue into the gap between the bridge and soundboard and clamp it down, but applying a little additional heat to the bridge will help. Hide glue is rarely used

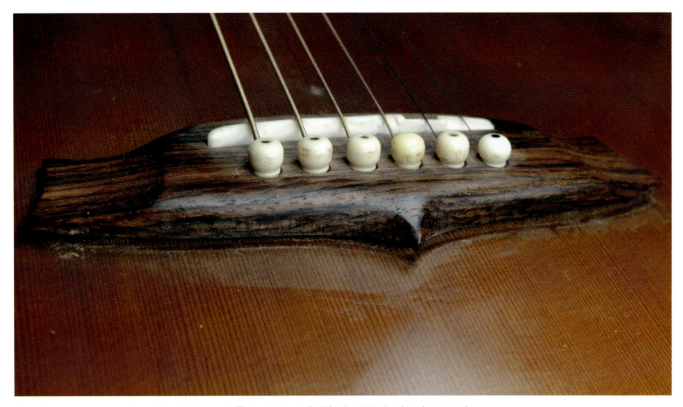

The lifting bridge as seen in the previous repair. This one is too far lifted to simply glue down again.

on modern guitars, and probably never on factory-made instruments. Even on older guitars it can be very difficult to determine what type of glue has been used, at least until you try to remove the bridge.

In all cases, making a well-fitted caul for the inside of the guitar (as described in the previous section) will spread the clamping pressure evenly and improve the chances of a successful repair.

I usually avoid using epoxy resin for repair work, but if the guitar is not of great value, it can be appropriate in some cases. If the bridge is lifting, and the complete removal of the bridge is not justified, then epoxy might be the best option, especially if the gap cannot be easily closed by clamping. The advantage of epoxy is that it will not shrink as it cures, making it more effective than water-based glue when gaps need to be filled. Use a good-quality epoxy, preferably a slow setting type, and work it as far into the gap as possible. Clamp the bridge down firmly but without using excessive pressure, and clean up any glue squeeze-out using a suitable solvent (one which will not attack the finish).

If the bridge has lifted because of poor initial preparation and fitting of the surfaces, or poor gluing procedures, then it is unlikely that simply gluing the bridge down again will offer any more than a temporary solution. In this case removal of the bridge is the most reliable method of repair.

Fitting bridge pins

Bridge pins come in a variety of materials including wood, plastic, bone and metal. They can either be slotted or plain, and the taper of the pin can vary. Oversized pins are also available, which can be used when the bridge pin holes become too worn for standard size pins.

When fitting new pins, it is important to use pins of the same taper. The most common taper is 5 degrees, but 3-degree pins can be found, for example on early Martin acoustics. Older guitars usually had slots cut into the front edge of the bridge holes for the strings, but it's now more common to find plain holes, and slotted bridge pins. This change was probably due to ease of manufacturing, but claims that unslotted pins 'sound better' are unsupported. When replacing pins, all you need to know is that if the bridge holes are slotted, plain pins can be used, but otherwise slotted pins are needed.

Plastic pins are best avoided, particularly slotted ones, as they tend to wear quickly. Bone or hardwood pins are preferred, with metal ones obviously being harder, but also heavier. You will find plenty of discussions on the internet about the different sound properties of wood versus bone, plastic or metal, but any difference is likely to be small, and most likely due to the different weights of the materials.

Unless the bridge pin holes are badly damaged, or you're making a new bridge, it is generally best to avoid using a reamer. If the existing pins are standard sized, then it is possible to ream the holes out to fit oversized pins, but once this has been done, any further reaming will make the holes too big for any normally available pins. At this point, the only options are to make your own pins, or fill the existing

A white, plastic slotted bridge pin (top), a wooden slotted one (middle) and a plain ebony pin.

Bridge pin reamers need to have a taper matched to the pins being fitted. This one has a 5-degree taper.

LEFT: The tape marks the depth to cut to for a particular pin. Final precise fitting should be done using the pin itself.

BELOW: Two of the pins fitted. These pins look very low as the pin holes have been countersunk. This can make removing tight pins difficult.

holes, and re-drill and ream new ones, either being a lot of work.

The fit of the bridge pins is very sensitive to the hole size, and it is very easy to go too far with the reamer, so it is worth practising on a scrap piece of hardwood. Drill a hole in the hardwood piece slightly larger than the smallest diameter of the tapered reamer (at the tip). Gradually ream out the hole, testing regularly with the pin you are fitting. Wooden pins can vary slightly in size, so each hole should be reamed for the individual pin.

Take care to keep the reamer perpendicular to the workpiece. Aim to have a gap of 1–2mm between the top of the bridge and the head of the pin. When you have achieved a perfect fit, mark the reamer with a piece of tape to show the depth needed for that pin.

Once you have practised this a few times, move on to the actual bridge, remembering to check the size of each pin, and adjust the depth marker on the reamer if necessary.

Bridge Repairs

Worn tie-blocks

Classical guitar bridges are commonly made from hardwoods, and these are fairly resistant to wear. Some cheaper instruments use softer hardwoods, and on these and very old instruments, you will often see a significant amount of wear around the string holes in the tie-block. Some wear is acceptable and will not affect the function of the bridge, but if the wear is excessive, it is advisable to carry out a repair.

It is possible to replace the whole tie-block, but this has the disadvantage that any tie-block decoration will either be lost or will have to be reproduced. There is also a risk that anything other than a very good glue joint between the new tie-block and the bridge will be a weak point that could fail.

The best solution is to drill out the worn holes over-sized, make dowels using a comparable (or harder) wood to fill the holes, and then drill new ones. I have also used brass tube as a reinforcement, which in some ways is easier, as you don't have to make the hardwood dowels. This is usually appropriate for bridges with softer woods, as it will prevent any recurrence of the problem. If brass tubes are used, great care should be taken to ensure the internal edges of the tube ends are rounded and smoothed, otherwise they will easily cut through the nylon strings.

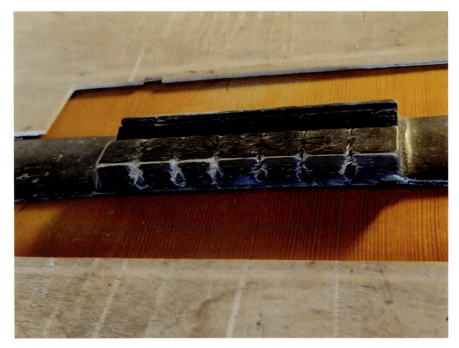

Badly worn tie-block holes on a classical bridge. This is common on instruments where a cheap, soft bridge material has been used, and stained to look like ebony.

These brass inserts look elegant and prevent wear from the strings. This bridge is walnut, which is a good bridge material, but not as hard as rosewood.

Remedying low break angles

The break angle of the strings at the bridge is the angle the string deviates by as it passes over the saddle. The angle is determined by the height of the saddle relative to the tie-block, the horizontal distance between the saddle and the tie-block, and by how the strings are tied.

It is commonly said that the break angle has a significant effect on the tone and volume of the guitar, but this is not really the case. Provided the break angle is above a certain minimum, any variation will not significantly change how the string vibrations are transmitted through the saddle and bridge to the soundboard.

If the break angle of the strings falls below about 12 degrees, the string is not firmly anchored, and can move sideways across the saddle. If this is the case, then the break angle needs to be increased. Simply raising the height of the saddle will increase the break angle, but will also increase the action, reducing playability. In extreme cases, some form of neck angle resetting will be needed, but if the problem is only in the break angle, then this can be remedied in a few different ways, depending on the type of bridge.

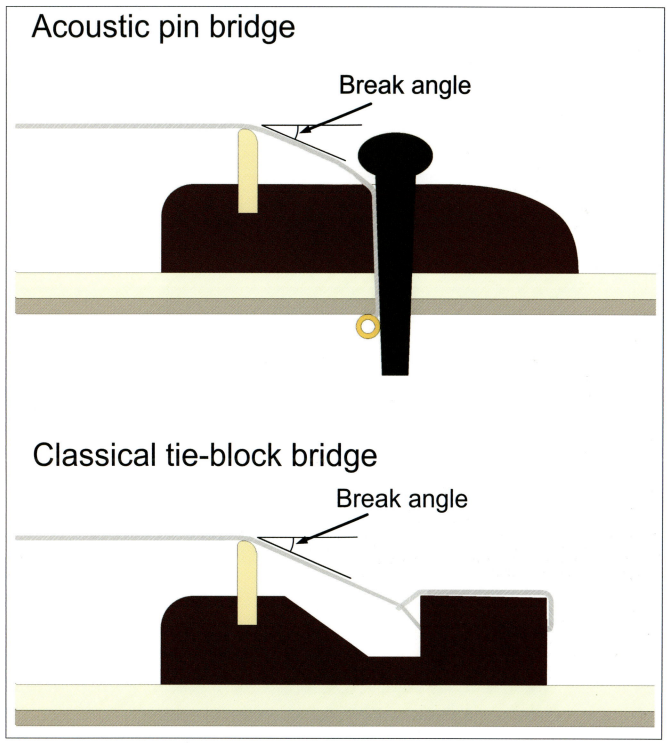

Break angles for an acoustic guitar and a classical guitar. The traditional 6-hole tie-block does not provide the best break angle.

Bridge Repairs

Classical 12-hole tie-block conversion

Nowadays 12-hole tie-blocks are becoming more common in classical guitars. They give a greater and more consistent break angle for the strings, and also look neater.

It is relatively straightforward to convert an existing 6-hole tie-block to a 12-hole tie-block without removing or replacing the bridge. The original six holes will be in the correct place, so all that is required is to drill an additional six secondary holes.

The reason for the improvement in break angle achieved with a 12-hole tie-block is that the angle of the string is not entirely dependent on the position of the string holes in the tie-block. In fact, the string leaves a normal 6-hole tie-block about halfway between the string hole and the top of the tie-block. This is due to the way the string is wrapped around the tie block, and the problem tends to be worse for the bass strings. In the photo, you can see that the bass E string in fact leaves the tie-block closer to the top of the tie-block than to the string hole. This can be improved a little by pressing the loop of the string downwards, but with a 12-hole block, the string comes directly from the lower primary hole.

Before drilling the additional holes, their positions need to be carefully marked on the back of the tie-block. In fact, the exact positions of these holes are not critical, but to do a professional job, you want to make them as accurate as possible.

A traditional 6-hole classical tie-block.

This 12-hole tie-block gives an improved break angle and looks neater when tied correctly.

With a traditional tie-block, the string does not follow a straight line from the saddle to the hole, and the break angle is reduced.

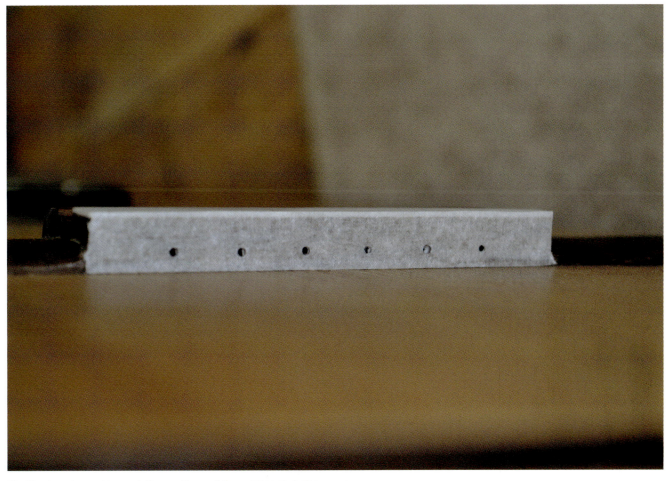

Masking tape is used to mark the positions of the existing six holes.

Bridge Repairs

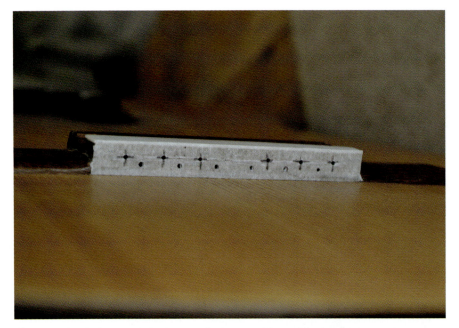

The secondary holes are marked out on the tape, and then with a bradawl.

Begin by applying masking tape to the back of the tie-block, and punch through the tape into the existing holes. These will be your reference for the placement of the secondary holes.

Now use a marking gauge, or just an accurately drawn pencil line, to mark the height of the secondary holes. This line should be between 1.5–2mm above the primary holes, but be careful not to place the holes too close to the top surface of the tie-block, and certainly at least 1.5mm below any decorative cap.

There are two options for the placement of the secondary holes – they can either all be on the same side of their respective primary holes, or can be positioned symmetrically, with the bass secondaries to the left of the primaries, and the treble secondaries to the right. I generally opt for the latter, as I prefer the symmetry, but there is no functional difference. The secondary holes should be placed between 4–5mm horizontally from each primary hole.

Using a bradawl to mark the hole positions will give greater accuracy of positioning when you start to drill.

In order to reach the bridge from the end of the guitar, you will need to buy or make a drill bit extender. Even if it is possible to obtain 1.5mm drill bits of sufficient length, these will be very fragile and difficult to control. A drill bit extender with a small chuck can be bought, but it is very simple to make your own extender, using either some dowel or (in this case) a length of fibreglass rod. I use an offcut from one of my go-bar rods. Simply drill a 1.5mm hole accurately centred in one end of the rod/dowel, and glue in a standard 1.5mm drill bit.

You are now ready to start drilling the holes. You can use a hand-cranked drill, but a battery drill/driver with a variable speed will give far greater control, allowing you to use your other hand to steady the drill bit/extender. Protect the soundboard with thin plywood or similar taped below the bridge.

Now start drilling each hole in turn. Use a slow speed, and if the bridge is made of rosewood or similar hardwood, clear the flutes of the drill bit regularly, as they tend to clog. Take care as the drill bit exits the tie block, as it

Drill bit extenders can be bought with small chucks, but a homemade one is more compact. The drill bit is simply glued into a hole drilled in the end of a dowel, or in this case a carbon fibre rod.

The extender allows the new holes to be drilled parallel to the soundboard with the drill itself away from the body of the guitar.

The bradawl mark locates the end of the drill bit. Drill carefully, and clean out the flutes of the drill bit regularly, as they can clog easily.

Bridge Repairs

Drilling complete, and the masking tape removed.

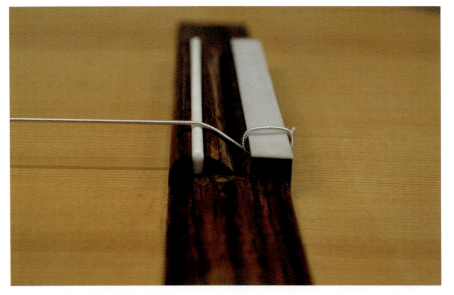

The string now follows a straight line to the tie-block hole, giving an increased and more consistent break angle.

is easy for it to mark the ramp of the saddle slot. If necessary, place a piece of scrap wood in the slot between the tie-block and the saddle slot ramp to protect it.

Once all holes are drilled, remove the masking tape, and clean up any debris from the drilling.

With a new bass string tied, it is easy to see the improvement in the break angle. In this case, with a low saddle, the string is in contact with the wood behind the saddle slot. Provided this does not limit the break angle too much it is not a problem, but if necessary, some material can be removed from the ramp until the string has a clear path from the saddle to the tie-block hole.

Bridge string ties

A simpler alternative to the 12-hole tie-block conversion is to use some form of string ties. These have the same effect on the break angle as the 12-hole conversion. There are two things to consider if going this route. Firstly, the bridge ties will add a small amount of mass to the bridge, which may have an impact on the sound of the guitar. Secondly, the bridge ties are not to everyone's taste aesthetically.

These bridge string ties perform the same function as the 12-hole tie-block, but are not as aesthetically pleasing.

Steel-string pin bridge

To increase the break angle on a pin-type bridge, you simply need to file slots in the edge of the bridge pin holes on the side towards the saddle, or extend the existing ones. This moves the point at which the string leaves the top surface of the bridge closer to the saddle, hence increasing the break angle.

Take a small round file, and carefully file a slot at an angle of about 45 degrees. The slot does not have to be the same size as the string, but it needs to be wide enough for the string not to bind, and the repair will be neater if the slot is not too much wider than the string.

How far you need to file the slots will depend on how much the break angle needs to be increased. As a rough guide, the gap between the end of the slot and the back edge of the saddle should be around two to three times the height of the saddle from the top surface of the bridge at that string position.

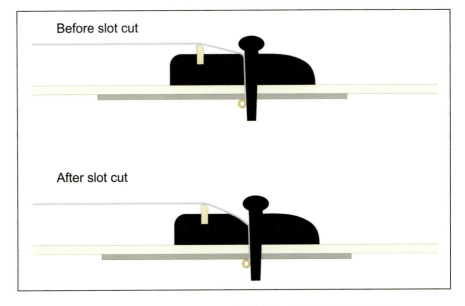

RIGHT: Section through an acoustic guitar bridge, showing how filing a string slot from the bridge pin hole increases the break angle.

BELOW LEFT: Filing the slots with a tapered round file.

BELOW RIGHT: The filed slots will be covered once the strings are in place.

Saddle replacement

If the saddle is damaged and needs replacing, follow the procedure described in Chapter 4 'Making a new saddle'.

CHAPTER 10

Inlay and Binding Repairs

Types of inlay

The decorative elements of a guitar can massively increase the amount of time it takes to construct a musical instrument. The picture facing the start of this chapter shows a good example of a highly decorated instrument made by one of my students, Sofia Johnston Suarez. The instrument was based on the famous FE08 classical guitar made by Antonio Torres in the latter half of the nineteenth century.

There are so many types of inlay and materials used that it would be impossible to cover everything in this chapter. A few examples will give an overview of most of the procedures that will be used when repairing or replacing damaged/missing inlays.

Rosette inlay replacement

The nineteenth century guitar described in this repair came into the workshop with a few cracks, and one mother-of-pearl (MOP) inlay missing from the rosette. As is often the case with instruments from this period, the inlays themselves were fairly roughly cut, and each one slightly different.

The MOP pieces were inlaid into a black mastic, which over the years has

This nice but rather worn looking nineteenth-century guitar has the common problem of a missing mother-of-pearl inlay. The black mastic the inlays are set into has shrunk, and one piece has fallen out and been lost.

shrunk slightly, causing some cracks, and allowing one piece to fall out and be lost.

On more modern instruments, the inlays are likely to be mass-produced, and it is sometimes possible to find an exact match to the existing inlays. On older instruments like this one, where each piece was individually made by hand, all the pieces have a slightly different shape.

Safety note

Mother-of-pearl and abalone are commonly used types of shell inlay, and the dust from these products can be hazardous. The dust can be an irritant, and any fine dust is hazardous when inhaled. The dust is often claimed to be carcinogenic, but I have not been able to find any evidence for this. Normal precautions against dust inhalation are strongly recommended. Wear a close-fitting dust mask and use extraction to remove any airborne dust. If using a vacuum system, fitting a fine mesh over the nozzle will prevent small parts disappearing up the hose!

Making the replacement inlay

The first job is to reproduce the size and shape of the missing piece. This is easily done by using the space left in the mastic as a template. I find the best way to do this accurately is to take a photograph of the empty space, alongside a steel rule for scale.

The image is first modified using photo editing software to give a good contrast to the edges of the missing piece. The image is then printed out, with the scale adjusted to match the reference rule. The image on the paper is then glued to a suitably matched piece of MOP. In this case, the various inlays in the rosette were quite varied in whiteness, so it was not necessary to try to obtain a close match to any particular piece. The thickness of the new piece should be slightly greater than the depth of the space in the rosette.

The MOP piece is then carefully cut out and filed down to match the printed shape. When close to the final dimensions, the piece can be test fitted in the space and adjusted to achieve a good fit. Because of the nature and colour of the mastic filler used, any slight gaps can be easily filled after the piece has been glued in, but it is good practice to get as close a fit as possible.

Taking a photo of the hole is an effective way to reproduce the shape of the missing piece, especially when no two inlays are exactly the same size and shape. The rule is used to ensure the correct scale when the image is printed.

Inlay and Binding Repairs

Photoshop or a similar image editing software package enables you to modify the image taken of the hole to provide good contrast, which when glued to the new inlay will make it easier to cut precisely to shape.

Gluing the replacement inlay

To glue the piece into the rosette, a mixture of epoxy resin and ebony dust or lampblack is used. This will both glue the piece in place securely and fill any small gaps from imperfect fitting.

The epoxy mix is spread into the space left by the missing piece, and the new MOP piece pressed firmly into place. If much epoxy is squeezed out, this can be wiped away before it sets, but it is best to leave a little on the surface to ensure there are no gaps left after levelling.

Once the epoxy has fully cured, the new piece and any epoxy can be carefully

An authentic, if slightly irregular, handmade look matches well with the rest of the inlays.

Epoxy resin mixed with ebony dust is used to both glue the new piece in place and fill any small gaps. An alternative is a CA glue-based filler, which can be made to match a wide range of colours.

Inlay and Binding Repairs

The blackened epoxy is spread over the surrounding area to help fill some of the cracks in the mastic. To give a more even look, the epoxy can be used to fill the cracks all around the rosette, but care is needed not to get any on the worn soundboard, which would be difficult to remove.

The new mother-of-pearl inlay and the epoxy fill do not really need any further finish applied, and making the rosette perfectly flat and shiny would be too much of a contrast to the surrounding soundboard, making the repair stand out more.

sanded level. Take care to protect the surrounding inlays around the rosette, and the soundboard itself. Work through to the required grade of abrasive (400 or 500 grit) before applying a matching finish over the repair work.

Fret marker replacement

Fret marker inlays are almost universal on acoustic guitars, both on the edge of the fingerboard facing the player, and on the top surface. These inlays range from very simple circular dots to highly elaborate decorations. Classical guitars usually only have edge marker dots, and often not even those.

In Chapter 6 the fingerboard of an acoustic guitar was removed to replace a damaged truss rod. The guitar only had two MOP fret markers on the top of the fingerboard at the 12th fret. The other fret markers were simple dots on the edge. Before the original fingerboard was planed down, the 12th fret marker inlays were carefully removed and stored.

Having replaced the truss rod and fitted a new fingerboard, the fret markers needed to be replaced.

As this fingerboard was being removed anyway, the rosewood could be cut away around the MOP fret marker inlays. This makes it easier to remove the inlays without risk of damaging them.

These simple square markers are relatively easy to inlay cleanly. The slots in the inlays would originally have been filled, probably with the same glue used to set them in place. Provided the fills are a reasonable match to the fingerboard material, they can be left in place.

First the MOP markers are carefully cleaned up to remove any glue and old bits of fingerboard that were stuck to them. The black fill that was originally used in the inlay slots is left in place.

Cutting the cavities for the inlays

First mark the position of the fret markers on the fingerboard in pencil, making sure that they are on the correct fret! The markers are then tack-glued in position using a small dot of CA gel glue, which should allow plenty of time to accurately adjust the position before it sets. Gluing the markers in place allows the position to be accurately scribed around the inlays without fear of them moving.

The position, size and shape of the inlay is now marked using a sharp scalpel, being sure to keep it tight up against the edge of the inlays to ensure a perfect fit. The inlays in this case were very simple, and hence the shape was quite easy to mark, and subsequently to cut out from the fingerboard. More complex shapes can be attempted using the same method described here, but will take a lot more time and care, and use of finer chisels, knives, or scalpels to excavate the holes for the inlays. For larger inlays, a Dremel or similar rotary cutting tool with a base fitted can be used to excavate the hole

The MOP markers tack-glued in position on the fingerboard. Note that the frets have not been installed at this stage. This makes levelling and cleaning up the inlays easier after they have been glued in place.

Inlay and Binding Repairs

Ideally, you would cut along the edges of the inlay with the grain, rather than against it as shown here. Provided the scalpel blade is sharp and you only cut lightly, it should not be a problem.

The scribed lines should accurately fall on the pencil line marking the centre between the frets.

A sharp chisel aligned to the scalpel marks, and a firm push is all that is required. Pushing too hard will result in compressing the wood on the outside of the marked area, and a poorly fitting inlay.

for the inlay, or at least the bulk of it. In general, I find I have greater control using hand tools.

Once the inlays have been accurately marked with the scalpel, they can be easily removed, provided not too much CA was used to glue them. Normally a light tap with a hammer and punch will release them, but if necessary, you can use a CA glue de-bonding agent.

A sharp chisel is now used to deepen the edges of the hole. It should be possible to locate the chisel accurately in the scalpel cuts before applying downward pressure. Do not attempt to cut down to the full depth needed in one go, as this can compress the wood on the outer edges of the hole. Depending on the hardness of the wood, you may only be able to cut easily down about half a millimetre. The wood now needs to be excavated from the holes, taking great care not to cut into the surrounding wood.

The wood is cut out only to the depth of the edge cuts, and then the edge cuts can be further deepened. The process is then repeated until the required depth is reached. It is best to aim for the inlays to be just a fraction proud of the surface when they are glued in place, so that they can be levelled perfectly with the surrounding wood. Again, more complex shaped inlays will take a lot more time and will require a variety of fine cutting tools.

Once the holes are excavated and the bottom of the holes is flat, the edges and corners can be cleaned up with a sharp scalpel if required. The inlays are now inserted into the hole without glue to test the fit. They should be a close fit, but not so tight that they are difficult to remove.

Care is needed when chiselling the wood out from the hole not to dent or compress the wood with the back of the chisel bevel.

Note the marks on the inlays. These inlays should in theory be perfectly square, but just in case they are not, they are marked to ensure correct orientation when glued in.

Inlay and Binding Repairs

Gluing and levelling the inlays

The inlays should be a good, close fit in the holes with no obvious gaps. In this case, CA glue is very effective for gluing the inlays in place and filling any very fine gaps. If there are any larger gaps, then epoxy resin can be used, mixed with wood dust to match the surrounding wood – in this case rosewood. The fills will not be completely invisible, but will usually bear any but the closest inspection.

The inlays are then levelled by sanding, taking care to maintain the flatness (or radius) of the fingerboard in the process. A vacuum/extraction system should be used whilst sanding to remove any harmful dust.

The whole area is finally finished to the desired level. In this case, abrasives were used up to 1,000 grit. When the new frets are installed, the fingerboard should be taped up between all the frets so that the frets can be dressed and polished without marking the fingerboard and inlays.

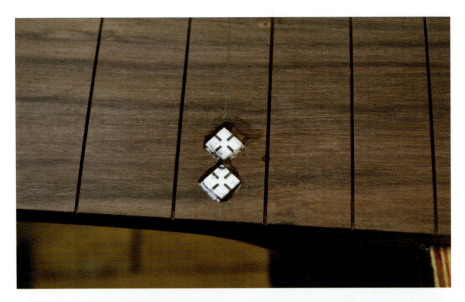

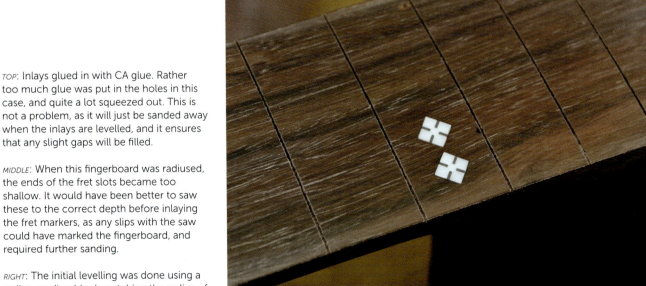

TOP: Inlays glued in with CA glue. Rather too much glue was put in the holes in this case, and quite a lot squeezed out. This is not a problem, as it will just be sanded away when the inlays are levelled, and it ensures that any slight gaps will be filled.

MIDDLE: When this fingerboard was radiused, the ends of the fret slots became too shallow. It would have been better to saw these to the correct depth before inlaying the fret markers, as any slips with the saw could have marked the fingerboard, and required further sanding.

RIGHT: The initial levelling was done using a radius sanding block matching the radius of the fingerboard to maintain the shape and flatness. A flat block can be used for the finer grades.

Replacing the side fret marker dots

Step 1: This fingerboard only had top inlays at the twelfth fret, but the side marker dots also needed replacing. Here the positions have been accurately marked on masking tape in pencil, and then with a bradawl. Double check the positions are marked at the correct frets and are well centred.

Step 2: The tape can be removed once the marks have been made with the bradawl. These marks are used to centre the drill bit. Use a slow speed, and only drill to the depth you need for the inlay, usually 2–3mm.

Step 3: To drill the marker holes above the body join, a drill bit extension will be needed. Note the thick card protecting the soundboard.

Step 4: The drill bit used needs to match the size of the inlays – 2mm in this case. A drop of CA glue is worked into the holes, then the inlays are pressed in. The excess glue will be removed when the inlays are levelled.

Step 5: The inlays are filed almost level, and then a flat sanding block is used to make them completely flush. Some finish has also been removed from the edge of the neck, which will need to be touched up after the frets have been installed and the ends levelled and smoothed.

Inlay and Binding Repairs

Binding repairs

One of the functions of the bindings on a guitar is to protect the relatively delicate edges of the soundboard. The corners and edges of an instrument are more likely to get knocked, so damage to bindings is fairly common. Small dents can be left, but players who like to keep their guitars looking at their best might prefer to have damaged bindings repaired, or in rare cases replaced.

Removal and replacement of plastic bindings is covered in Chapter 12 under back removal. Wood bindings are generally easier to repair, re-glue and replace than plastic ones.

Binding damage

Small dents in bindings can often be steamed using the same methods described in Chapter 5. Filling dents in bindings is a little more difficult because the dent is not on a flat surface, but it is still possible. In the case described here, the rosewood binding has been dented by an impact, and the purfling on the back is also slightly damaged. Always try to steam out a dent first, and if that is not successful, or only partly successful, then resort to filling.

Before steaming the binding, first remove the finish around the area – the heat will lift off this shellac finish anyway. Try to avoid touching the finish on the back and the sides. A small scraper is ideal, but a sanding stick can also be used. Extra care was needed here to avoid further damaging the back purfling.

Apply some clean water to the dent and allow it to soak in. Next apply a clean wet cloth to the dent and heat it with the clothes iron. This process can be repeated a few times, making sure the cloth is kept wet, but if the dent is still there after three attempts, it is unlikely to improve further.

In this case a significant improvement was made, but there is still a slight indentation that will need to be filled. There are a few options for filling the remaining depression. If the dent were still quite large, then the best solution might be a fill with epoxy resin, mixed with wood dust to match the material of the binding. As only a very small amount of material needed to be added for this repair, a CA glue fill was chosen.

Any CA glue can be used to build up a surface to fill an indentation, but Glu Boost is specifically formulated for this sort of application. Care is needed to avoid the glue running onto the surfaces of either the back or the sides, so it is better to apply the glue in small amounts. After each application, spray the fill with the Glu Boost accelerator and wait for it to harden.

This type of impact damage to the bindings is common. Repair of wood bindings is usually straightforward, although in this case the damage to the purfling could make it a bit trickier.

This scraper is ideal for removing a small area of finish. It was made from an old Japanese saw blade, cut to size, and then filed to clean the edges, and a burr created on one edge.

The tip of this clothes iron is ideal for applying heat to a small area without damaging any of the surrounding finish. The cloth will dry quickly, and needs to be kept wet.

Inlay and Binding Repairs

Steaming a dent almost always yields some improvement, and very occasionally removes the dent without need for any filling. In this case, some filling is required.

Applying a CA filler to the remaining indentation. A fine nozzle like this works well, but the fill will often need some 'adjustment' to pull it up to the edges of the dent.

Keep going until the fill is just slightly proud of both the back and the side surfaces. In this case a single application was enough. One of the advantages of using a clear fill is that the colour of the wood below the fill will be seen, making it less noticeable than a colour-matched fill.

The filled dent now needs to be levelled with the surrounding wood on both the back and the sides. The single-edge razor that was used for levelling fills on flat surfaces can still be effective, but more care is needed as only one side of the taped part of the razor will be resting on the surface. By keeping the pressure on the side where the tape is in contact with the back or the side, it should still be possible to make the fill almost perfectly level.

Keep going with the scraper until you *just* touch the surrounding finish. Now switch to a flat sanding block with a fine abrasive to make the fill completely smooth and flat.

At this stage you could simply use a burnishing cream on the repair area to

A slightly overfilled dent. I prefer to overfill and have to scrape back more than to underfill and have to add more CA glue.

bring it back to a gloss, but for a better finish, work over the affected area with a few sessions of French polishing to blend in the repair perfectly. Both the back and the side will need touching up, and working over a larger area than just that surrounding the repair will make the repaired area less noticeable.

Using the single edge razor scraper is more difficult on this curved surface compared to a flat one. Pressure is applied to the taped area of the blade in my right hand (lower side of the image) to prevent the blade tipping over and rounding the corner.

Inlay and Binding Repairs **213**

A fairly clean repair, which will become less visible when polished over. Not seen here, the damaged purfling on the back was pressed back into position when the CA fill was applied.

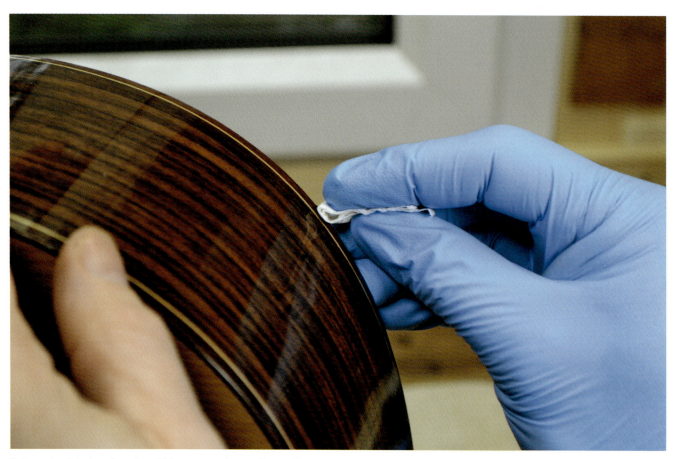

Patience is vital when French polishing over such a small area. The temptation is to keep applying the polish, but it needs to dry slightly between applications. Just a couple of passes with a small piece of cloth dampened with shellac, then leave for 5–10 minutes before repeating.

The reflected light shows that the repair is perfectly flat. Viewed from a different angle, the colour of the wood below the fill is seen. There was a slight darkening of the fibres where the CA had penetrated the wood, but given the variation of colour present anyway, it was barely noticeable.

In some cases where the finish over the rest of the plates is in poor condition, it is worth doing one polishing session over the whole of the plates affected by the repair – in this case all of the back and sides. It will not take much longer to do, and the result will be better.

If a lubricating oil has been used when applying the shellac, remove any residual oil with a burnishing cream after the shellac has fully hardened – ideally after a week. On a dark wood like rosewood, this type of repair should be almost invisible.

Binding removal and replacement

Wood bindings will rarely need to be removed, but if they are badly damaged, or if the back needs to be taken off, then it is usually not too difficult to do.

Start by scraping away the finish along the length of binding to be removed. Try not to touch the finish on the sides, but don't worry too much, as the bindings will need to be refinished anyway.

Apply a little water to the join between the bindings and the back (or front), and then heat the binding using the tip of the clothes iron.

As soon as the binding is warm, start inserting a thin palette knife into the join between the purfling and the back of the guitar. With a single purfling like this, there is usually a single rebate for both the purfling and the binding, and the join between the purfling and back will be easier to separate than the one between the binding and the purfling. Multiple purflings will usually have their own, shallower rebate. In such cases it will be necessary to just remove the bindings, and then remove the purflings after (if required).

Work slowly, using the heat to weaken the glue joint, and not forcing the palette knife to cut into the join, just using it to ease the binding away. Take care not to damage the purfling.

As soon as the gap is big enough, switch to the slightly thicker knife, and

The finish has been scraped off the bindings, and a little off the sides as well.

The clothes iron is slightly angled to avoid burning the finish on the sides. Start heating just beyond the join between the two halves of the binding.

ABOVE: Inserting the palette knife between the purflings and the back. It should not be necessary to use the knife in the join between the ends of the two bindings, as this end grain join will be weak.

RIGHT: Slightly rotating the knife will help prise the binding away from the rebate. If applying heat at the same time as using the knife, it helps to have the guitar firmly clamped by the neck.

add some water into the opening. It helps to continue to apply heat with the iron at the same time as working the knife along the joint. Try to peel the bindings away, rather than cut into the joint, as this is less likely to cause any damage. If the bindings are to be replaced anyway, you do not need to worry about damaging or breaking them, but it is good practice to try to keep them intact.

Once the binding has started to come loose, it should be relatively easy to continue to release it from the rebate, continuing to apply heat and working around as far as you need to go. If the binding is being completely removed, the other end will often be held between the back and the heel cap. This makes applying heat more difficult, particularly if you are trying not to damage the finish on the back. The alternative is to remove the heel cap first, but in this case some refinishing will be needed anyway. The top bindings will almost certainly be captive below the fingerboard. If they are to be replaced, the best approach is to remove the last, captive section with a small chisel. Extracting the ends of the bindings from beneath the fingerboard is likely to be very difficult without damaging at least the finish. It is generally better to leave a small section in place and join it to the new bindings with a scarf joint, which can easily be made invisible if the wood is dark in colour. The same approach can be used if just replacing a damaged section of the binding.

Continue to remove as much of the binding as required. If removing the back, continue as described in Chapter 12. The rebate will need to be cleaned up, removing any old glue or binding material that has remained in place. There are a few options for holding the binding in place when re-gluing, but I find masking tape gives the most control. If the guitar has a delicate finish, however, you will need a tape that has enough tack to hold well, but not so much as to risk damaging the finish. The alternative is to secure the bindings by wrapping around the whole guitar. Some makers use rope for this, but for a delicate finish a better option is lengths of bicycle inner tube.

The bindings and purflings have come away from the rebate very cleanly and without any damage. The glue join between the purflings and the back is likely to be easier to release than the one between the purflings and the bindings. This is because much of the join to the back is end grain, and hence weaker.

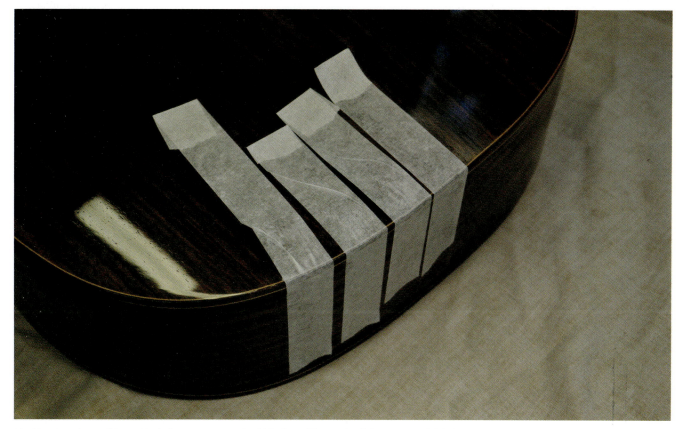

Masking tape is used to reattach the new or repaired bindings. The ends of the tape are folded over to make removal easier.

CHAPTER 11

Wolf Notes and Resonances

What are wolf notes?

Wolf notes are most problematic in the bowed instrument world – particularly in cellos. They occur when the frequency of the note being played matches, or is very close to, a natural resonant frequency in the body of the instrument. Although people often refer to wolf notes in guitars, the problem is actually slightly different, and the term can be a bit misleading. In a cello, the string has a constant input of energy from the bow, and the vibrations of the string can repeatedly shift in pitch by an octave, producing a 'howl' that gives the wolf note its name.

In a guitar, the situation is different. The cause of the problem note is the same, with the frequency of the played note coinciding with one of the many resonances in the body of the guitar. The result is different, however, largely because the input to the string is a single pluck. What tends to happen on a guitar is that you get an initial 'thud' followed by a shorter sustain than usual. There can also be a slight shift in pitch away from the desired note.

An acoustic guitar body has a large number of resonances. Some of these will be from the top or the back, with each plate having many different resonance frequencies. Others will be from the air volume within the body of the guitar. The first or main air resonance is also known as the Helmholtz resonance. Most of these resonances have an insignificant effect on the sound of the played notes, but the first body resonance and the first few top resonances can be problematic. The exact frequencies of the resonances will vary depending on the construction of the guitar. The volume of air in the body, the size of the soundhole, the mass and stiffness of the soundboard will all influence the resonant frequencies, and these resonances will also interact with each other. On classical guitars the first body resonance is most commonly somewhere between F and G# (87–104Hz) on the bass E string, and is usually a bit higher on steel-string guitars. The first top resonance is normally about an octave higher than this.

Can wolf notes be eliminated?

It is often said that better-quality, more expensive guitars have stronger resonances, potentially making them more of an issue. Whether or not these resonances are a problem depends largely on how close the resonant frequencies lie to the played notes, but also on the sensitivity of the player to these problem notes. If a resonance falls exactly between two notes, then both notes will be impacted (because the resonance has a certain bandwidth, or frequency range), but at a much lower level than if the resonance is at exactly the frequency of the played note. It is *not* possible to eliminate resonances altogether. At best, their impact can be reduced by shifting the frequency of resonances slightly to fall between two notes. As we will see, there can also be unwanted consequences to adjusting resonances. The overall output of the guitar may be reduced, other resonances may become more of a problem, or the overall character of the guitar may be changed. It is therefore recommended that any adjustments attempted should only be undertaken if they are easily reversible, or if any of the resonances are completely unacceptable for the player.

Before we can do anything about a problem resonance, the frequency of all the significant resonances present in the guitar must be measured.

Measuring resonances

There are a number of ways to measure resonant frequencies. Just singing into the soundhole of the guitar will produce an obvious 'boom' in sound when you hit the main air resonance frequency. Not everyone has a vocal range that extends low enough for this, and there are more reliable methods.

A more scientific approach is to either drive the resonances with a signal generator, amplifier and speaker, or to use a microphone to record the 'tap-tones' of the top, and frequency analysis software to find the resonances. The first method has the advantage of providing a visual representation of the soundboard resonances in the form of Chladni patterns.

Chladni patterns

In the eighteenth century the German physicist Ernst Chladni performed experiments investigating vibrating plates and their associated nodal patterns. Similar experiments are often performed by luthiers as part of the soundboard tuning process, either before the soundboard is attached to the body, or on the completed instrument. On a finished guitar, the patterns can help identify where adjustments might be made. The frequencies at which the patterns occur will identify the resonances.

The equipment needed is simple. A frequency generator capable of producing a sine-wave output over the range of frequencies to be investigated (from 60Hz up to 1kHz is plenty), connected to a suitable amplifier, and a reasonably sized, good-quality speaker. You will also need some tea leaves.

These days, a frequency generator could simply be a phone app, of which there are a number available. I use an old 40W guitar amp as an amplifier, which has the added benefit of having a built-in speaker. You will need to dismount the speaker and add some long extension cables to make the speaker easy to move around above the soundboard.

Support the guitar so that the soundboard is fairly level, and scatter some tea leaves sparsely over the soundboard. The strings can either be left on the guitar, or removed, but the tension of the strings

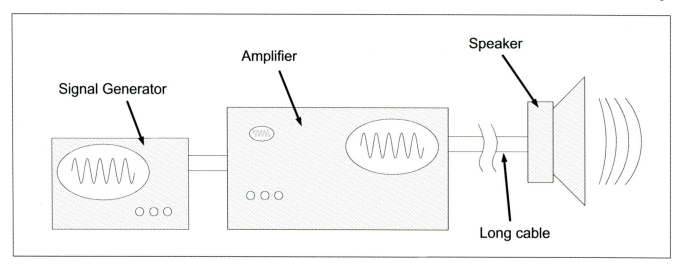

ABOVE: Diagram showing the setup I use for generating Chladni patterns. The signal generator can be a phone app that connects to an amplifier, preferably 20W or more. The output from the amp is connected to the speaker with a cable long enough to allow movement around the guitar.

LEFT: Fine tea leaves scattered on the soundboard. The guitar needs to be supported so that the soundboard is level, otherwise the tea leaves tend to migrate down the slope.

acting on the soundboard will slightly shift the resonances. If the strings are left on, they should be damped by inserting some felt or a piece of cloth between the strings and the fingerboard.

Set the frequency generator to around 70Hz and turn on the amplifier at a modest volume. The lower resonant modes do not need much power, but for some of the higher ones the volume will need to be set quite loud, so a good pair of ear defenders will be needed. Hold the speaker over the soundboard and gradually increase the frequency of the signal generator. At some point, usually at around 85–110Hz, the tea leaves will start to vibrate on the surface of the soundboard. This is the main air resonance, or first body resonance. If you hold the speaker near to the soundhole, the vibrations will increase. Don't hold the speaker directly over the soundhole, as this will shift the resonance slightly.

Continue to gradually increase the frequency, and the vibrations will increase until they reach a maximum, and then die down again. If the vibrations get too loud, move the speaker further away from the soundboard. This will avoid the vibrations causing any damage, and also increase the sensitivity of the measurement. Scan back and forth past the point of maximum vibrations to identify the exact peak. Take a note of the frequency – this is the main body resonance. If you keep driving the soundboard at this frequency, the tea leaves will form a pattern, moving away from the antinodes (points of maximum vibration) and collecting at the nodes (points of minimum vibration). For this classical guitar, the main body resonance occurred at about 95Hz (between F# and G on the 6th string). In general terms, the resonances of acoustic guitars will be higher than those found on classical guitars, due to the higher stiffness of the soundboard.

Now increase the frequency of the signal generator to find the next resonance – the first top (soundboard) resonance. This is usually about an octave higher than the body resonance – for this guitar at around 190Hz. The pattern of the tea leaves will be another monopole mode, very similar in appearance to that of the main body resonance.

Continue to increase the signal frequency until the next mode is found. This is usually the transverse dipole, occurring at around 230Hz for this guitar.

The next resonant mode found is the longitudinal dipole.

Continuing up the frequency range, we find the transverse tripole.

At higher frequencies, we start to see a lot of more complex modes, some with less clearly defined patterns, and some that merge into each other. Note that the

The first body resonance at around 90Hz. The antinode is roughly centred on the bridge. The pattern was disturbed slightly just before the photo was taken.

ABOVE: The transverse dipole at about 230Hz. The antinode running along the centreline of the soundboard would be displaced if the soundboard and bracing were very asymmetric.

LEFT: The longitudinal dipole is often the only low-frequency resonance that extends beyond the lower harmonic bar of a classical guitar.

RIGHT: Transverse tripole. The antinodes of the higher frequency resonances extend further out towards the edges of the lower bout.

BELOW: This higher order mode looks like it might give a clue as to the bracing pattern used in this guitar, but in fact it has five fan braces, which do not align with the antinodes of this Chladni pattern.

Wolf Notes and Resonances   **223**

At above 1kHz the upper bout once again becomes active. The guitar has to be driven with quite a high amplitude for this mode to be seen clearly.

shapes of the modes bear little relation to the bracing pattern used on the soundboard. However, as we will see below, the patterns are useful in terms of how we might modify the bracing or otherwise adjust the resonant frequencies.

The higher modes are of less interest in terms of any adjustments we might make, but it is worth noting that on a classical guitar with traditional construction, the upper bout of the guitar shows virtually no vibrations until we reach 1kHz or more.

Frequency response curves

Another way to find the resonant frequencies of the guitar is to plot a frequency response curve. You will need a good-quality microphone with a reasonably flat response curve, and software to record and analyse the signals.

There are various ways to obtain a spectrum showing the response of the guitar, but the easiest is to simply tap the bridge with a suitable 'hammer', record the audio output from the guitar with a microphone connected to a laptop, and analyse the resulting audio file using suitable software. 'Audacity' is a free, open source piece of software that will allow you to record audio samples and analyse them.

A simple impact hammer can be made in various ways. Mine is rather crude – a hard piece of rubber wedged into a hex socket, attached to an Allen key! A more reproduceable impulse can be obtained using the wire-break method. A thin copper wire is tied around one of the strings hard against the saddle. The wire is pulled until it breaks, imparting a sudden impulse to the bridge. The wire will break with a repeatable force, giving a more consistent result than a tap with

a hammer. I use the hammer method because it is quicker and easier, and gives satisfactory results.

The microphone is positioned about 20cm from the soundboard and pointed roughly at the bridge. The bridge is tapped lightly and repeatedly with the hammer, whilst the audio signal is recorded on the laptop via Audacity. Recording multiple taps gives the software more data to work with, and can give a cleaner spectrum, making it easier to identify the resonances.

Once the audio has been recorded, a series of taps is selected in the software, and a frequency analysis function is used to plot the spectrum. If using Audacity, once the spectrum is displayed, adjust the 'Size' parameter to get a plot with enough resolution to see the peaks clearly, but without too much noise. I find a value of 16,000 usually works best.

A makeshift impulse hammer. I have since switched to using a hammer with a softer head, which gives results for the spectrum that are a closer match to the frequencies found using Chladni patterns.

Tapping the bridge repeatedly with the hammer and recording the output with a microphone connected to a laptop. The position of the microphone is not critical, but placing it too close to the soundhole will result in a spectrum dominated by the main air resonance mode.

Wolf Notes and Resonances

Again, the dots mark the antinodes, this time for the long dipole mode.

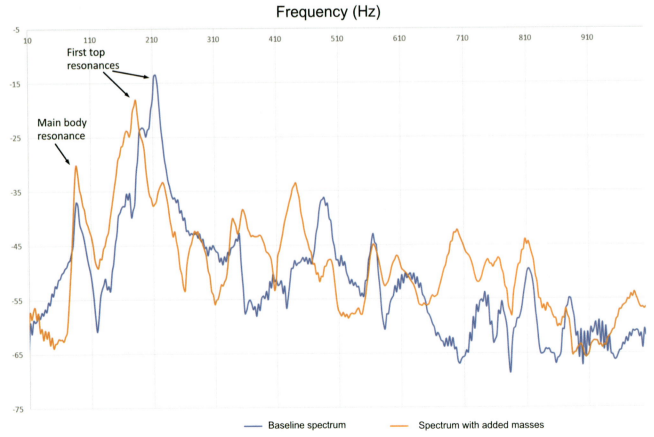

Graph showing the shift in resonant frequencies when a relatively large mass of 8g is added close to the centre of the soundboard.

We can see that when masses are added on the transverse dipole antinodes, there is a significant shift in the resonant frequency of that mode, but very little change (within the experimental error) in the long dipole resonance. The converse is true when mass is added to the long dipole antinodes.

From these results it is clear that a useful shift in resonant frequency can be achieved with just a few grams of added mass if the position is chosen carefully.

Adding mass in the centre of the soundboard will have less effect on the dipoles than on the monopole, as both dipoles have antinodes in this position. Adding mass under the bridge will not shift the main body resonance by much, but should affect the first top resonance significantly.

In the example below, a piece of Blu Tack of 8g in mass was added to the centre of the soundboard to assess the impact on the frequency of the first few resonances of a classical guitar. This is a larger mass than would normally be needed, but it clearly shows the impact of the added mass on the resonant frequency.

The main body resonance and the first top resonance (both monopoles) are easily identified. Before the mass was added, these can be seen as peaks at around 85Hz and 215Hz respectively. After adding the mass, the main body resonance shifts only slightly, reducing by 1–2Hz, but the first top resonance has moved from 215Hz to 184Hz.

Adding or reducing bracing/stiffness

Gluing an additional brace to the soundboard will add mass as well as stiffness. The added mass will tend to lower the resonance frequency, but the added stiffness will increase it. For thin, light braces, the overall result should be an increase in resonant frequency, provided the position of the brace is chosen correctly. A new brace glued along the line of the node of a resonance will have little impact in terms of added stiffness for that mode, as the soundboard will not be vibrating significantly along that line at that frequency. As we found in the case of adding mass to the soundboard, braces can be added in such a position to significantly shift one resonance whilst having much less impact on others.

In general, the most efficient position to add a brace to adjust a particular resonance will be perpendicular to a node line of that resonance. For the longitudinal dipole, this might be along the centre line of the lower bout, which on most classical guitars would correspond to the position of the centre fan brace. Reducing the height of this brace might be an efficient way to lower that resonance, but when removing material from braces it is important to remember that they also support the tension of the strings acting on the bridge, so removing too much material from longitudinal braces can have structural implications.

A good position (theoretically) to add a brace to shift the long dipole resonance without affecting the transverse dipole. Of course, there is usually already a brace here on a classical guitar. Lowering the centre brace might be effective but could result in increased bridge rotation.

CHAPTER 12

Catastrophic Damage

What counts as catastrophic?

You might think that catastrophic damage would mean irreparable, but almost anything can be repaired given enough time (and money). The main problem with really serious damage is the question of whether the guitar is beyond economic repair – that is, a write-off. The cost of carrying out repairs on guitars can be high, and it does not take a huge amount of damage before your average guitar isn't worth the expense. More valuable instruments are, of course, more worthwhile repairing, and there is also the question of sentimental value. For the purposes of this chapter, I am defining catastrophic as damage that at first sight, a customer is likely to think is either impossible, or at least very expensive, to repair.

Occasionally, of course, there is really nothing that can be done. In fact, this 1950 Martin was a restoration project taken on by one of my braver students. (Photo: Chris Snow)

Broken neck/headstock

A break at the join between the head and the neck is fairly common. It can be a weak point, especially on acoustic guitars with a truss rod adjuster at the head end. The combination of a thin and narrow neck, along with the weakening caused by the channel for the truss rod, makes it prone to breakage. Add that to the fact that many guitar owners rest their beloved instruments against a table rather than in a proper stand (or safely stored in the case), and you have a recipe for disaster.

In fact, a broken headstock is not always a very difficult repair, provided it has not been left in a broken condition for too long. If the head is not completely detached from the neck, which is often the case thanks to the reinforcement provided by the head plate, then the repair can be a little easier. If the head becomes completely detached, then it is quite common for a few pieces of wood to be missing, and this isn't always obvious until you start work on the repair.

Preparation

The broken headstock repair described here is on a classical guitar. Although the Spanish cedar of the neck is completely broken through, the head is being held on by the rosewood headplate.

Applying gentle pressure gives an indication of how far the break goes. The separation of the join between the white veneer and the head itself extends slightly beyond the centre tuner hole. Look for any loose fibres of wood inside the break. If there are, then remove these with a pair

The rosewood head veneer is holding everything together, which makes realignment easier, and reduces the risk of parts getting lost.

Headstock breaks like this are fairly common, although more frequently seen on steel-string acoustics.

The splinter seen near the bottom edge of the image will be repositioned prior to gluing the joint back together. The missing piece at the bottom of the slot will need replacing using some matching wood.

LEFT: These flat clamping blocks will spread the pressure evenly when the repair is glued up. The cork-faced block will be used on the back surface of the head to protect the relatively soft Spanish cedar.

of tweezers. If left, there is a risk that they will not go back in the correct position and prevent the join closing up perfectly.

Fortunately, most of the wood was still present in this break, apart from a small piece missing from the back of the head. This will be relatively easy to replace invisibly with a well-matched piece of cedar.

Prepare two clamping blocks to hold the break firmly closed whilst gluing. A cork lining will help prevent damage to the surfaces, and both should have clear tape covering to prevent them being glued to the head.

Before applying any glue, perform a test clamp-up to check everything is in place and closes up correctly. Note the additional small clamping block. This is used so that the area with the missing piece is exposed, which will allow you to clean up the glue. If any glue is left in the space to dry, it will be difficult to remove, and hence to fit the repair piece perfectly.

A dry run is advisable when clamping a repair to ensure everything closes up as you expect before any glue is applied.

Catastrophic Damage **233**

Re-gluing the headstock

You are now ready to start gluing. Have the clamps and clamping cauls ready to put in place as soon as you have glue in all the fractures.

Step 1: Squeeze Titebond glue into the break. Other glues can be used, but it will take some time to work the glue well into all the gaps, so a slow setting one is preferred.

Step 2: Now work the glue into the break using a brush, adding more glue as needed. Do not worry about using too much glue – it will be easy to clean up later.

Step 3: Keep flexing the break, which will help to work the glue right into the cracks. Check carefully all the way around the head, and in the tuner slots, making sure glue has been applied to all fractures in the wood, and to any open joins.

Step 4: When you have enough glue in the break, clean off the worst of the excess glue and position the clamping cauls. Place the clamps evenly around the cauls, and gradually tighten them.

Step 5: Clean up the worst of the glue squeeze-out using a brush and some water. Any remaining dried glue can be cleaned up later after the clamps have been removed. For this repair, the additional small clamping caul and clamp need to be positioned and tightened.

Step 6: Now the glue needs to be cleaned out from any gaps left by missing pieces of wood, using a brush and water. Also clean up any other squeeze-out that you can get to.

Step 7: Leave the clamps in place for at least 4 hours. With the clamps removed, we can see some dried glue in the tuner slots that could not be cleaned up when the clamps were in place. This dry glue can be cut away with a sharp chisel, filed, or sanded flat.

Small patch repairs

Now move on to replacing any missing pieces. Although it would be possible to make a piece to fit perfectly into this gap as it is, it will be much easier to get a perfect fit if we straighten the sides of the gap, leaving a wedged shape with straight edges, roughly along the lines of the grain. Using a steel rule as a guide, carefully cut into the wood just far enough in from the gap to give a straight cut, without removing any more wood than necessary. Make sure that the cuts are vertical.

Cutting straight edges around the missing piece of the head. The rule could be clamped in position to leave both hands free to make the cut.

Catastrophic Damage

The gap now has straight edges, making the fitting of the inlay piece much easier. As the cuts run roughly parallel to the grain, the repair should be invisible.

When both sides have been cut, and any excess material removed, you should be left with a clean, wedged gap ready for the insert.

Find a piece of wood for the insert that matches the original as closely as possible and cut it roughly to shape.

Start trimming the piece to get a close fit in the gap.

Test the piece for fit. Because the piece is wedged in shape, and longer than the space it needs to fill, adjustments can be made to perfect the angle, and the piece can be pushed into the wedged gap until it is tight. Continue to adjust and test until the fit is perfect, and then glue the piece in. Hide glue will be best here, and it should not need to be clamped, but just held firmly in place for a minute.

When the glue has dried, use a sharp chisel to carefully trim back the top of the inlaid repair piece until it is perfectly flush with the surrounding wood. Finish this with a sanding block if you are not confident with a chisel, or if the grain is difficult.

LEFT: The repair piece is initially cut to approximately the correct angle, and longer than needed. This allows the angle of the taper to be gradually adjusted until a perfect fit is obtained.

Holding such a small piece while adjusting it with a chisel or place can be difficult, so a scalpel is my preferred tool for this.

236   Catastrophic Damage

Final test fit. If the fit had not been right at this stage, it would have been necessary to make a new piece, as there isn't much length left.

A sharp chisel is the best tool for levelling the repair patch. Provided you follow the grain direction, you will be able to get it perfectly flush without damaging the surrounding area.

Catastrophic Damage

The inlay piece glued in place. It is best to trim the ends after the glue has fully dried.

Once flush, the ends need to be trimmed.

Gradually trim the ends back until they are flush, taking care to match the angles of the surfaces.

A sharp knife or scalpel is used to trim the ends of the repair patch. You need to take very fine cuts when working across the grain like this.

238　Catastrophic Damage

Refinishing

If the finish is French polish or lacquer, then it is best to just touch up the finish on the newly inlaid piece. In this case the guitar was finished with oil, and it was easy just to sand back all the surfaces affected by the break. After sanding, but before finishing, the repair should already be almost invisible. After two coats of Danish oil, the repair looks very good.

Back removal

Applying some oil finish to this repair was enough to blend the repair patch in with the surrounding wood. In some cases, some colour touch-up might be required.

Removing the back of a guitar can be quite challenging and is rarely called for. In previous chapters we have seen how many body repairs can be successfully completed by working through the soundhole. For more extensive repairs, or where access just isn't possible, the only option may be to remove the back completely. This involves removing the bindings and opening the glue joint between the linings and the back, and also between the heel and end blocks and the back. There will probably be some damage to the linings and back braces, and possibly to the back itself. In most cases you will need to make and fit new bindings and purflings. Some refinishing will also be required. A detailed assessment of all the work required, and the time it will take (and hence the cost), should be made before deciding to proceed.

Removing the bindings

The first job is to remove the bindings. The glue holding wooden bindings can be released by applying heat and water to the joins, and it is usually worth first attempting removal (*see* Chapter 10: Binding removal). In the case shown

With a lacquer finish, cutting the bindings away with a chisel will almost certainly chip the finish on the sides. Cutting through the finish with a sharp scalpel will help minimise the chipping, and hence the amount of finish touch-up required.

Catastrophic Damage **239**

here, the bindings were plastic, and heating them enough to loosen the glue would also melt them.

The alternative is to just cut away the bindings with a chisel, and this method was used for the plastic bindings on this guitar. First use a sharp scalpel to cut through the finish at the join between the binding and the sides. This will help to prevent the finish chipping when the bindings are cut away. This step would not be required for a French polish or an oil finish.

Now start to cut into the bindings with a sharp chisel. Work carefully and slowly until you have cut right through the binding.

If you're lucky, the binding will start to peel away from the rebate, but in this case, it simply broke off in small sections.

Continue to work the chisel under the exposed end of the binding, cutting along the line of the join, and taking care not to cut into the side. Continue all the way around the guitar until the binding has been completely removed.

If the ends of the bindings at the heel are tucked in between the heel and the sides, use a narrow chisel (no wider than the binding width) to cut the bindings out from the recess.

You should now be able to see the join between the linings and the back all around the guitar body, and also the ends of the back braces. If the height of the ends of the braces are lower than the depth of the bindings, it will be relatively easy to release the back bars from the linings.

LEFT: Using a chisel to start to cut through the plastic bindings.

BELOW: Once the bindings have been cut right through, the chisel must be guided accurately along the join between the bindings and the back of the guitar.

From this point on, the bindings broke off in chunks as the chisel was worked under the end. Wood bindings are much easier to remove using a combination of heat and moisture to release the glue.

With the binding removed, and the rebate cleaned up, the join between the back and the linings is easy to identify. This is the join that will be separated to remove the back.

Catastrophic Damage **241**

Removing the back

Now move on to removing the back itself. Start at a point away from the widest point of the upper and lower bouts, as there is a greater risk here of cracking the back plate when you work the knife through the joint. Apply water along the binding rebate, and allow it to soak in.

Now apply heat to the edge of the back over the linings using a clothes iron. This will almost certainly damage the finish on the back, but is usually necessary to get enough heat into the join to release it.

You can try applying the heat just in the rebate, which might help to minimise damage to the finish, but is usually less effective.

Now work a thin palette knife into the join between the linings and the back. Getting started is the trickiest part, so

ABOVE: Applying water into the rebate to soften the glue in the join between back and linings.

LEFT: Applying the heat directly to the back will damage the finish, but is usually necessary to get enough heat into the joint to soften the glue.

Applying the heat into the rebate will do less damage, but is less effective at getting the heat to where it is needed.

Getting the palette knife started in the joint is often the hardest part, particularly if the lining wood is quite soft.

Catastrophic Damage

work slowly, and make sure you are not just cutting into the linings, which are usually relatively soft. Apply more water and heat frequently. Heating the knife on the iron can help, but take care not to burn yourself on the blade.

Wiggle the knife back and forth, and gradually push it through the join. Once it is all the way through, start to work it sideways along the join, applying water into the section already opened, and heating with the iron as necessary.

Once a slight gap has been opened, switch to a knife with a slightly thicker and stronger blade. Here I'm using an old kitchen knife, which is not sharp, but is tapered across the width of the blade, making it fairly strong, and easy to get into small gaps. When you reach a back brace, move the knife to cut through between the top of the brace and the lining, rather than continuing along the line of the back.

Work alternately on either side of the brace between the back and the linings, and between the brace and the linings. Once the end of the brace is free from the linings, continue around the back as before.

There are usually three or four back braces, so there will be six or eight brace ends to release. Identify their positions and be sure to separate each one from the linings, and not cut through between the brace and the back.

The end block of the guitar should not be any more difficult to release than the linings, but the heel block is usually

LEFT: Once the palette knife is right through the join, things get a little easier. Note that there is some scorching of the wood in the binding rebate.

BELOW: The stiffer kitchen knife is here being inserted between the spruce back brace and the pocket in the lining.

A clear gap where the join has been opened, with very little damage to the linings or the back.

Working the knife to release the next back brace. A slightly narrower knife matched to the width of the brace would be better, but the damage to the linings was minimal.

somewhat bigger, especially in the case of a classical guitar with a Spanish heel. You will need to heat a larger area of the back and continue to apply water into the gaps already opened up. Heating the knife will help for this part. I usually try to open up a shallow gap across the end of the block, before pushing the knife straight into the join.

Work the knife back and forth, adding more water frequently, and applying more heat. Don't try to force the knife, just keep working it slowly into the joint. When you are almost through the joint, it is tempting to just pull the back off, but be patient, and continue working with the knife until it has completely released the heel block.

The back should now come free, but take care lifting it off, checking for any sections that are still hanging on, releasing them with heat and the knife. Depending on the type of glue used, and the material used for the back and for the bindings, you may get away with no damage at all. In most cases, particularly if the linings are made from a relatively soft wood like spruce or Spanish cedar, some repair will be needed.

On acoustic guitars the heel cap is usually below the level of the back, making back removal a little easier. On classical guitars the heel cap is generally flush with the back and will probably have to be removed first.

Catastrophic Damage

The knife is almost through the join with the heel block. Being the largest gluing area, this is the hardest part to separate.

There will inevitably be some damage to either the linings or the back, but with care this can be kept to a minimum. Damaged linings will be easy to repair, and not visible on the outside of the guitar.

Repairing damage and preparation

Hopefully, the outside of the back itself will be undamaged (as in this case), although the finish will certainly need some work.

The back of this guitar was removed to make some major changes to the bracing. The guitar was somewhat over-built, and it was hoped that taking some material from the braces, and improving their shape, would result in a more responsive instrument. The details of the adjustments need not be described, as here we are focussing on the process of removal and re-fitting of the back.

While the back is off, inspect the inside of the guitar for any problems not necessarily related to the main reason

ABOVE: The outside of the back was undamaged. Surprisingly, even the finish survived relatively unscathed from the heat of the iron.

RIGHT: The X-braces and finger braces have been lowered on this guitar in an attempt to make it more responsive. It remains to be seen whether any improvement was worth the number of hours put into the job.

Catastrophic Damage **247**

The gap between the linings and sides is not a major problem, but worth fixing as the back is already off.

Working Titebond glue into the gap.

Lining clamped using a small triangular block to prevent the clamp slipping off. The gap did not close completely but was an improvement.

for removing the back. On this guitar, there was a section of lining that was very poorly glued to the side.

Clearly this should be remedied whilst the back is off. Titebond glue was worked into the gap using a brush.

The linings were clamped to the side using a long reach clamp, and a triangular shaped block of wood so that the clamp would not slide off the angled linings.

Once all necessary work has been carried out on the inside of the guitar, prepare the surfaces for re-gluing. It is inevitable that there will be at least some glue residue on the linings, heel block, end block and the back. It is also possible that the back and/or linings will have been damaged in the process of removing the back. In the case of this repair, some sections of linings were damaged. Also, the area of the back where it was glued to the heel block was damaged. This is a common problem with guitars with laminated backs and sides – the inner (and outer) laminations are quite fragile, and very easy to damage with the knife when removing the back.

Clean up the back, removing any trace of glue and bits of lining material. Any large pieces can be removed with a chisel, before scraping and sanding to leave a clean, flat surface all around the edge of the back. The damaged section of the back has been simply filled and levelled using a mix of wood dust and glue. A cleaner repair could be achieved by replacing the missing layer of the lamination with a suitable piece of veneer.

Now move on to cleaning up the linings. Remove all traces of old glue, taking care to maintain the correct angle of the linings to match the curvature of the back. Any damaged sections of lining will need to be repaired or replaced.

In this case, there was one section that was badly damaged near the heel. This section was completely removed using a chisel, followed by scraping and sanding to give a clean gluing surface.

The back cleaned up to remove residual glue and a few bits of lining. The dark patch to the left is where the damaged inner lamination was filled.

The gluing surface of the linings has been cleaned up, but there is some damage near the heel block that will need to be repaired.

Catastrophic Damage

A new section of kerfed lining was made from a similar material used for the original linings.

The new kerfed lining section is cut to length and glued in place clamped with clothes pegs. It should be glued just slightly proud of the original linings and then levelled after the glue has dried.

When cleaning up the gluing surface of the linings, some material will have been removed. Check that the back brace pockets in the linings are still deep enough for the back brace ends. Test fit the back and carefully inspect the areas around the back bar ends. If the back bars are preventing the back from sitting completely flush with the linings, the pockets will have to be deepened slightly. Another option is to reduce the height of the ends of the back braces where needed.

ABOVE: The damaged lining section has been removed, and the gluing surface scraped and sanded clean.

LEFT: New section of kerfed lining made. When trimmed to length it can be glued in place.

Homemade lining clamps. Wooden clothes pegs reinforced with elastic bands.

Lining pockets for the back braces deepened slightly. The braces should contact the bottom of this pocket when the back is in contact with the top of the linings.

Catastrophic Damage

Re-gluing the back

Now prepare all the required clamps for gluing the back on again. I use mostly spool clamps, which have a cork padding to help prevent damage to the top and back plates, and also help them to grip. The curvature of the back tends to make unlined spool clamps slip off. At the heel block end, an F-clamp is used together with a cork-lined caul. A smaller caul is used for the end block.

When gluing the back on, it is important that it is aligned correctly. Once the back has been removed, the sides can move slightly, so that the shape of the sides do not exactly match that of the back. Small errors can be corrected as you apply the clamps, but if the shape is a long way off, it is better to devise a way of holding them in the correct shape until all the clamps are in place. Perfectly aligning the back will also ensure that the correct neck angle is reproduced. Removing the back allows the body to flex in the same way described later in this chapter under 'Soundboard replacement', and potentially change the neck angle, but this will not happen if the back is aligned exactly as it was before.

When ready, apply glue all the way around the linings, and to the heel and end blocks. If you are not confident about getting all the clamps on correctly and quickly, or if you need to adjust the sides a lot to match the back shape, using Titebond Extend will give you more time to work.

Position the back accurately onto the linings and start by clamping the large caul at the heel block. Check carefully that the edge of the back is perfectly aligned with the binding rebate – if not, release the clamp and adjust the position. Now work around the guitar, checking the alignment as you tighten each clamp.

When all the clamps are applied, make a final check of the alignment and then clean up any glue squeeze-out.

When the glue has dried, the clamps can be removed, and the binding rebates then cleaned up with a file or sanding stick.

BELOW: Glue applied all around the linings, and on the end and heel blocks. Not seen is a block supporting the end of the guitar to help maintain the correct neck alignment.

OPPOSITE ABOVE: The back glued and clamped. The alignment between the edges of the back and the linings should be perfect. This will minimise the work needed fitting the new bindings and purflings, and also ensure the correct neck angle is retained.

OPPOSITE BELOW: A sanding stick being used to clean up the binding rebates. A file could be used, but the tapered sides of this sanding stick make it easier to avoid damaging the bottom edge of the rebate.

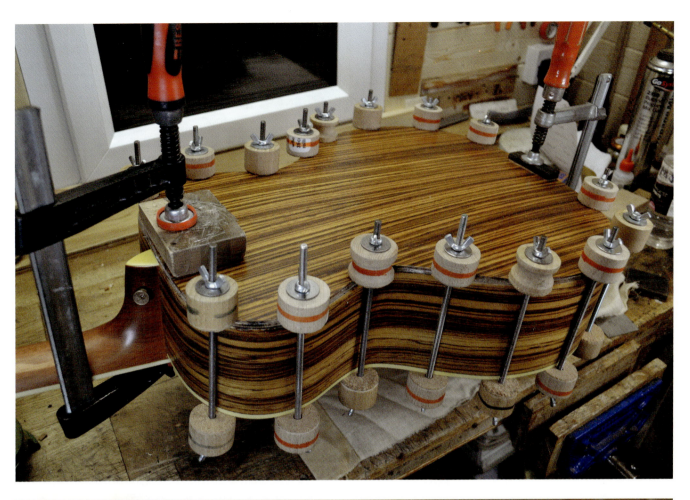

Replacing the bindings and purflings

There are a few different ways to hold the bindings in position whilst gluing, but I find masking tape the easiest and quickest. Stick lengths of tape to the sides all the way around the guitar, so that they are ready and in position when you glue in the bindings.

The replacement plastic binding piece is long enough to go all the way round the guitar without a join. The original black purflings were plastic, but here I have used black wood veneer. Before gluing down the last section of binding and purfling, mark them accurately to the correct length and trim them so that they meet perfectly on the centre line at the heel. Titebond and other similar water-based glues are not reliable for use with plastics. Epoxy resin was used for this repair, and to minimise difficult clean-up, any excess glue was removed by wiping with a paper towel as the binding was taped into position.

Once the glue has dried (24 hours in this case, as a slow setting epoxy was used), the tape can be removed. The bindings and purflings now need to be scraped and sanded flush with the back and sides. If you have managed to do minimal damage to the finish when cutting out the old bindings, you will want to take care not to damage the finish when scraping. Hold the cabinet scraper

ABOVE: When using tape, it is not necessary to completely cover the bindings. Small gaps between the pieces of tape are fine, but should be minimised at the waist.

BELOW: Masking tape stuck to the sides in preparation for gluing the new bindings and purflings. Preparation of this sort reduces the stress of long glue-ups.

Catastrophic Damage

ABOVE: A cabinet scraper works well on plastic bindings. Angle the scraper slightly downwards away from the back and stop as soon as you hit the finish.

RIGHT: The finished replacement bindings and purflings.

BELOW RIGHT: The replacement plastic binding was whiter in colour than the original. This will be improved when some coloured finish is applied.

at a very slight angle to the surface of the back, and work very slowly, stopping as soon as you hit the finish on the back. Marking the finish very slightly with the scraper is acceptable if the finish will need touching up anyway.

Once the bindings and purflings have been scraped flush on both the back and the sides, use some very fine abrasive (Micro-Mesh or similar) with a sanding block to smooth the surfaces and remove any slight marks left by the scraper.

Go around and very lightly sand the corner of the bindings to remove the sharp edge. The back removal and replacement is now complete, but any damage to the finish will need to be repaired appropriately.

Catastrophic Damage

Soundboard replacement

As we saw in Chapter 5, a cracked soundboard is relatively easy to repair, even if there are multiple cracks. Repairs become a lot more difficult if there are any fractures across the grain. A structurally satisfactory repair is often still possible, but it is unlikely to be cosmetically perfect. Occasionally, a soundboard will be so badly damaged that it just isn't practical to repair, with multiple cracks along the grain, and significant fractures across the grain. If the cost is not prohibitive, the best approach may be complete replacement of the soundboard. Consideration should be given to the fact that a new soundboard will not be exactly the same as the original one. Accurate measurements can be made of the soundboard thickness, bracing dimensions and even the average density of the tonewoods used, but no two pieces of wood are identical, and there needs to be an understanding that the guitar will not play exactly as it did before the damage occurred.

One of the problems encountered when attempting to replace a soundboard is the fingerboard. Whichever type of construction has been used (Spanish method or separate body/neck construction), the fingerboard will have been glued on after assembly of the soundbox. This leaves the repairer with three options:

- Remove the fingerboard entirely before attempting to remove the soundboard.
- Cut through the fingerboard at the body join (usually at the 12th or 14th fret).
- Fit the new soundboard *under* the fingerboard without removing it.

The last of these sounds the most complex, but it does have advantages, and is the method that will be used here.

Cutting through the fingerboard at the body join is fairly common practice, but is my least preferred method. The fingerboard contributes a significant part of the structural integrity of the guitar, and cutting through it and simply gluing the cut piece back onto the new soundboard will reduce the strength of the body/neck joint.

Removing the fingerboard entirely is perhaps the most satisfactory solution, but it does involve a lot of extra work for a job that is already going to be very time-consuming.

I have carried out the 'under the fingerboard' top replacement on three guitars, all very successfully. All were classical guitars with traditional bracing, but I believe the method can be applied to X-braced acoustic guitars equally well. In order to be able to insert the replacement soundboard under the fingerboard, the soundboard will need to flex in the upper bout. This should not be a problem for a classical soundboard, but an acoustic soundboard with X-bracing might be too stiff. There will be some flex in the body itself once the original top has been removed, but for some guitars there might not be enough flex in the soundboard and body for this method to work. If this is the case, then completely removing the fingerboard is recommended.

Removing the damaged soundboard

Given that the soundboard itself will be scrapped, you will not need to worry about damaging it further when removing it. The bridge will need to be reused, and possibly also the rosette.

Start by drilling small holes in the soundboard at each corner of the bridge, and about 10mm from it. The holes should be large enough to allow the tip of a saw to go through. I used a Japanese saw with teeth extending up to the tip for this. Starting at the hole, saw along a line parallel with the bridge starting at one corner, all the way to the next hole. Work around the bridge until the whole bridge and section of soundboard come away. Remember that there will be braces that need to be sawn through.

Put the bridge to one side – later you will need to remove all of the soundboard material from the underside so that it can be glued to the new soundboard.

If the rosette is a simple inlay, then it is often easier just to make a new one. If the existing rosette is to be saved, then cut through it as close to the edge of the fingerboard as possible using a sharp scalpel and using the edge of the fingerboard as a guide. You will inevitably lose a small amount of material, which will require some filling after the rosette has been inlaid in the new soundboard. If this is not acceptable, then the fingerboard will need to be removed completely in order to remove the whole rosette intact.

Starting at the hole left by the bridge, make further cuts up to and around the rosette and continue these up to the cuts next to the fingerboard. Again, you will have to cut through some bracing.

Once the bridge and the rosette have been recovered, the rest of the soundboard can be removed. There are two options here: either completely remove the top, the purflings and the bindings, or cut through the purflings and retain the original bindings. It is not practical to try to retain the purflings, as the replacement soundboard outline would need to be cut perfectly to fit. By sacrificing the purflings, the new soundboard can be cut anywhere between the bindings and the join between the purflings and the soundboard. Retaining the bindings has the added advantage that no refinishing work will be needed to the sides of the guitar.

In this case, the purflings and binding were removed along with the top. Start by cutting through the top flush with the inner edge of the linings, all the way around the perimeter, and then along the edges of the fingerboard. The exact method used to separate the remaining parts of the soundboard from the linings will depend on the glue used, but a combination of heat and moisture can be used to soften the glue and allow you to

ABOVE: Removing the soundboard. The bridge has been cut out and stored to be used on the replacement. Cuts have also been made around the rosette up to the edges of the fingerboard to allow it to be removed intact. As this was a simple rosette to make, the existing one was not used.

RIGHT: For this repair, the top bindings were also removed. On more recent repairs I have switched to retaining the bindings, which reduces the time needed for the whole job.

Catastrophic Damage

prise it away with a spatula. Alternatively, the remaining soundboard material can be carefully cut away with a chisel.

If the bindings are to be removed, this is done next. Either carefully chisel them away from the linings, taking particular care as you approach the sides, or use a combination of heat and moisture to release the glue, and pull the bindings away starting at the join at the end of the guitar. When you reach the neck, cut enough of the bindings out from the pocket between the neck and the linings/neck block to allow the new bindings to be located.

The replacement soundboard

It is now time to make the new soundboard. Unless you are aiming to change the sound of the guitar, you will need to take accurate measurements of the thickness of the original soundboard, and the dimensions and positions of the braces, and reproduce these as accurately as possible. If reusing the original rosette, then this must be cut out of the removed section of soundboard, including removing the soundboard material underneath the rosette. To cut the channel in the new soundboard, tack glue the rosette in position on the top, and carefully mark around it into the soundboard with a sharp scalpel. Remove the rosette, and then deepen the cuts to the required depth. Now excavate the channel using a hand router (Granny's tooth) or a Dremel. The depth should

RIGHT: The new soundboard is as close a match as possible to the original.

BELOW: The old soundboard laid out next to the replacement.

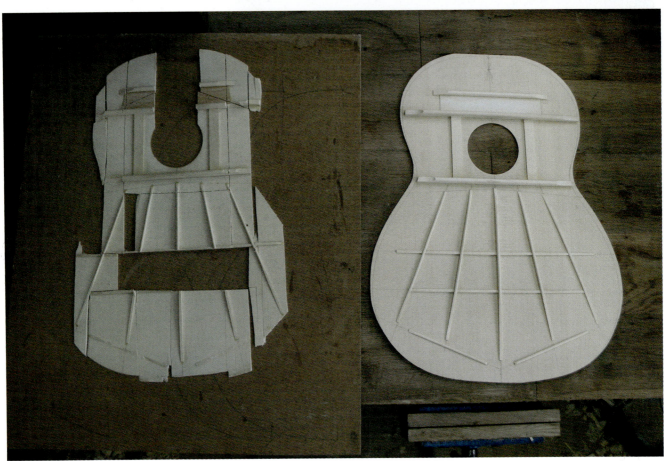

be a fraction less than the depth of the rosette. This will allow a small amount of clean-up on the top to level it perfectly.

At this stage, apart from the original being cut into pieces, the two soundboards should be as close a match as possible. A few adjustments will need to be made to the new soundboard before it can be fitted. Whilst you have good access to the inside of the new soundboard, it is worth taking the time to make a clamping caul for the bridge, which can be perfectly fitted over the bracing to help when re-gluing the existing bridge to the new soundboard.

Preparing to glue the new soundboard

Now remove the remains of the soundboard from the underside of the fingerboard up to the heel block using a chisel. It can be tricky working under the fingerboard as it is difficult to see what you are doing. If necessary, use a rasp and a sanding block, but in either case, take care not to remove any material from the fingerboard, particularly at the edges. In order to fit the new soundboard cleanly under the fingerboard, a rebate must be cut by removing material from the part of the old soundboard left between the fingerboard and the heel block to a depth of 3mm. This can be done with a narrow, sharp chisel, and should not be too difficult as the soundboard material is much softer than the fingerboard, and any slight damage to the wood of the heel block is not critical.

As some of the original soundboard has been left between the fingerboard and the heel block, we need to cut this part away from the new soundboard. Measure carefully the dimensions of the fingerboard at the body join and up to the end of the heel block, and mark this on the underside of the soundboard. Now mark just under 3mm inside this marked line and cut the soundboard away to this new line. The new soundboard should now fit under the fingerboard leaving no visible gaps.

The soundboard will have to be flexed to insert it under the fingerboard. The amount of flex needed depends on the thickness of the soundboard, but will also depend on the height of any braces that are fitted into the linings in the upper bout. In the case of a typical classical guitar, this will be both of the transverse harmonic bars, and for a typical acoustic guitar the upper ends of the X-braces. For this classical guitar, I reduced the height of the upper harmonic bar ends to about 2mm, and the lower harmonic bar ends to about 4mm. The corresponding

The remains of the old soundboard have been removed from the underside of the fingerboard, and from between the fingerboard and heel block to a depth of about 3mm. Note also one of the two new supporting blocks to match the lowered upper harmonic bar ends.

ABOVE: A section of the new soundboard has been cut out to fit around the heel block. The width of the cut-out is less than the width of the fingerboard, as it will be recessed under it to get a perfect finish.

LEFT: The original harmonic bar ends were about 6mm high and could not be worked into position. On the new soundboard they have been lowered, and the corresponding supports in the linings modified to match.

A dry-run fit of the new soundboard. This is essential to check that everything can be worked into place correctly before any glue is applied.

cut-outs in the linings were adjusted to match these heights, so that when assembled, the harmonic bar ends are supported by the linings.

Before applying any glue, it is very important to carry out a dry fit. Insert the top end of the soundboard under the end of the fingerboard, and gradually work it into position. You will need to flex the soundboard, and also the body. Watch out for the harmonic bar ends catching on the linings. If the soundboard cannot be worked into position without excessive flexing, then the ends of the bars will need to be lowered further.

Checking the neck angle

With the soundboard removed, the body of the guitar is no longer rigid, and this flexibility is what allows you to insert the new soundboard underneath the existing fingerboard. Unfortunately, it also means that the neck angle is no longer fixed, and will potentially be changed when the new soundboard is glued in place. You will therefore need a setup that holds the neck at the correct angle to the body when the soundboard is being glued. This can be accomplished by holding the neck of the guitar firmly in a pattern-maker's vice secured to the bench, with the back of the guitar clear of the bench surface. Now place some support under the body of the guitar and adjust the height of this support until the correct neck angle is achieved. This support will need to be removed to allow the body to flex when the new soundboard is inserted, but should be replaced in exactly the same position before the soundboard is clamped.

Gluing the new soundboard in place

When you are satisfied that the soundboard can be fully inserted into the correct position, prepare the required clamps. In addition to the spool clamps used to clamp the soundboard to the linings, a G-clamp will be needed to secure the fingerboard to the new soundboard. If the bindings have been left in place, make sure that the clamps are exerting pressure on the edges of the soundboard, and not just on the bindings. In theory, the new soundboard should be perfectly flush with the existing bindings, but if any material was removed from the linings during clean up, it will be very slightly lower.

Apply glue to the linings, the end block, the underside of the fingerboard and into the recess cut between the fingerboard and the heel block. Insert the soundboard into position, trying not to scrape too much glue from the linings of the upper bout in the process. Check the position carefully, and make sure the body support is securely in position to hold the neck at the correct angle. The support should be left in place until after the new soundboard has been glued. Now apply the clamps, starting with the fingerboard clamp and working

Catastrophic Damage **261**

The guitar was mounted on a solera to glue the new soundboard on. Normally, the guitar would be the other way up during construction, with the soundboard facing down. The neck was clamped to the neck extension of the solera using spacing blocks adjusted to ensure the correct angle between the body and the neck was maintained when the soundboard was glued in place.

round to the end block. Clean up any glue squeeze-out and allow the glue to dry overnight before removing the clamps.

Replacing the bindings and purflings

If the bindings were removed along with the soundboard, then the procedure for replacing the bindings and purflings is mostly the same as when making a new guitar. Cut rebates for the purflings and the bindings using a purfling cutter (gramil), and a sharp chisel, but maintaining the original edge at the top of the sides where the bindings were previously removed.

The only significant difference when installing the purflings and bindings compared to a new guitar is that the

Having removed the original bindings with the soundboard, the edges of the new top are trimmed back flush with the linings, and then a new purfling rebate is marked and cut.

fingerboard will be in place, and so the ends will need to be trimmed to fit exactly into the space under the fingerboard where the original bindings and purflings were removed. The remainder of the bindings can be left slightly proud of both the top and the sides, but care will be needed when scraping or sanding the bindings flush with the sides not to damage the existing finish.

If the bindings have been kept, the next step is to trim the soundboard back to create a channel for the new purflings. This can be done using a purfling cutter in the same way as on a new guitar. Because the outside surface of the sides will be used as a reference for the purfling cutter, the new purfling channel will only be uniform in width if the bindings are uniform all the way around. If they are not, then some adjustment of the channel will be needed to obtain a perfect fit for the purflings. Small errors in the width of the channel can be accommodated by making the new purflings slightly over the required size, and then compressing them slightly. If hide glue is used, then the compressed wood should expand again when glued into the channel, filling any slight gaps.

The only remaining jobs are to apply the new finish to the soundboard, and to re-glue the bridge. The frets may need levelling, and it is also possible that the neck angle will not be perfect, so this should be checked, and adjustments made to the setup if necessary.

The finished repair. The only evidence that this is not the original soundboard is hidden away inside the guitar.

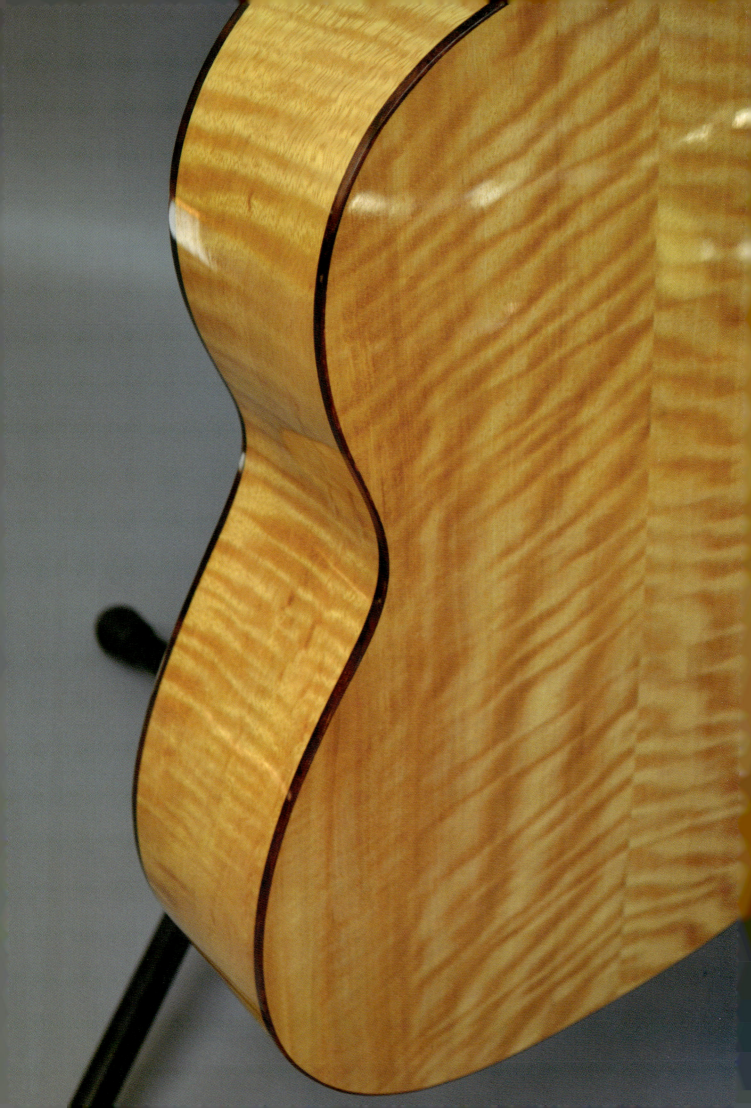

Glossary

Action: The height of the strings above the fingerboard. Lower action makes the guitar easier to play but increases the risk of the strings buzzing on the frets.

Adjustable neck: A neck that is not rigidly fixed to the body, with a mechanism allowing the angle of the neck to be adjusted relative to the body, hence adjusting the action.

Aliphatic resin glue: (yellow glue). A water-based glue, similar to PVA, but with a quicker grab time and better heat and water resistance.

Barbs: Small hooks on the sides of the fret tang that help hold it into the fret slot.

Bindings: Strips of wood (or plastic) that protect the corners of a guitar, particularly the edge of the soundboard where it meets the sides.

Bolt-on neck: A neck that is attached to the body using one or more bolts. The fingerboard may still be glued to the soundboard, or may be bolted as well, making the neck completely detachable.

Bound fingerboard: Bindings used on the edge of the fingerboard to hide the ends of the fret tangs. Can cause problems with lifting fret ends.

Bracing: (strutting). Tonewood bars used on the soundboard and back, and sometimes the sides. Provide structural strength, and also influence the sound of the guitar.

Break angle: The angle of the strings as they pass over the saddle. Too low a break angle can cause problems as the string is not firmly anchored.

Bridge pins: Pins that hold the strings to the bridge, usually found on steel-string acoustic guitars.

Bridge rotation: Tendency for the bridge to rotate around its long axis, tilting forwards towards the soundhole. Due to the tension of the strings.

Bridge string ties: Small blocks with holes that the strings are tied to on a classical type bridge, which will improve the break angle on 6-hole tie-block bridges.

Cabinet scraper: (card scraper). A tool steel plate, usually 1mm thick or less, used to 'scrape' wood surfaces, particularly those with difficult grains which may tear out when planed.

Caliper: Vernier, dial or digital. An accurate measuring device.

Capo: Device that clamps all strings across the fretboard at a particular fret, changing the pitch of the 'open' strings.

Chladni patterns: Patterns that give a visual representation of the vibration modes of the guitar soundboard.

Cleats: Small pieces of wood used to reinforce repairs. When glued across a crack repair the grain of the cleat should be perpendicular to the crack.

Compensation: An adjustment (increase) of the theoretical string length to ensure a guitar plays in tune at higher fret positions.

Crowning file: File used to remove flats from the top of a fret after levelling, and recreate a rounded crown.

Cyanoacrylate glue: (superglue, CA glue, crazy glue). A fast-bonding glue that is also useful for filling small dents and gaps in finishes.

Epoxy resin: A two-part adhesive that sets chemically when the resin is mixed with the hardener.

Fan-braced: A bracing pattern popularised by Torres and used primarily on classical and flamenco guitars. The braces in the lower bout form a fan shape, usually radiating from a point near the body join.

Flat-sawn: (plain or tangential sawn). Wood plate or plank that has been cut tangentially to the growth rings of the tree. Less dimensionally stable than a quarter-sawn plate.

frets
  clamping 132-133, 139
  end dressing 141
  fret hammer 22, 138
  fret marker replacement 204
  fret rocker 22, 46
  gluing frets 134
  installing 134, 137-140
  levelling 22, 45-48
  loose 131
  nippers 22
  polishing 49
  removal 135
  wear 134

G
German construction 99
glair 145
glossary 265
GluBoost 166
glues 24
gluing braces 91, 177
go-bar deck 21, 82-83
gouges 19, 20
grain matching 97

H
health and safety 9
heat resetting 100
Helmholtz resonance 219
hide glue 24, 68
humidity 39-40, 67
hygrometer 40
hygroscopic 39

I
impact damage 67, 210
impulse hammer 224-225
inlay repairs 201-204
inlays 201
inspection mirror 23
intonation 45, 63-65

J
Japanese paper 26, 27

K
Kevlar thread 82, 83
knives 19
Kremer pigments 89, 169

L
laminated plate repairs 87
lemon oil 31
levelling beam 22, 47
levelling inlays 204, 208
lifting bridges 178, 189
lighting 18
longitudinal modes 221-222, 226-227
loose braces 90
low break angles 193
low humidity 40, 67, 79
lubrication 43, 120

M
machine heads 41
magnets 21, 70-72, 75-77, 173, 177-178, 182
main air resonance 219, 221
mapping bracing 173-174, 182
mastic 201, 202
materials 24
measuring
  braces 176, 177
  bridge rotation 172
  resonances 219
modern construction methods 15
mother-of-pearl 201, 202
moving the saddle slot 65

N
naphtha 25, 26, 30
neck reinforcement 53, 100
neck removal 112-114
neck reset 112
nitrocellulose finishes 145, 167
notebook 26
nut
  adjustment 53
  clearances 53
  files 20
  replacement 56
  slot spacing 57-58
nylon-string 11, 12, 14

O
oil finishing 26, 146-147
open heel joints 118

P
patch repair 94-97, 235
pattern maker's vice 17, 18

personal protective equipment 9
pigments 26, 89, 168-169
pin bridges 179, 191, 199
planes 19, 108-109
plate repairs 67
polyester finishes 145, 161

Q
quarter-sawn 40

R
radial cut 39-40
rasps 20
razor scraper 96, 158, 166, 213
re-crowning 45, 48
refinishing 151, 165, 239
re-fretting 134
re-gluing the back 252
re-gluing the bridge 184, 189
relief 45-46, 50-53, 100
relief adjustment 50, 100
repairing fret slots 136
repairing finishes
  shellac 152
  nitrocellulose 167
  oil 146
  poly 161
repairing linings 248-251
replacing flat-head tuners 122
replacing slotted-head tuners 120
replacing strings 32
research 8
resonances 219-229
resonant frequency shift graph 228
rosette inlay replacement 201-204
routing 65

S
saddle
  adjustment 59
  profile 62
  replacement 61, 199
sanding finishes 148-150, 152-153, 162-164, 165
sanding sticks 20
scalpels 18, 19
scrapers 20
scraping finishes 148
scratch removing 165
setup 45

shelf life 153
shellac 26, 31, 89, 145, 152, 155, 169
shooting board 105
signal generator 220-221
slab cut 40
slotted bridge pins 190, 191
small patch repairs 94-97
sound box 11
soundboard bulge 172
soundboard replacement 256
Spanish heel 99
spectrum 224-226, 228
splinting 78
stains 81, 168
steaming a dent 93, 210-211
steel rules 18, 60
steel wool 25, 31
steel-string 8, 9, 99
storage 39
straightedge 46, 51, 109, 113, 129
string
   cutters 23
   lifter 55
   slots 53-54, 58-59, 62
   tension 14, 171, 172
   whips 94
   winder 23
Super Nikco 25, 26, 30, 156, 164
superglue 24
sustain 131, 219

T

tangential cut 39, 40
tapered dovetail joint 99, 112
terminology 9
tie blocks 35, 192, 194
tools 18
transverse modes 221-223, 227, 229
truss rod
   adjuster 51, 126
   replacement 123
tuning machines 41-43, 120-123
tuning pegs 21, 41
types of finish 145

U

under-saddle pickup 56, 186, 187
UV light 78

V

Van Dyck crystals 77, 78, 81, 168
violin peg clamp 21, 83, 85

W

water-based finishes 145
wire-break method 224
wolf notes 219
workbench 17
workshop facilities 17
worn tie-blocks 192

First published in 2024 by
The Crowood Press Ltd
Ramsbury, Marlborough
Wiltshire SN8 2HR

enquiries@crowood.com
www.crowood.com

© James Lister 2024

All rights reserved. No part of this publication may be reproduced or transmitted in any form or by any means, electronic or mechanical, including photocopy, recording, or any information storage and retrieval system, without permission in writing from the publishers.

British Library Cataloguing-in-Publication Data
A catalogue record for this book is available from the British Library.

ISBN 978 0 7198 4418 8

Cover design by Sergey Tsvetkov

James Lister has asserted their right under the Copyright, Designs and Patents Act 1988 to be identified as the author of this work.

Typeset by SJmagic DESIGN SERVICES, India
Printed and bound in India by Nutech Print Services - India

Acknowledgements

A comprehensive list of those who have helped me on the journey to the point where I could write this book would be very lengthy. Guitar makers are a generous group of people, who always seem willing to share their knowledge and experience with no thought of 'helping the competition'. I thank them all.

Particular thanks go to the tutors who inspired me as a student at Newark College, Roy Courtnall and Tony Johnson. Also, all tutors past and present, and all the many students I have known in my eighteen years (and counting) teaching at Newark.

Sofia Johnston Suarez provided the opening image for Chapter 10, the guitar she made in her final year at Newark. Thanks also to Stuart Christie, Chris Snow and Nick Pearson for providing additional photographs. Ask Eide carried out the work, provided notes and took the photographs of the neck reset in Chapter 6. Finale Guitars of Sheffield kindly provided two of the guitars used for the repairs in this book.

And finally, thanks to Ewan Cumming and Lesley Lister for reading the whole manuscript and providing feedback that has greatly improved the readability of the book.